A Centaur's Life 20

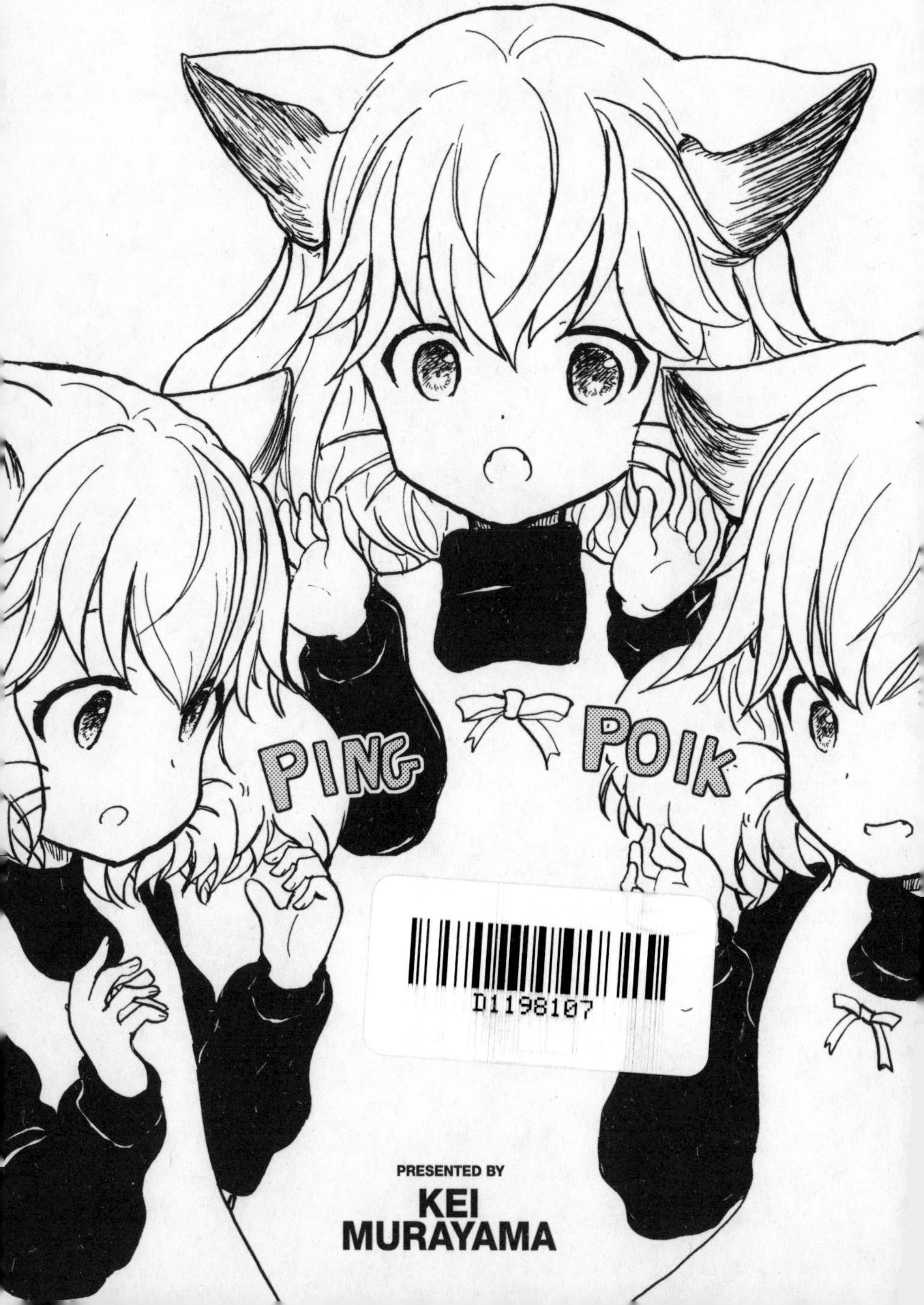
PING
POIK

PRESENTED BY
KEI
MURAYAMA

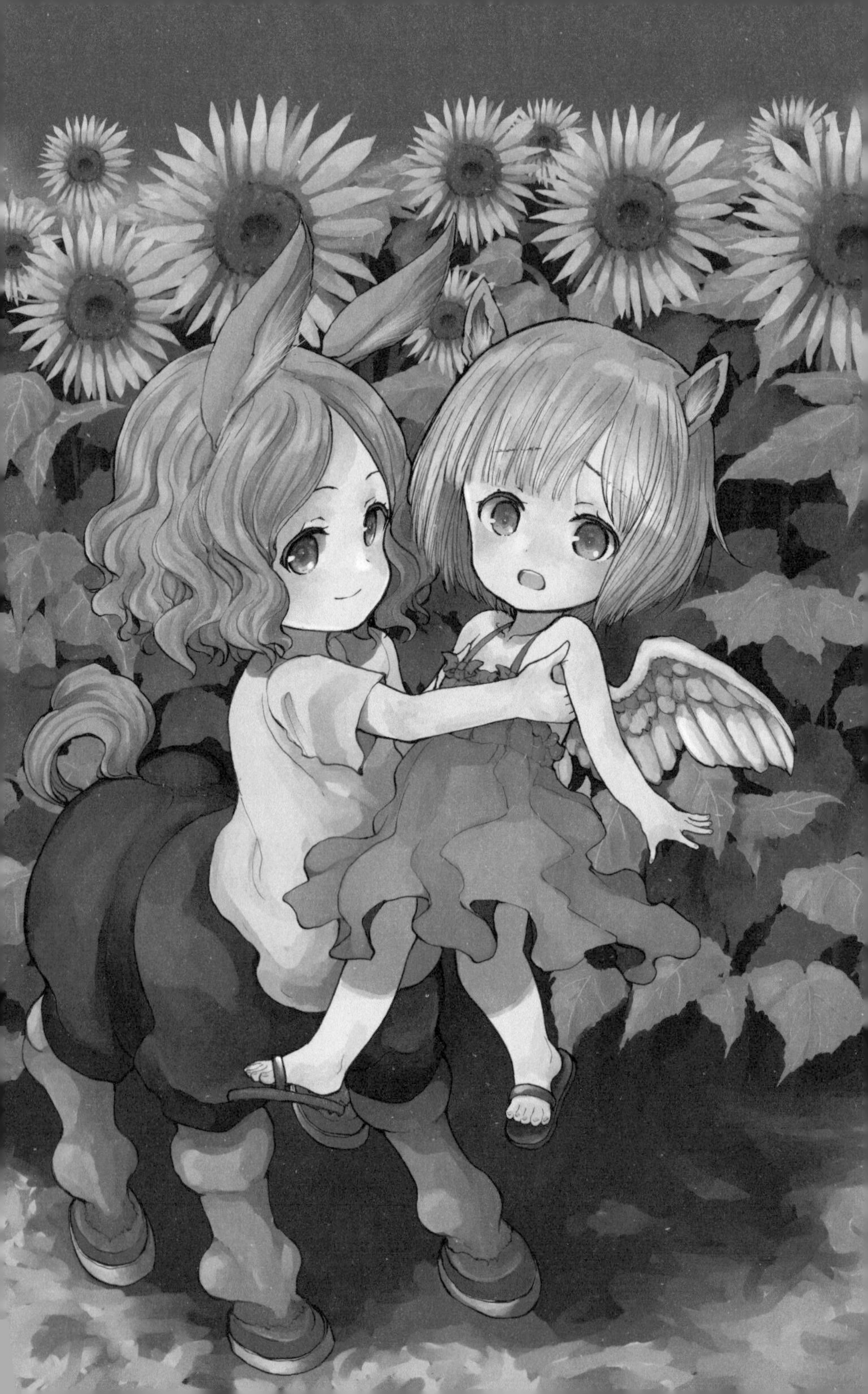

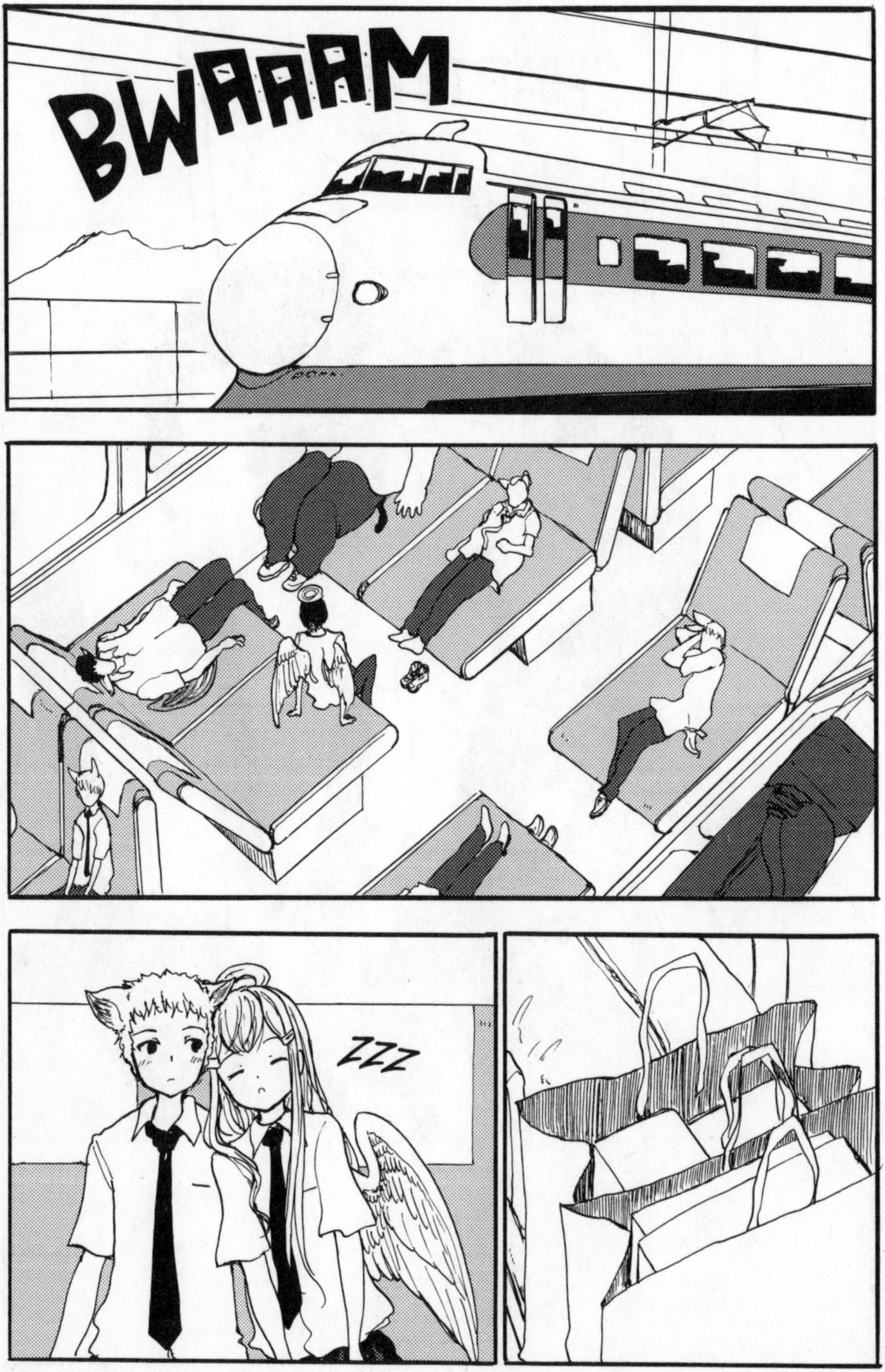
BWAAAM
ZZZ

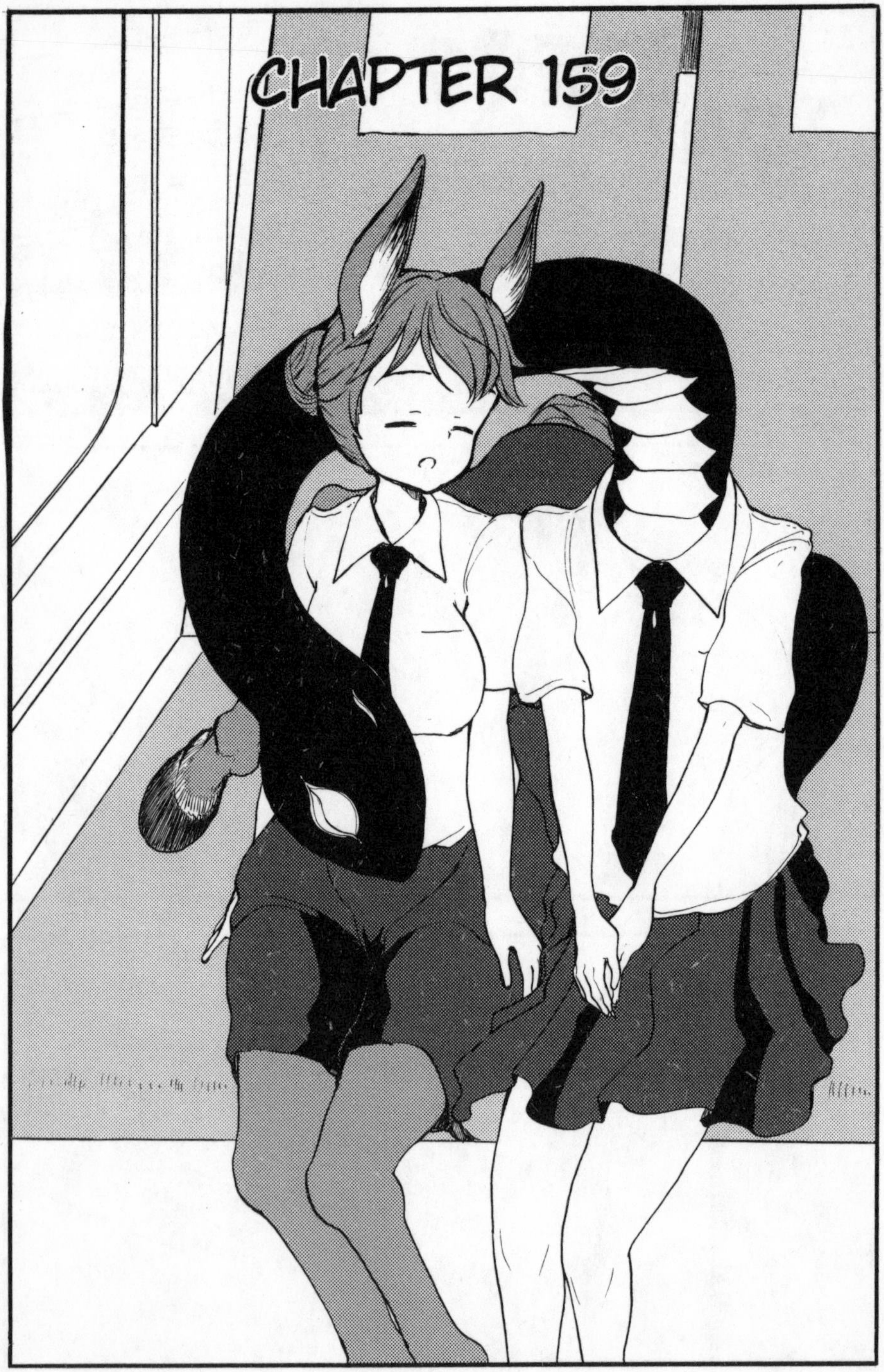
CHAPTER 159

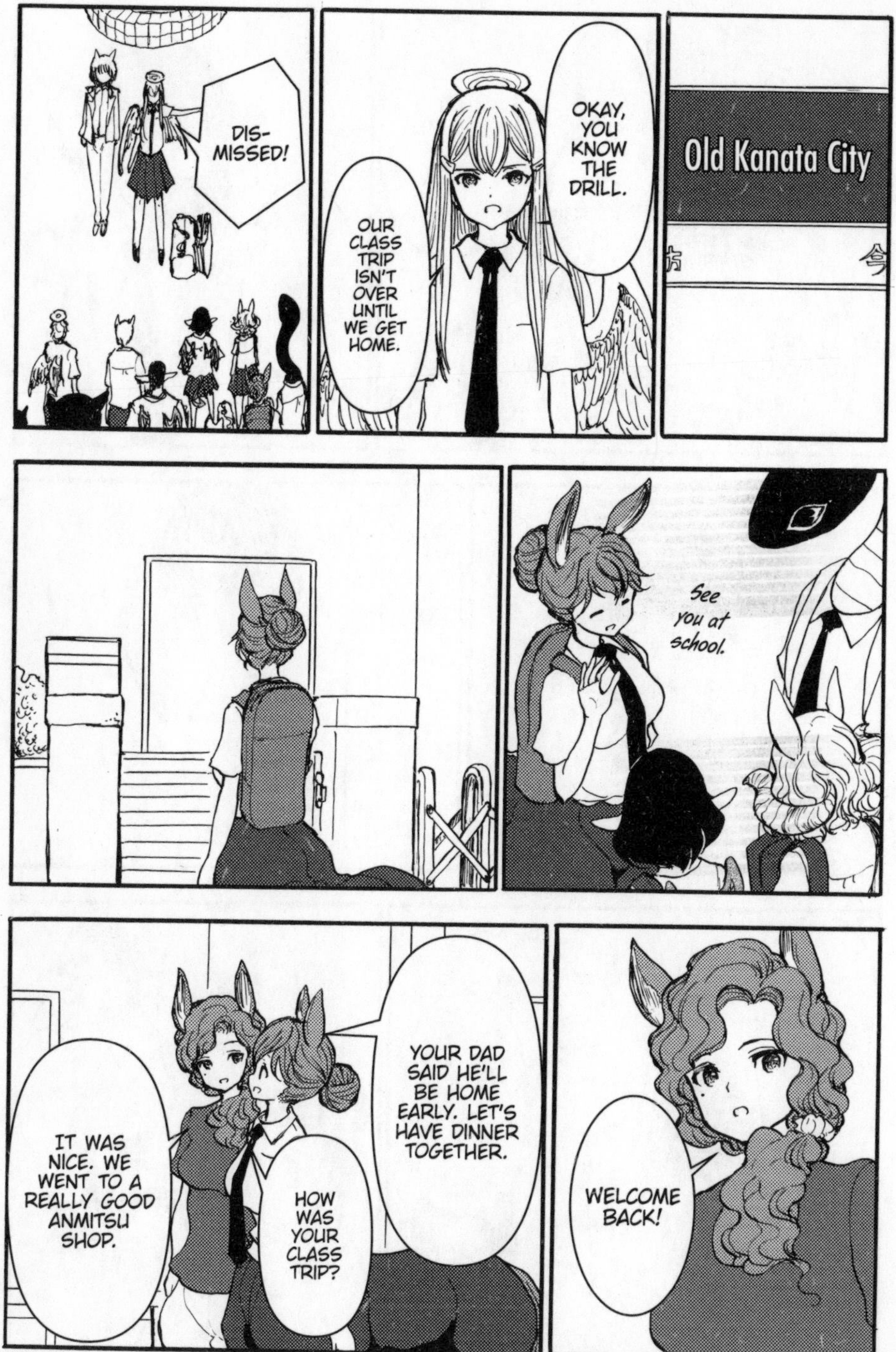
Old Kanata City
OKAY, YOU KNOW THE DRILL.
OUR CLASS TRIP ISN'T OVER UNTIL WE GET HOME.
DIS-MISSED!
See you at school.
WELCOME BACK!
YOUR DAD SAID HE'LL BE HOME EARLY. LET'S HAVE DINNER TOGETHER.
HOW WAS YOUR CLASS TRIP?
IT WAS NICE. WE WENT TO A REALLY GOOD ANMITSU SHOP.

I'M HOME.
HI! YOU'RE BACK EARLY.
I WOULD'VE PICKED YOU UP AT THE STATION.
THAT'S OKAY.
Here, a souvenir for you.
BIG BRO YASUMURA, I CAN TAKE IT FROM HERE.
OSU!
BIG SIS NOZOMI, YOU'RE BACK!
HEY, CALL ME "SHIHAN-DAI"* IN CLASS.
I knew, they'd prefer a girl.

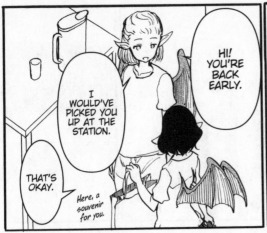

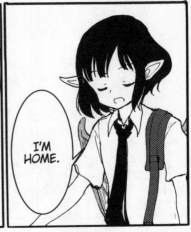

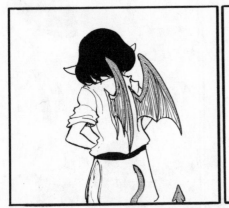

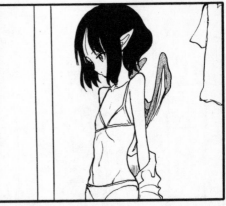

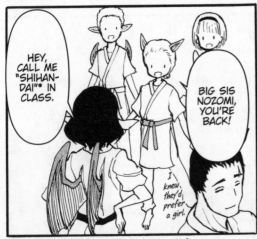

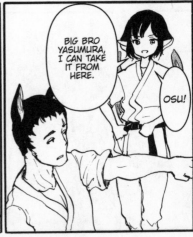

*Shihan-Dai is a karate title meaning "assistant master."

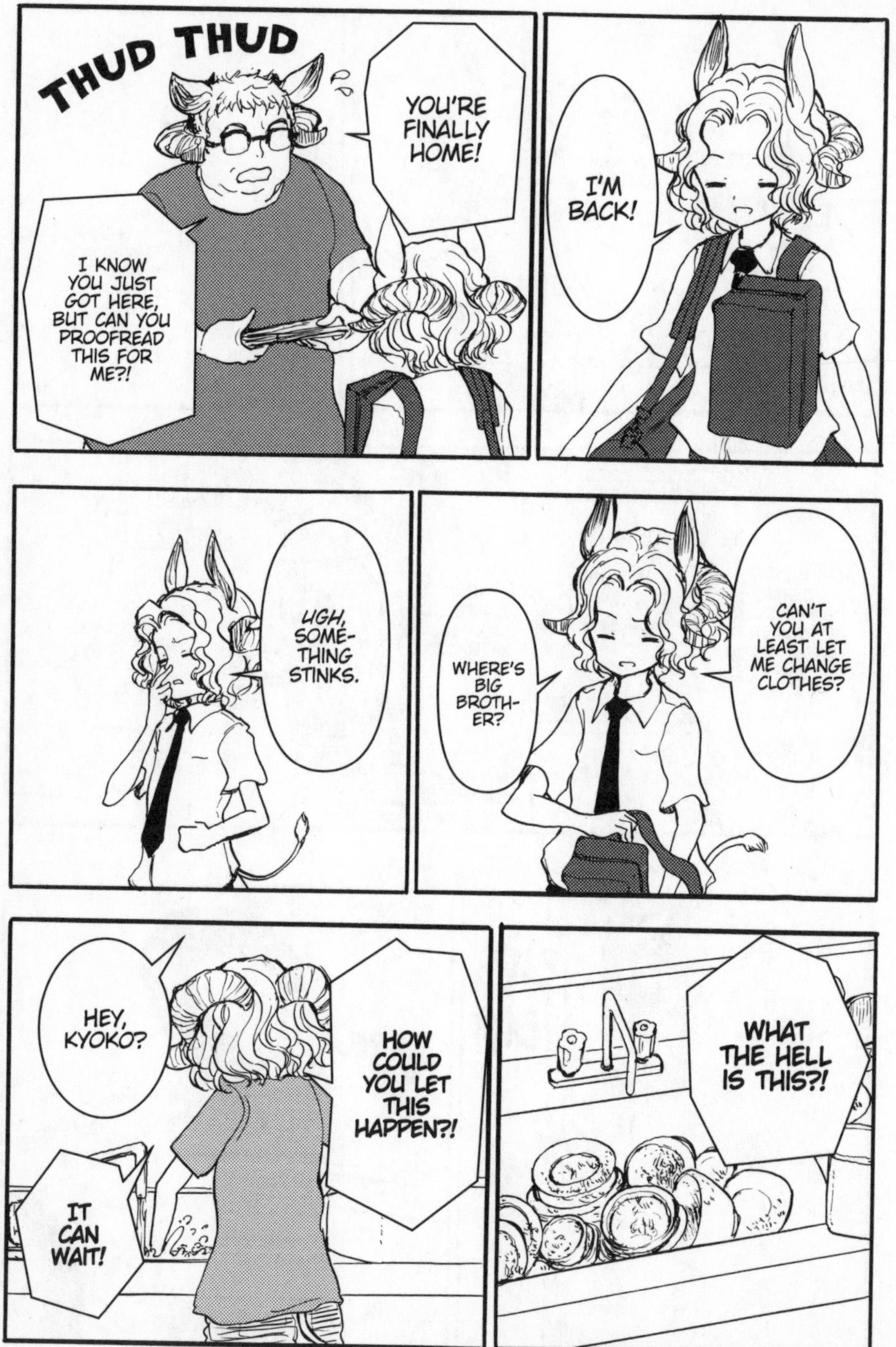
I'M BACK!
THUD THUD
YOU'RE FINALLY HOME!
I KNOW YOU JUST GOT HERE, BUT CAN YOU PROOFREAD THIS FOR ME?!
CAN'T YOU AT LEAST LET ME CHANGE CLOTHES?
WHERE'S BIG BROTHER?
UGH, SOMETHING STINKS.
WHAT THE HELL IS THIS?!
HOW COULD YOU LET THIS HAPPEN?!
HEY, KYOKO?
IT CAN WAIT!

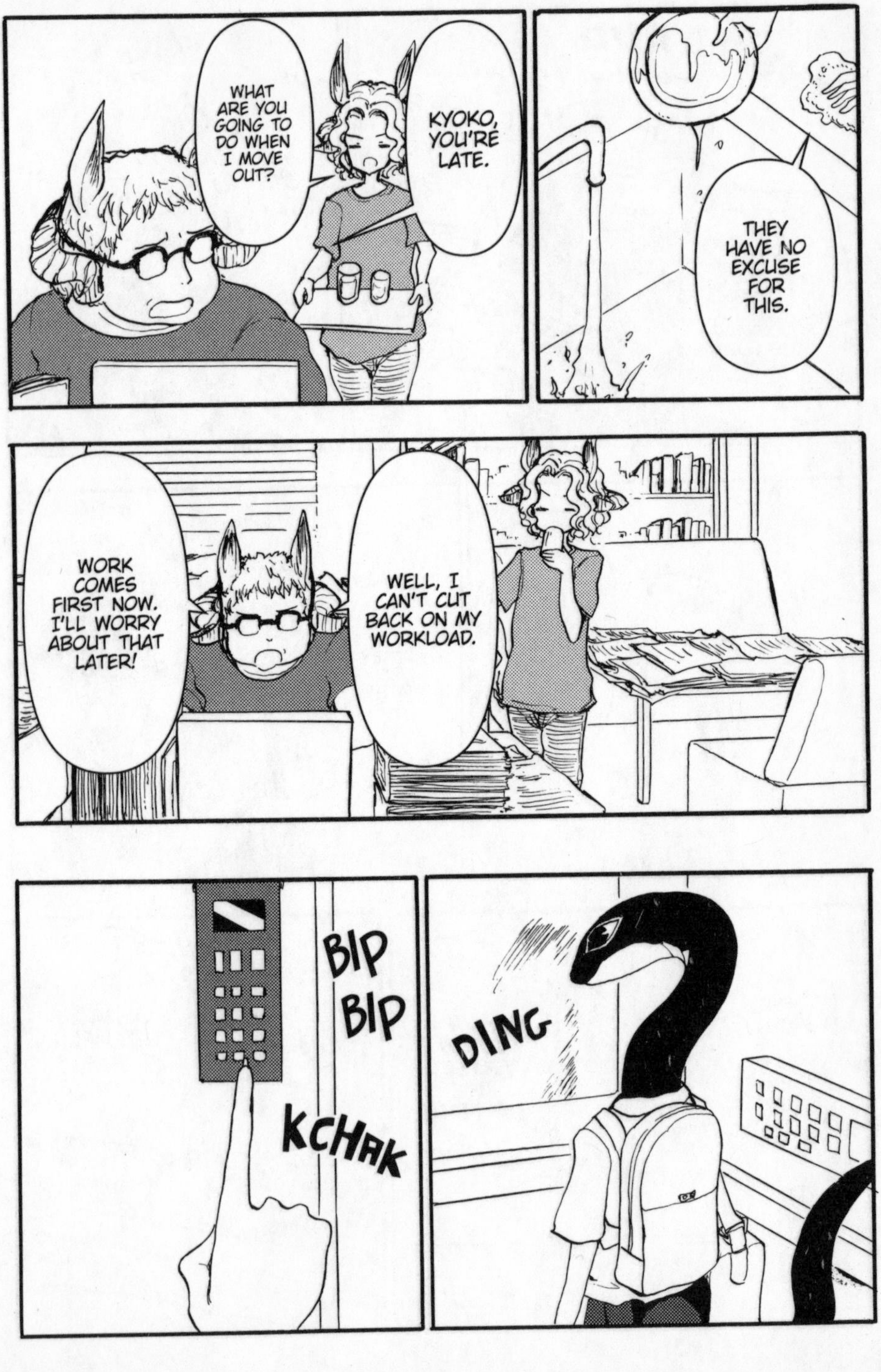
THEY HAVE NO EXCUSE FOR THIS.
KYOKO, YOU'RE LATE.
WHAT ARE YOU GOING TO DO WHEN I MOVE OUT?
WELL, I CAN'T CUT BACK ON MY WORKLOAD.
WORK COMES FIRST NOW. I'LL WORRY ABOUT THAT LATER!
DING
BIP BIP
KCHAK

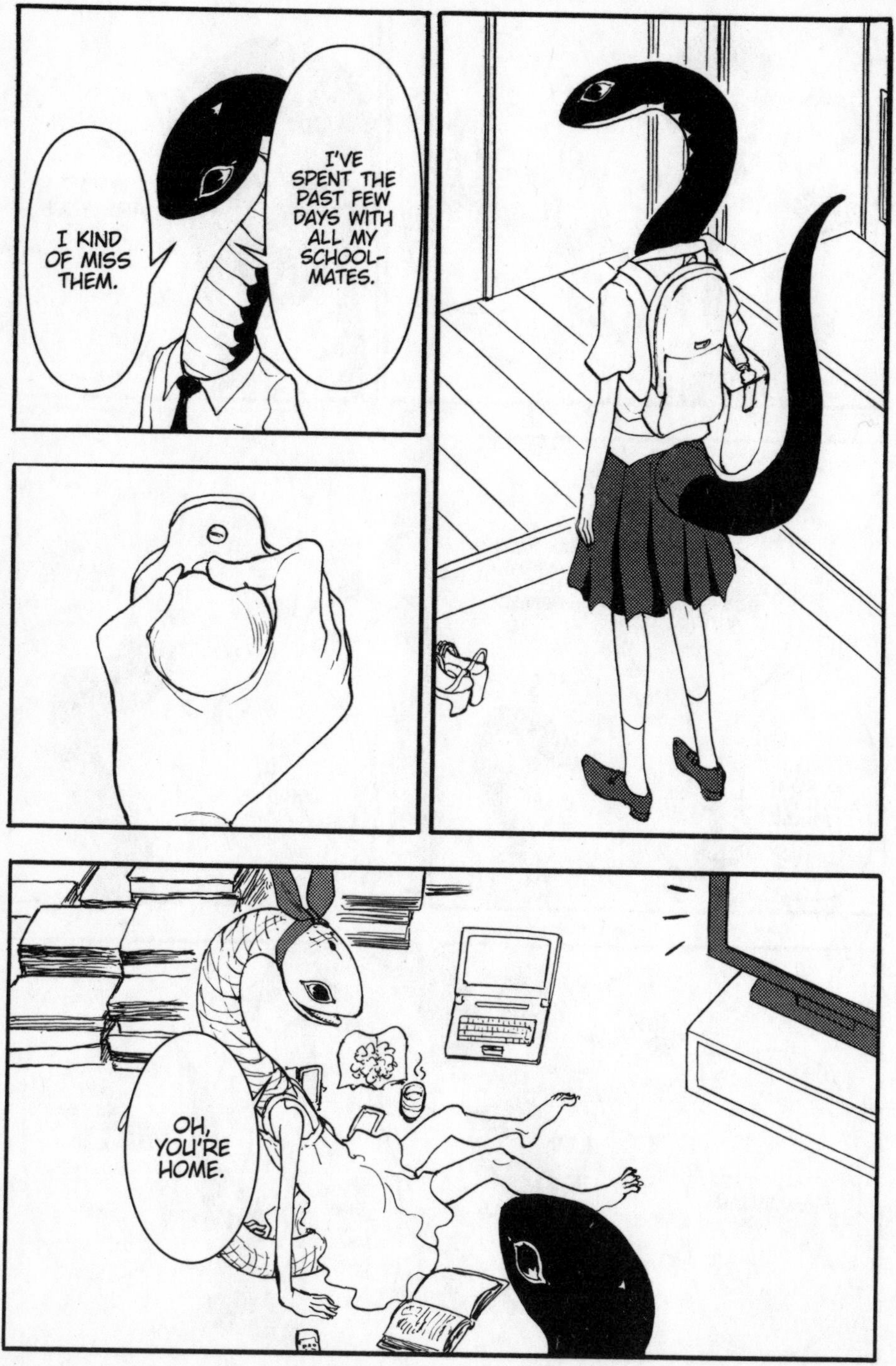
I'VE SPENT THE PAST FEW DAYS WITH ALL MY SCHOOL-MATES.
I KIND OF MISS THEM.
OH, YOU'RE HOME.

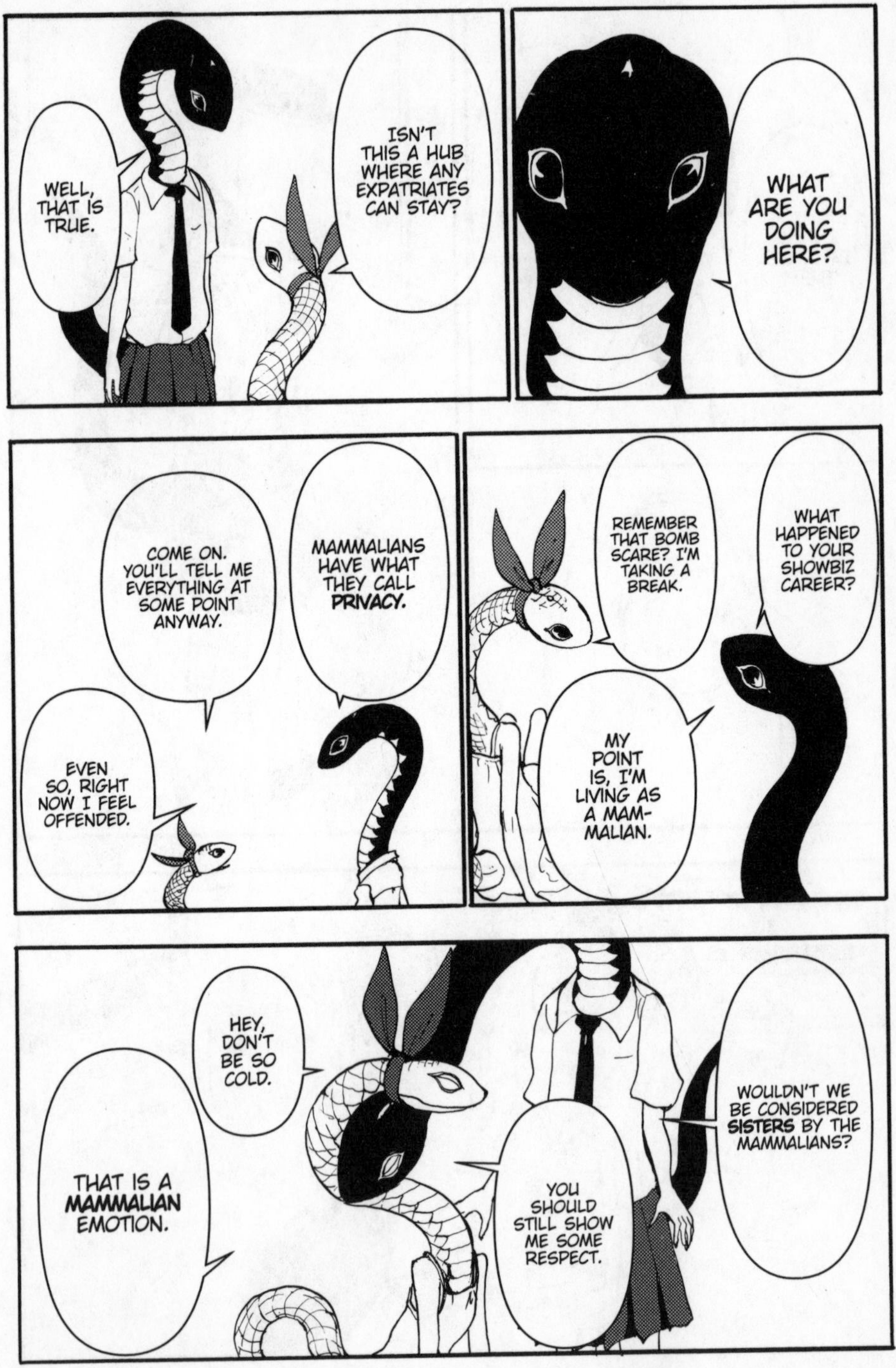
WHAT ARE YOU DOING HERE?
ISN'T THIS A HUB WHERE ANY EXPATRIATES CAN STAY?
WELL, THAT IS TRUE.
WHAT HAPPENED TO YOUR SHOWBIZ CAREER?
REMEMBER THAT BOMB SCARE? I'M TAKING A BREAK.
MY POINT IS, I'M LIVING AS A MAM-MALIAN.
MAMMALIANS HAVE WHAT THEY CALL **PRIVACY.**
COME ON. YOU'LL TELL ME EVERYTHING AT SOME POINT ANYWAY.
EVEN SO, RIGHT NOW I FEEL OFFENDED.
WOULDN'T WE BE CONSIDERED **SISTERS** BY THE MAMMALIANS?
YOU SHOULD STILL SHOW ME SOME RESPECT.
HEY, DON'T BE SO COLD.
THAT IS A **MAMMALIAN** EMOTION.

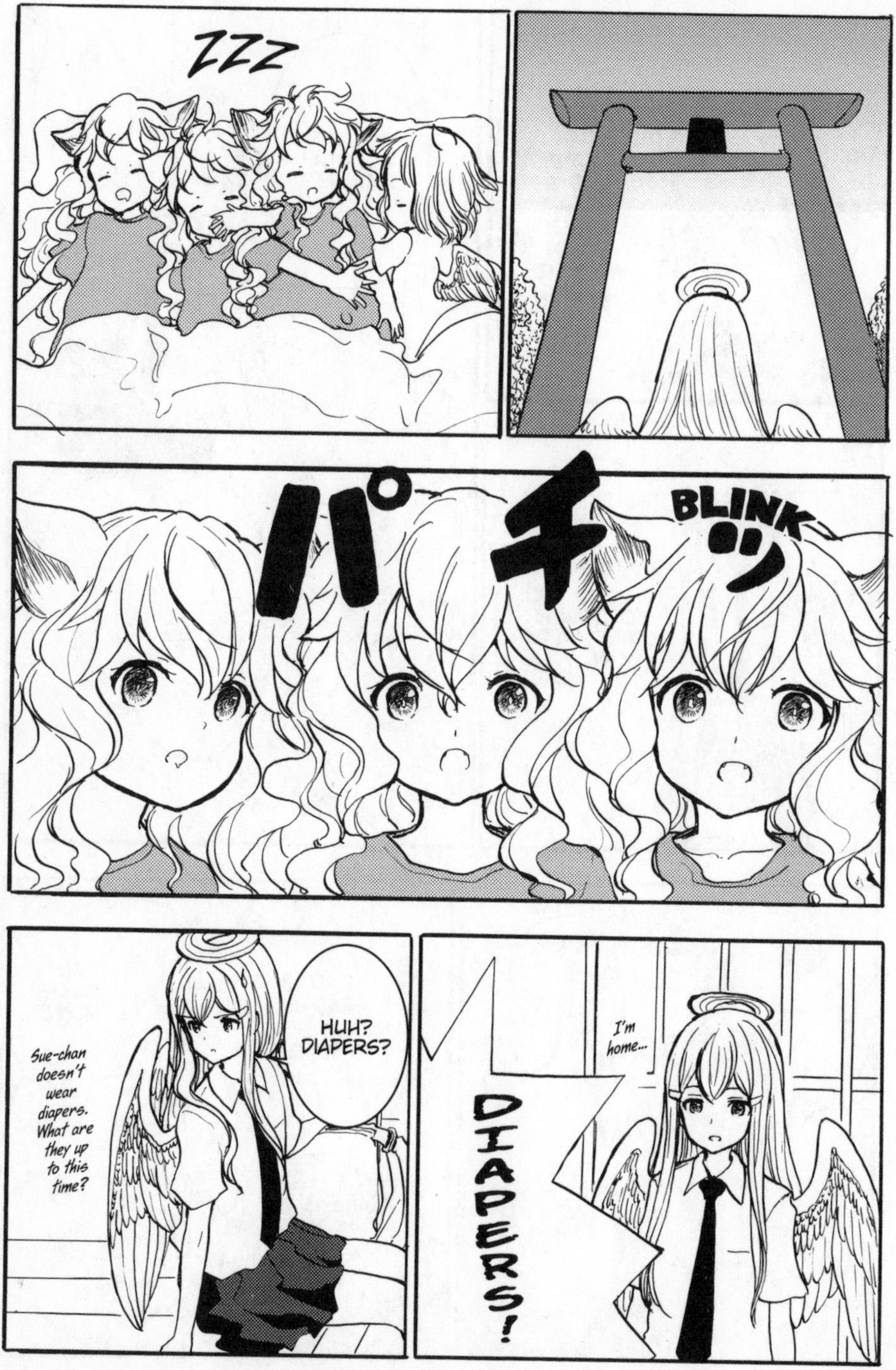
ZZZ
パチッ
BLINK
I'm home...
DIAPERS!
HUH? DIAPERS?
Sue-chan doesn't wear diapers. What are they up to this time?

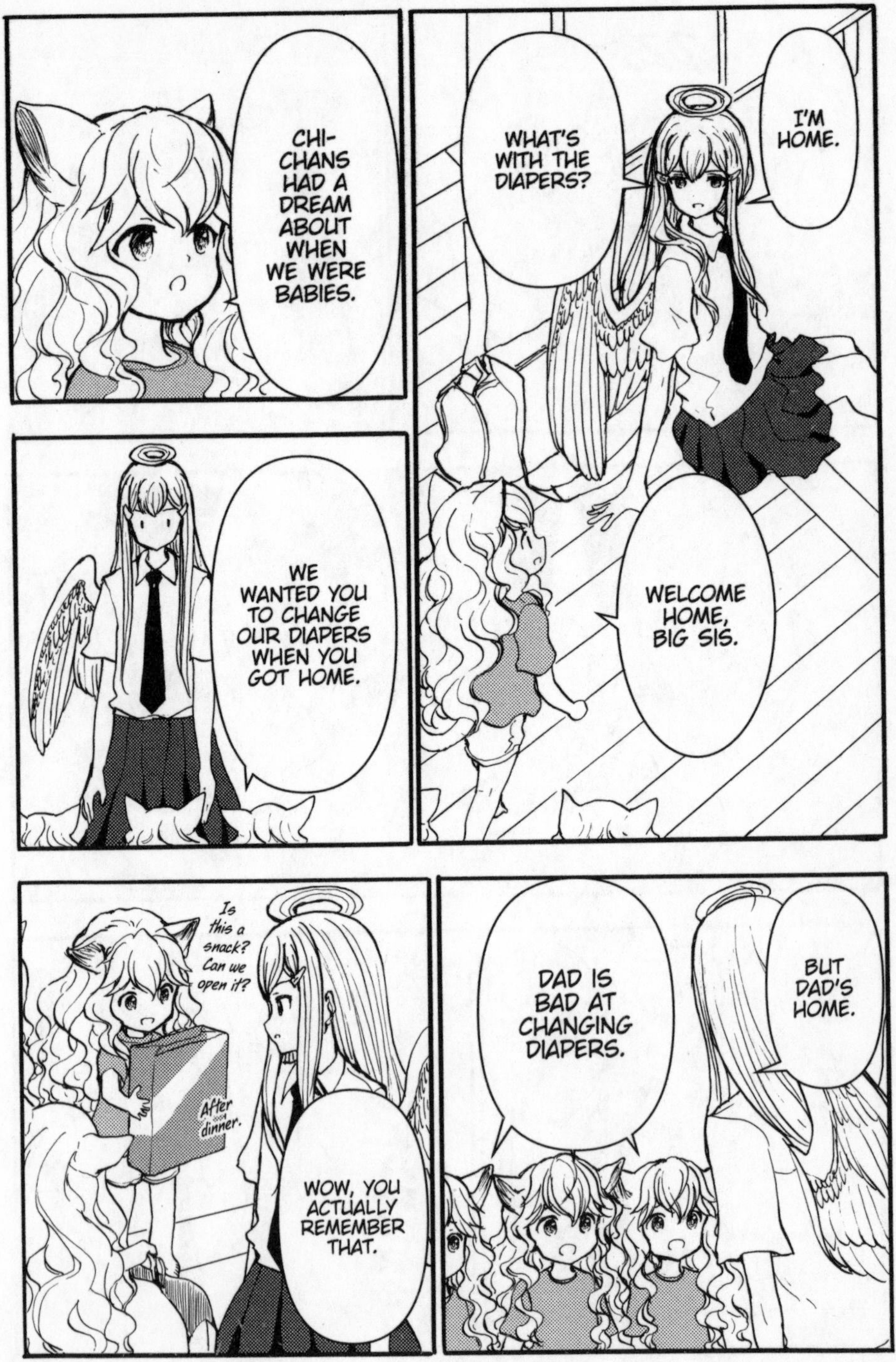
I'M HOME.
WHAT'S WITH THE DIAPERS?
WELCOME HOME, BIG SIS.
CHI-CHANS HAD A DREAM ABOUT WHEN WE WERE BABIES.
WE WANTED YOU TO CHANGE OUR DIAPERS WHEN YOU GOT HOME.
BUT DAD'S HOME.
DAD IS BAD AT CHANGING DIAPERS.
Is this a snack? Can we open it?
After dinner.
WOW, YOU ACTUALLY REMEMBER THAT.

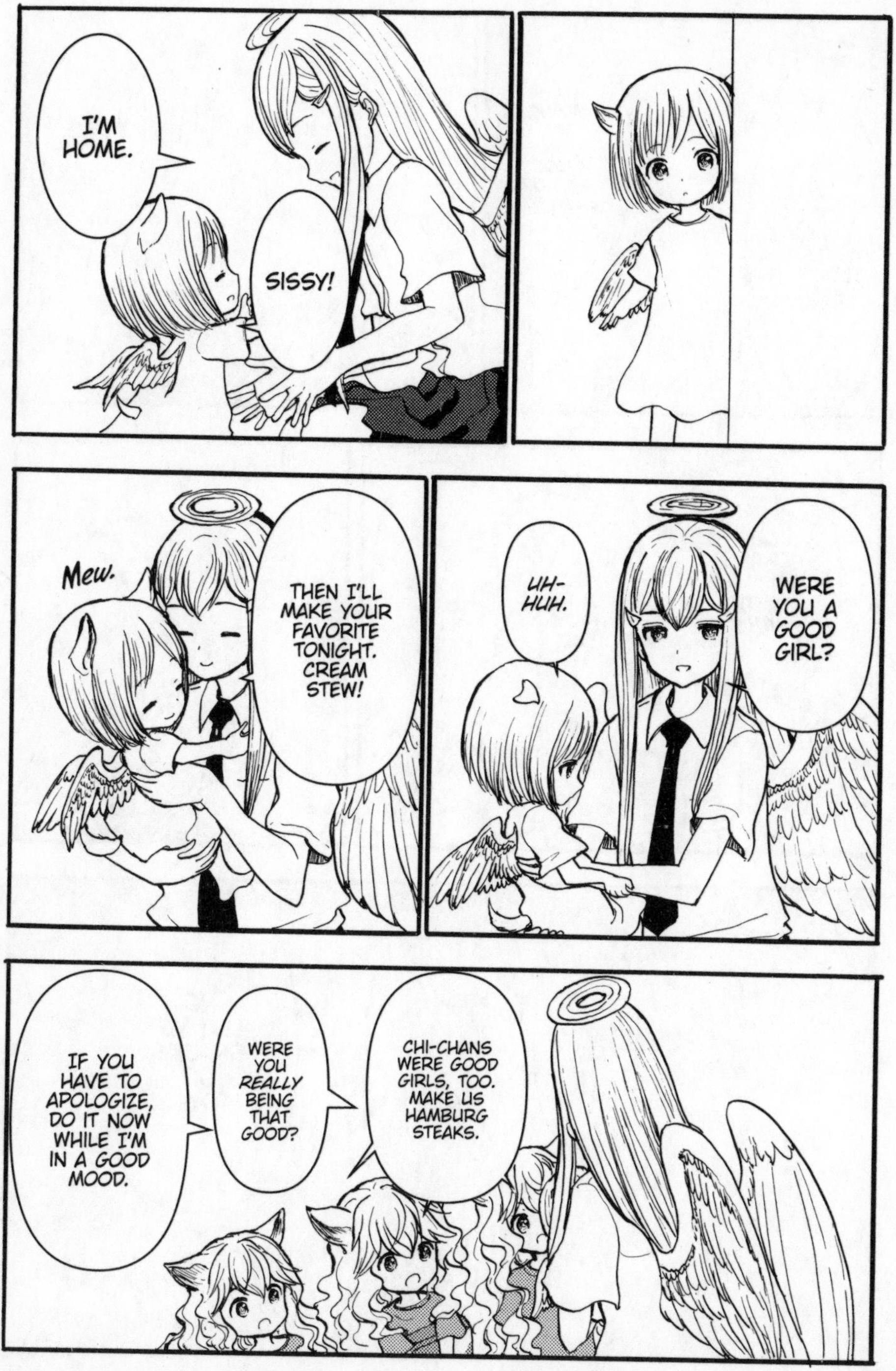
I'M HOME.
SISSY!
WERE YOU A GOOD GIRL?
UH-HUH.
THEN I'LL MAKE YOUR FAVORITE TONIGHT. CREAM STEW!
Mew.
CHI-CHANS WERE GOOD GIRLS, TOO. MAKE US HAMBURG STEAKS.
WERE YOU *REALLY* BEING THAT GOOD?
IF YOU HAVE TO APOLOGIZE, DO IT NOW WHILE I'M IN A GOOD MOOD.

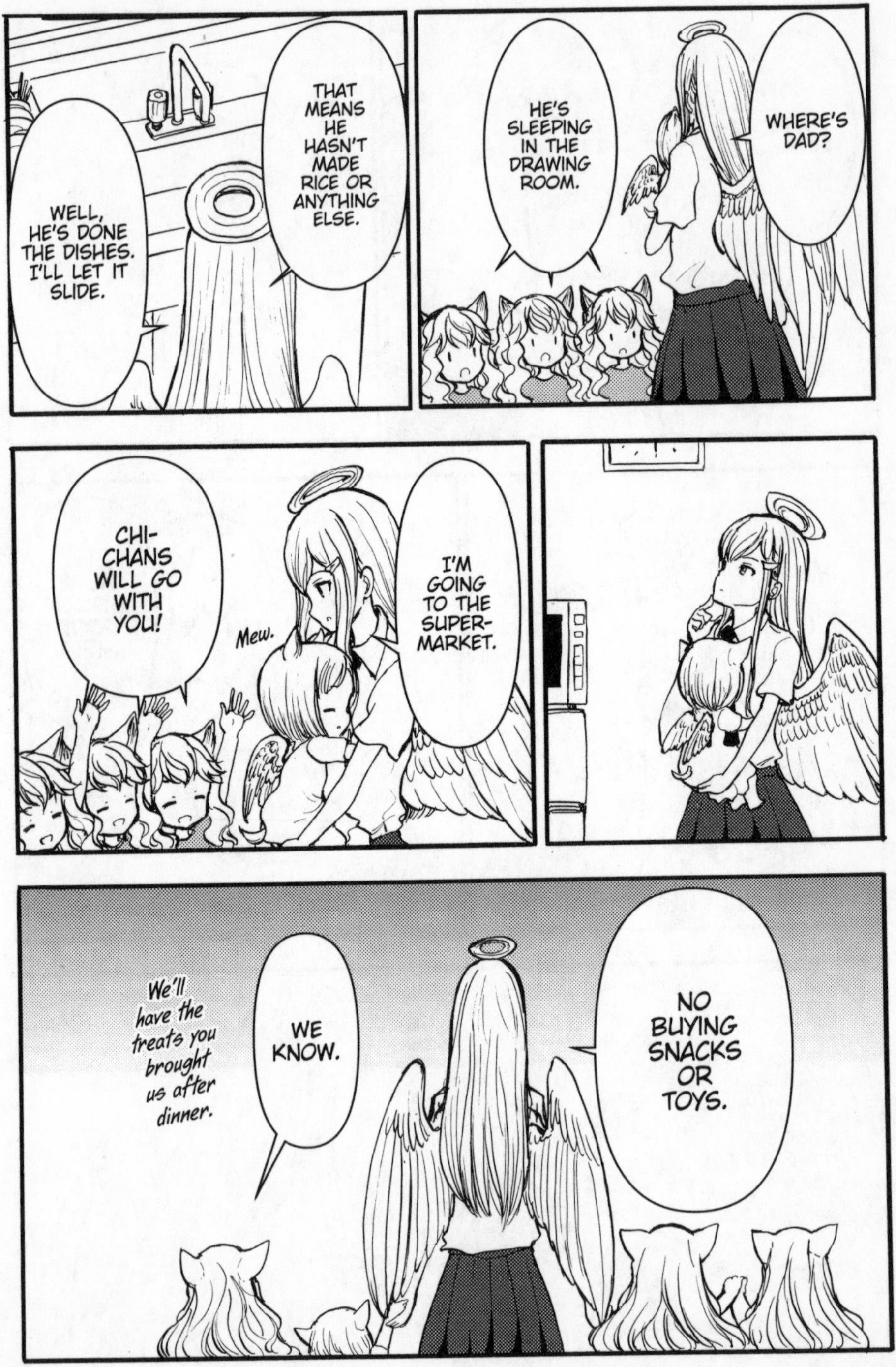
WHERE'S DAD?
HE'S SLEEPING IN THE DRAWING ROOM.
THAT MEANS HE HASN'T MADE RICE OR ANYTHING ELSE.
WELL, HE'S DONE THE DISHES. I'LL LET IT SLIDE.
I'M GOING TO THE SUPER-MARKET.
Mew.
CHI-CHANS WILL GO WITH YOU!
NO BUYING SNACKS OR TOYS.
WE KNOW.
We'll have the treats you brought us after dinner.

A Centaur's Life

RELEARNING THE ORIGIN OF MAMMALIAN HUMANS
1. WHY STUDY LOST CIVILIZATIONS?

WHERE DID WE COME FROM? WHY DO WE EXIST AS WE DO NOW? THROUGH SCIENTIFIC RESEARCH, ESPECIALLY OF FOSSILIZED MAMMALIAN HUMANS, NEW INFORMATION CONTINUES TO ACCUMULATE. HOWEVER, THIS HAS CAUSED DEVIATIONS--IN SOME CASES, DEADLY ONES--BETWEEN KNOWLEDGE FROM THE LATEST STUDIES AND WHAT'S TAUGHT IN SCHOOLS. MANY MEMBERS OF THE SCIENTIFIC COMMUNITY TEND NOT TO CONTINUE THEIR EDUCATION AFTER COMPLETING THEIR DEGREES. A GOOD EXAMPLE OF THIS IS THE BELIEF THAT CENTAURS AND DRACONIDS HAD DISTINCT ANCESTORS FOR THEIR RESPECTIVE RACES. THIS MAY BE BASED ON "COMMON KNOWLEDGE." HOWEVER, THE STUDY ON WHICH THIS BELIEF IS BASED WAS REJECTED BY THE SCIENTIFIC COMMUNITY A HUNDRED YEARS AGO, AS WELL AS BY EXPERTS IN EACH NEW FIELD OF SCIENCE THAT HAS SINCE EMERGED, SUCH AS GENETICS AND MOLECULAR BIOLOGY. DESPITE THIS, MANY AMONGST THE ELDERLY AND UNEDUCATED STILL BELIEVE IN THE OLD THEORY OF EVOLUTION BY SPECIES, AND THEY BASE THEIR POLITICAL BELIEFS ON FALSE SCIENCE. A CORRECT UNDERSTANDING OF POLITICS CAN ONLY COME FROM ACCURATE SCIENTIFIC KNOWLEDGE. BECAUSE OF THIS, IT'S IMPORTANT TO BE AWARE OF THE LATEST RESEARCH IN THE STUDY OF FOSSILIZED MAMMALIAN HUMANS.

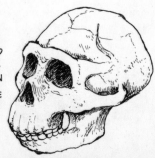

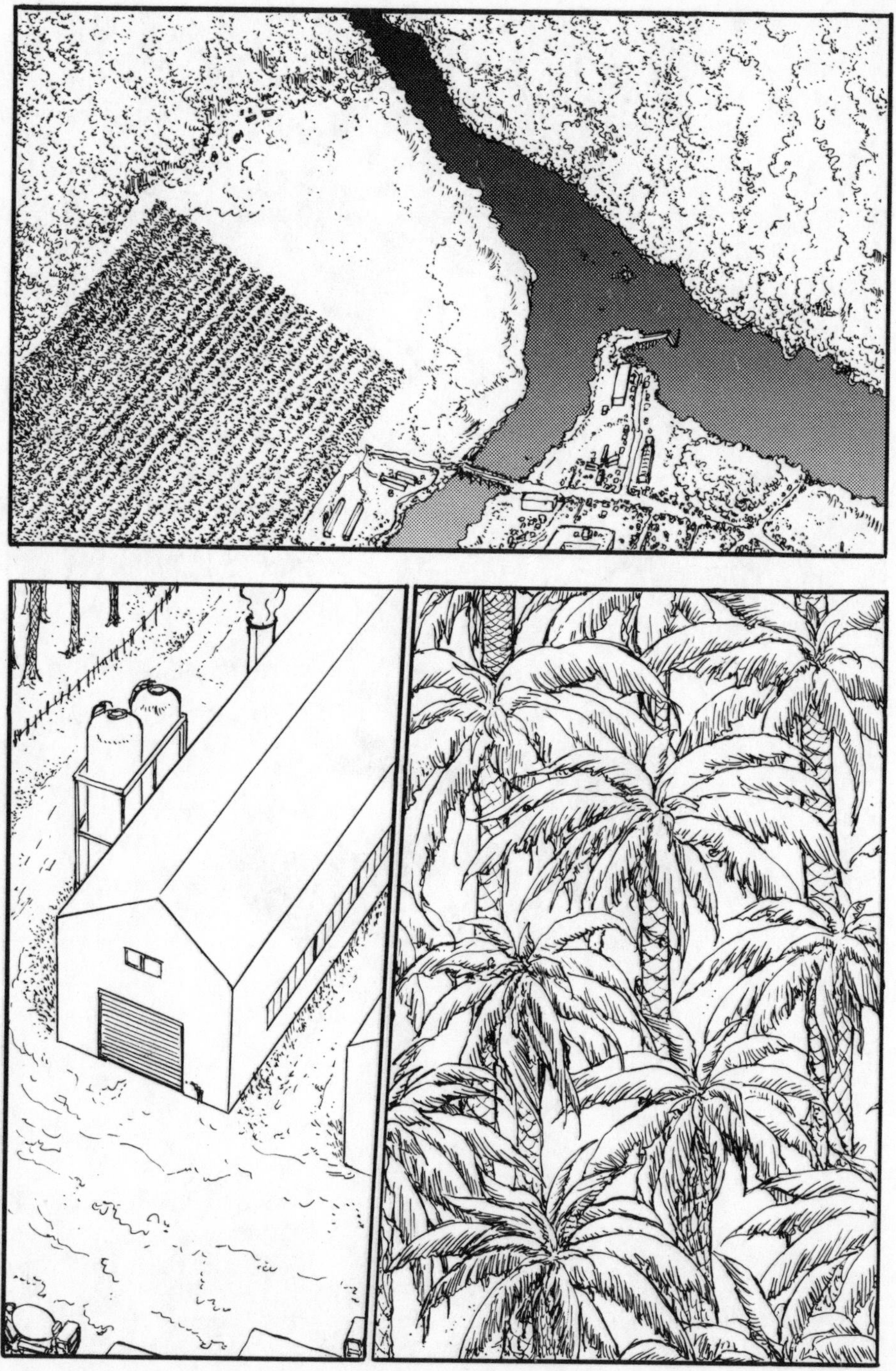

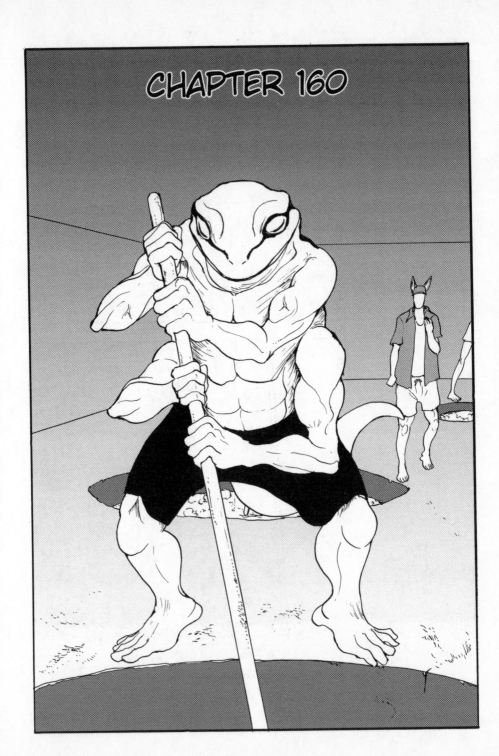

CHAPTER 160

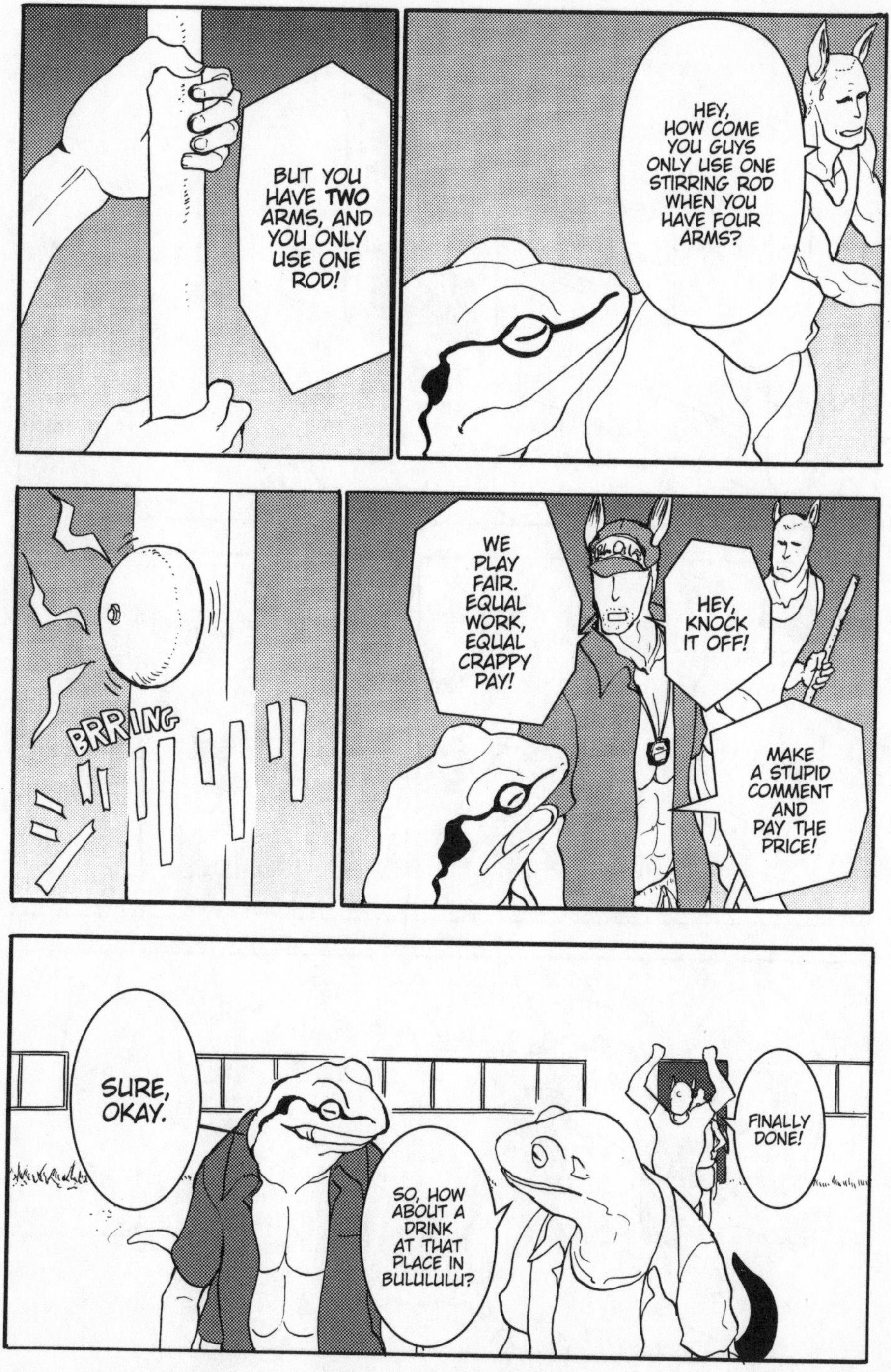
HEY, HOW COME YOU GUYS ONLY USE ONE STIRRING ROD WHEN YOU HAVE FOUR ARMS?
BUT YOU HAVE TWO ARMS, AND YOU ONLY USE ONE ROD!
WE PLAY FAIR. EQUAL WORK, EQUAL CRAPPY PAY!
HEY, KNOCK IT OFF!
MAKE A STUPID COMMENT AND PAY THE PRICE!
BRRING
FINALLY DONE!
SO, HOW ABOUT A DRINK AT THAT PLACE IN BULULULU?
SURE, OKAY.

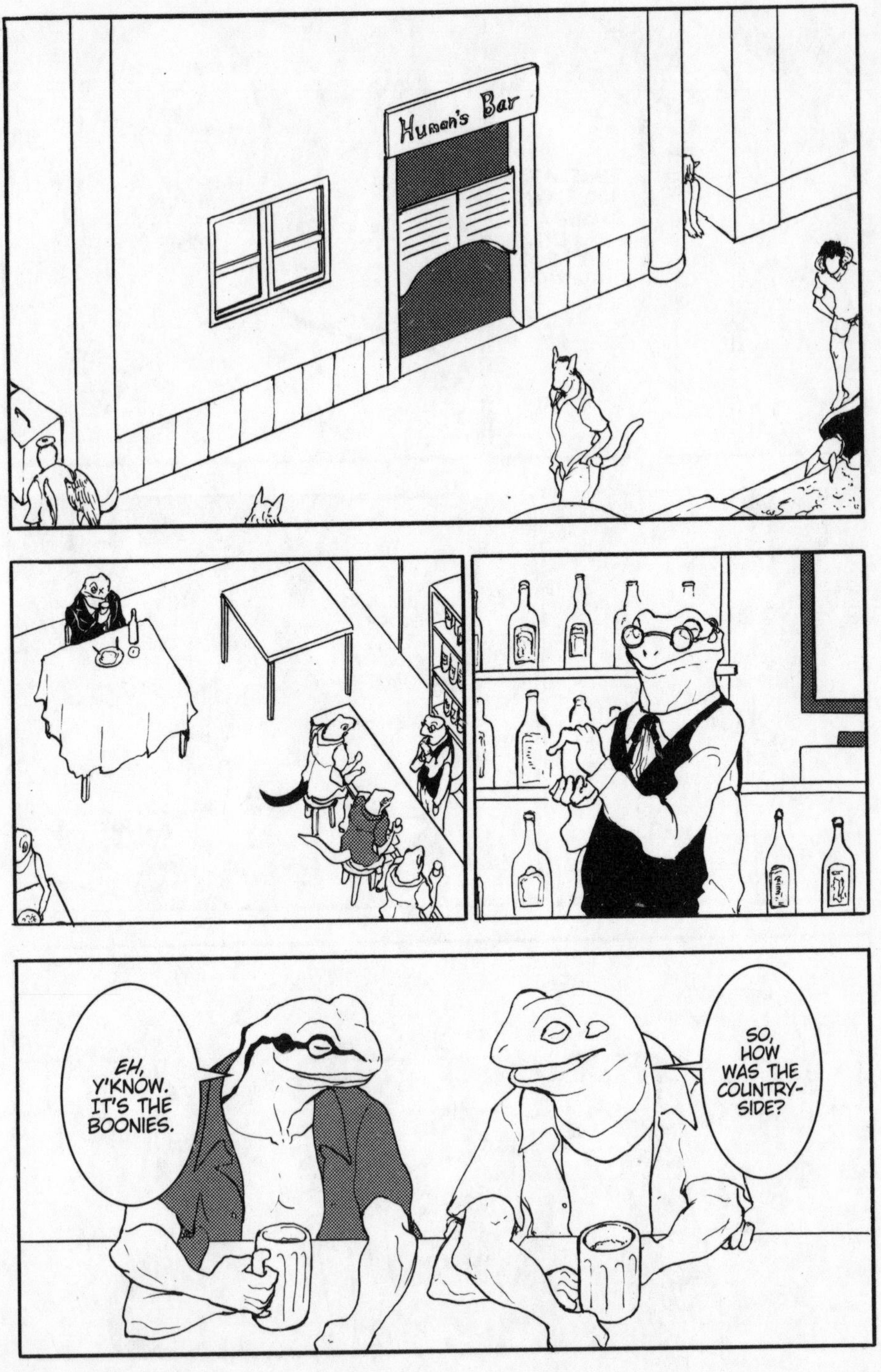
Human's Bar
SO, HOW WAS THE COUNTRY-SIDE?
EH, Y'KNOW. IT'S THE BOONIES.

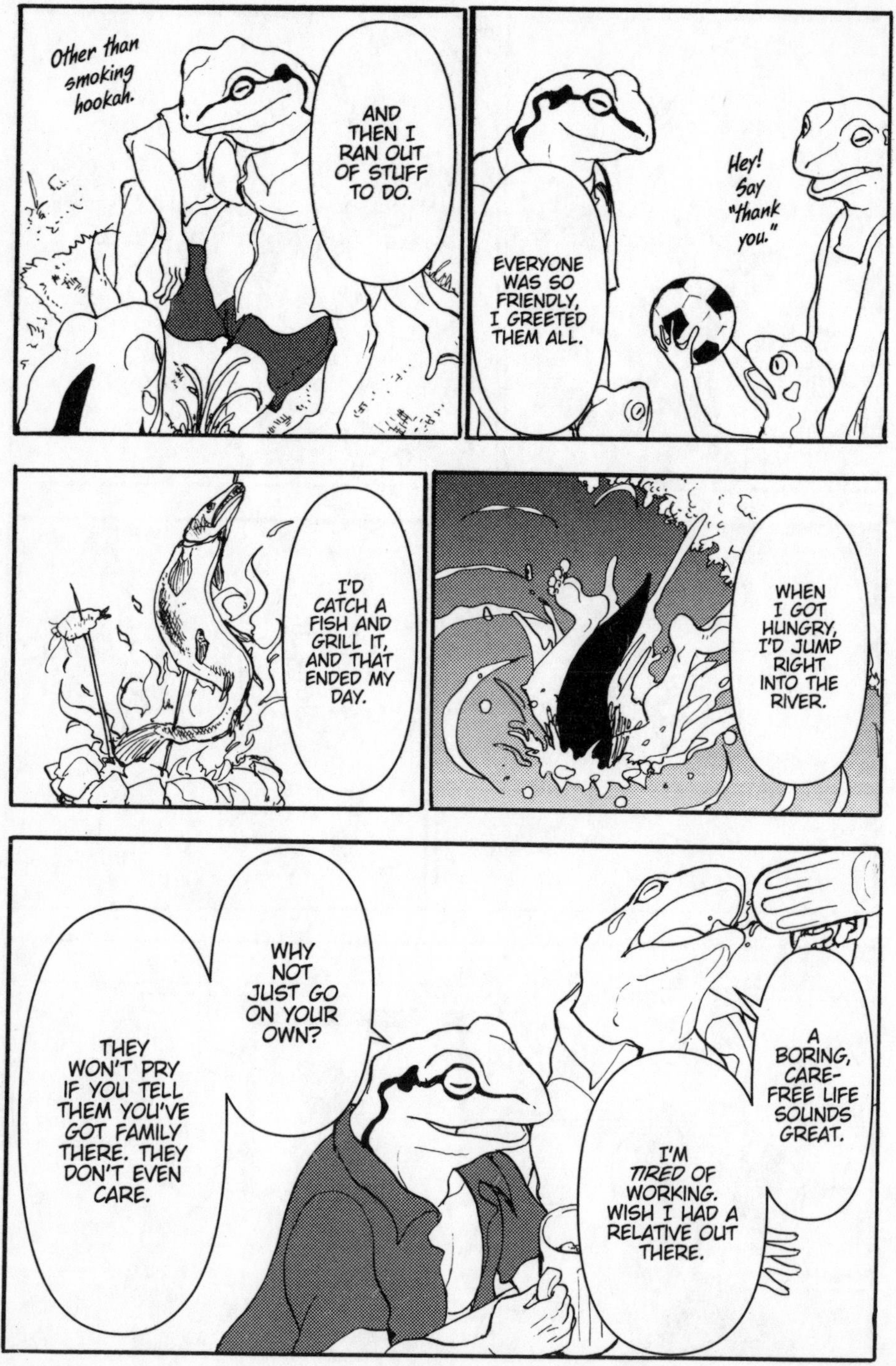
Hey! Say "thank you."
EVERYONE WAS SO FRIENDLY, I GREETED THEM ALL.
AND THEN I RAN OUT OF STUFF TO DO.
Other than smoking hookah.
WHEN I GOT HUNGRY, I'D JUMP RIGHT INTO THE RIVER.
I'D CATCH A FISH AND GRILL IT, AND THAT ENDED MY DAY.
A BORING, CARE-FREE LIFE SOUNDS GREAT.
I'M *TIRED* OF WORKING. WISH I HAD A RELATIVE OUT THERE.
WHY NOT JUST GO ON YOUR OWN?
THEY WON'T PRY IF YOU TELL THEM YOU'VE GOT FAMILY THERE. THEY DON'T EVEN CARE.

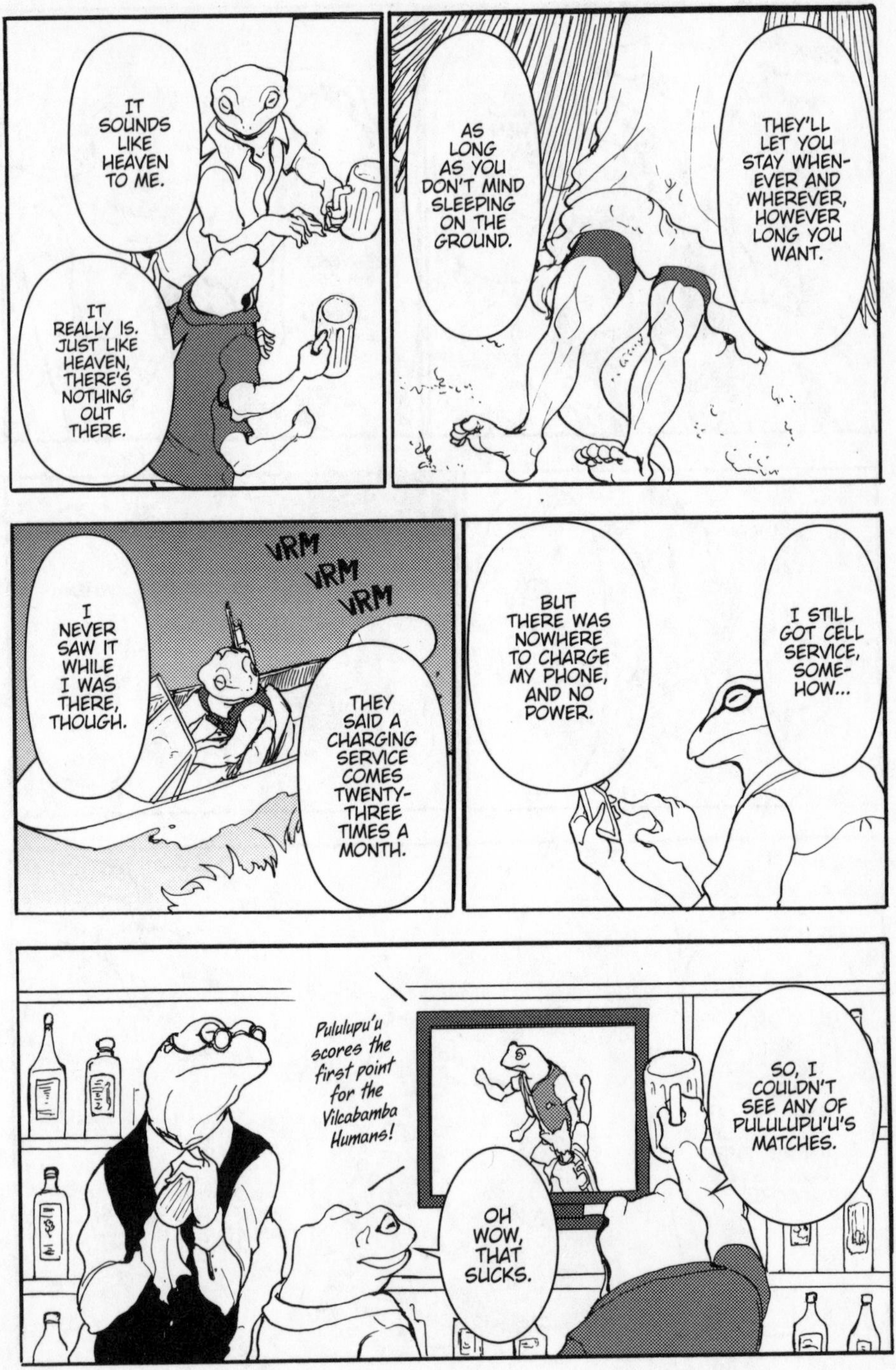
THEY'LL LET YOU STAY WHEN-EVER AND WHEREVER, HOWEVER LONG YOU WANT.
AS LONG AS YOU DON'T MIND SLEEPING ON THE GROUND.
IT SOUNDS LIKE HEAVEN TO ME.
IT REALLY IS. JUST LIKE HEAVEN, THERE'S NOTHING OUT THERE.
I STILL GOT CELL SERVICE, SOME-HOW...
BUT THERE WAS NOWHERE TO CHARGE MY PHONE, AND NO POWER.
VRM VRM VRM
THEY SAID A CHARGING SERVICE COMES TWENTY-THREE TIMES A MONTH.
I NEVER SAW IT WHILE I WAS THERE, THOUGH.
SO, I COULDN'T SEE ANY OF PULULUPU'U'S MATCHES.
Pululupu'u scores the first point for the Vilcabamba Humans!
OH WOW, THAT SUCKS.

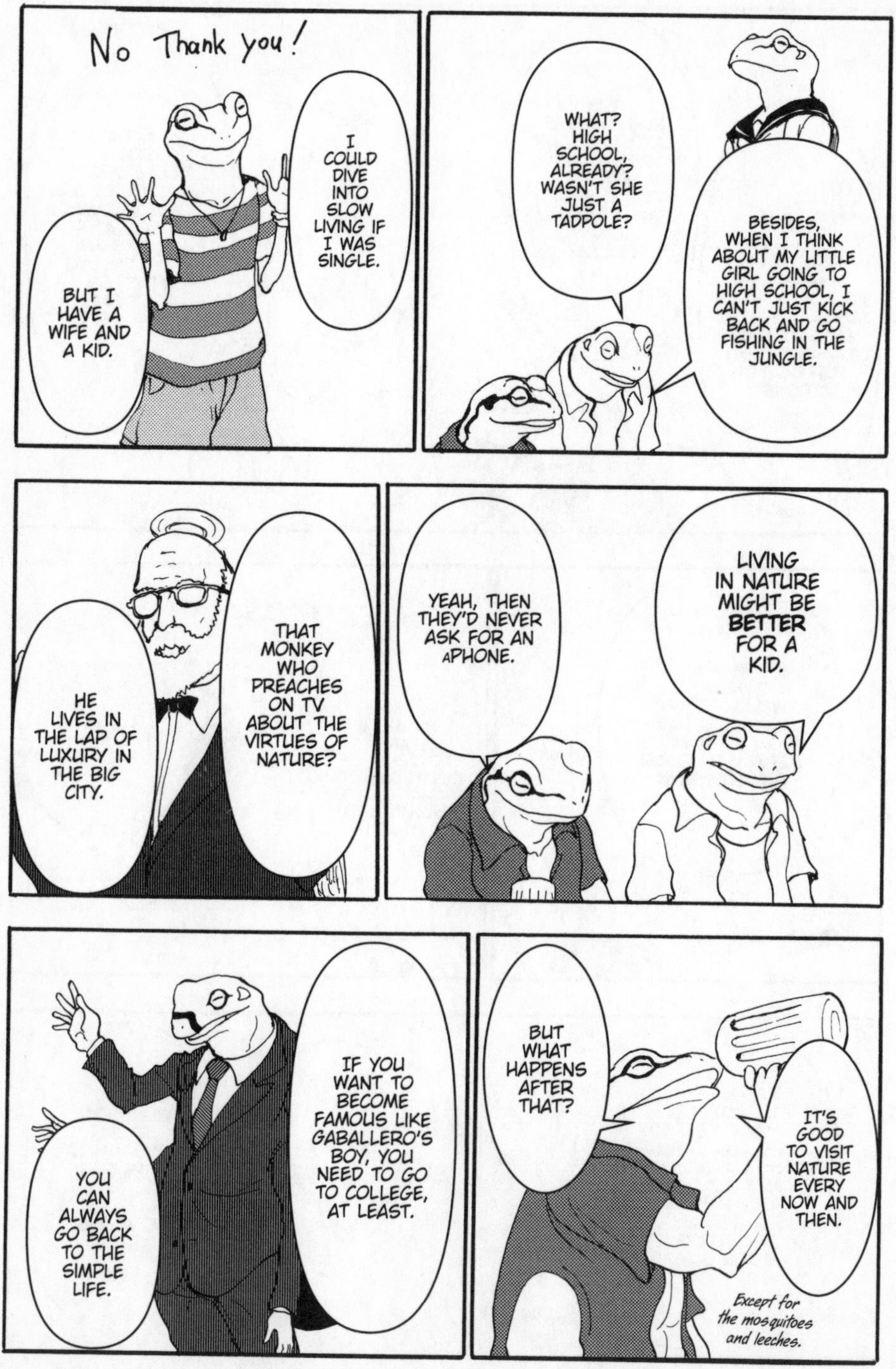
BESIDES, WHEN I THINK ABOUT MY LITTLE GIRL GOING TO HIGH SCHOOL, I CAN'T JUST KICK BACK AND GO FISHING IN THE JUNGLE.
WHAT? HIGH SCHOOL, ALREADY? WASN'T SHE JUST A TADPOLE?
No Thank you!
I COULD DIVE INTO SLOW LIVING IF I WAS SINGLE.
BUT I HAVE A WIFE AND A KID.
LIVING IN NATURE MIGHT BE BETTER FOR A KID.
YEAH, THEN THEY'D NEVER ASK FOR AN aPHONE.
THAT MONKEY WHO PREACHES ON TV ABOUT THE VIRTUES OF NATURE?
HE LIVES IN THE LAP OF LUXURY IN THE BIG CITY.
IT'S GOOD TO VISIT NATURE EVERY NOW AND THEN.
BUT WHAT HAPPENS AFTER THAT?
Except for the mosquitoes and leeches.
IF YOU WANT TO BECOME FAMOUS LIKE GABALLERO'S BOY, YOU NEED TO GO TO COLLEGE, AT LEAST.
YOU CAN ALWAYS GO BACK TO THE SIMPLE LIFE.

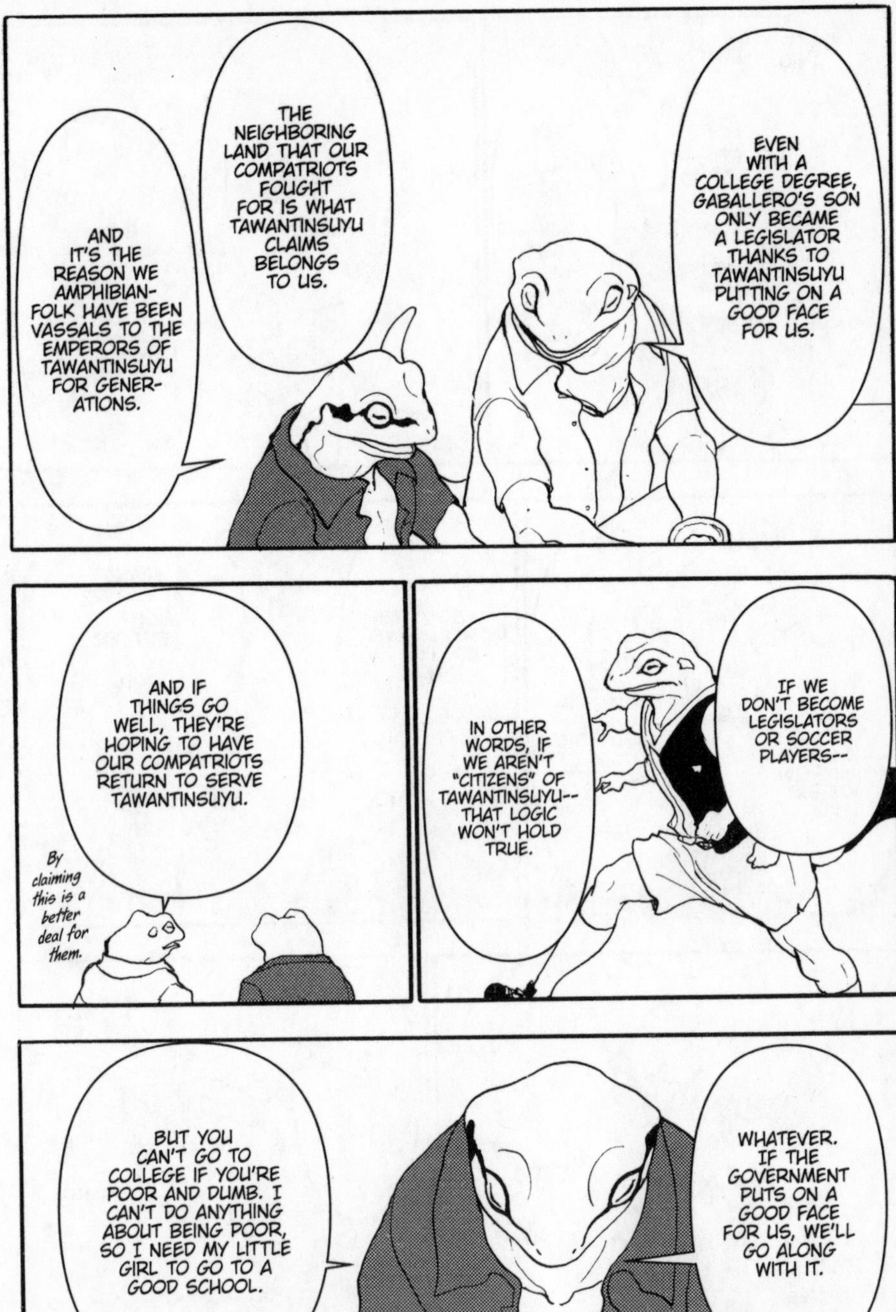
EVEN WITH A COLLEGE DEGREE, GABALLERO'S SON ONLY BECAME A LEGISLATOR THANKS TO TAWANTINSUYU PUTTING ON A GOOD FACE FOR US.
THE NEIGHBORING LAND THAT OUR COMPATRIOTS FOUGHT FOR IS WHAT TAWANTINSUYU CLAIMS BELONGS TO US.
AND IT'S THE REASON WE AMPHIBIAN-FOLK HAVE BEEN VASSALS TO THE EMPERORS OF TAWANTINSUYU FOR GENERATIONS.
IF WE DON'T BECOME LEGISLATORS OR SOCCER PLAYERS--
IN OTHER WORDS, IF WE AREN'T "CITIZENS" OF TAWANTINSUYU--THAT LOGIC WON'T HOLD TRUE.
AND IF THINGS GO WELL, THEY'RE HOPING TO HAVE OUR COMPATRIOTS RETURN TO SERVE TAWANTINSUYU.
By claiming this is a better deal for them.
WHATEVER. IF THE GOVERNMENT PUTS ON A GOOD FACE FOR US, WE'LL GO ALONG WITH IT.
BUT YOU CAN'T GO TO COLLEGE IF YOU'RE POOR AND DUMB. I CAN'T DO ANYTHING ABOUT BEING POOR, SO I NEED MY LITTLE GIRL TO GO TO A GOOD SCHOOL.

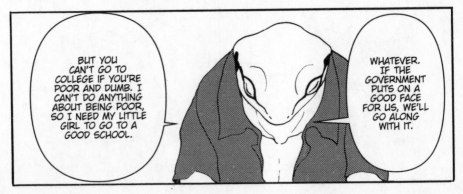

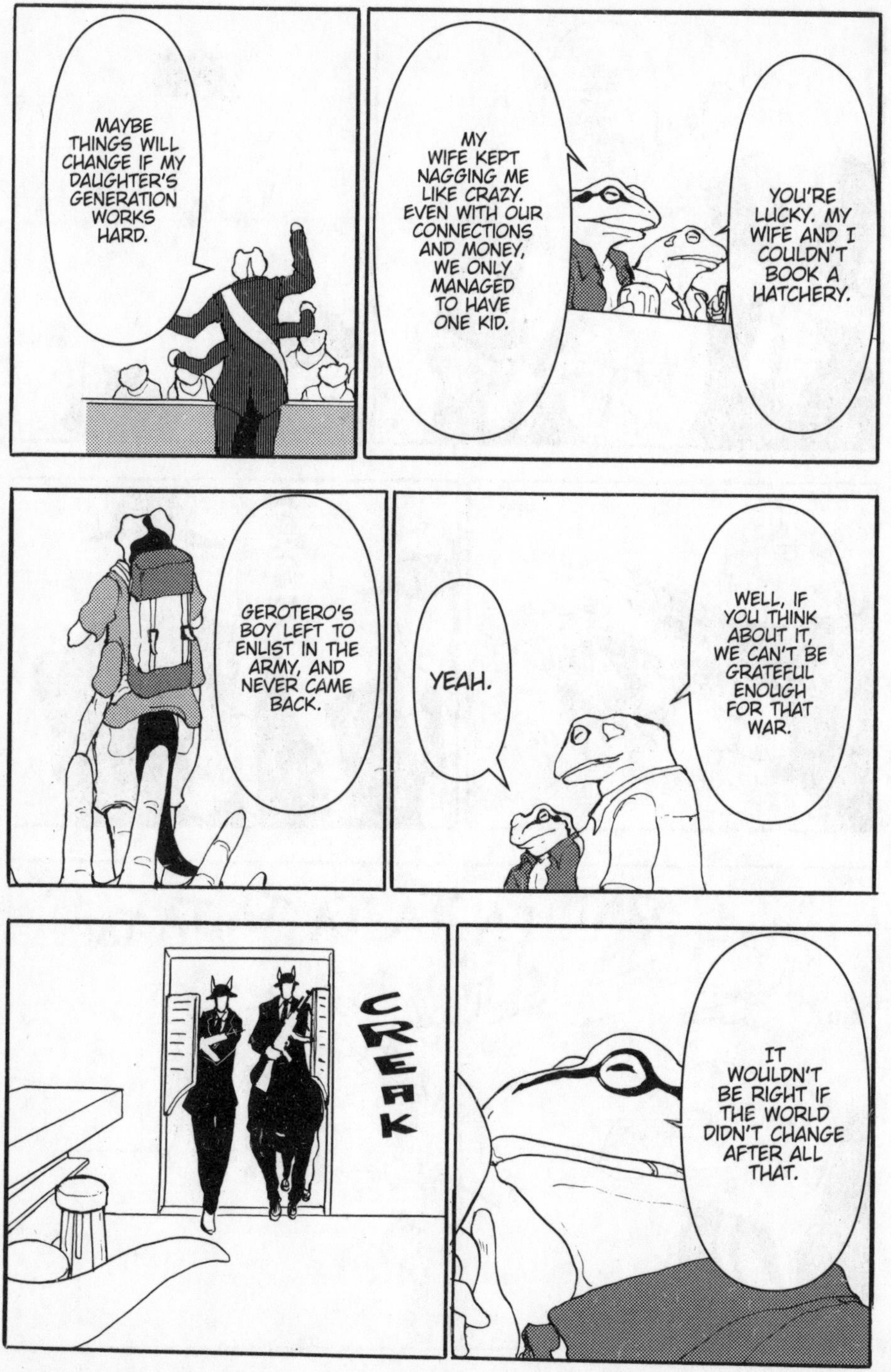
MY WIFE KEPT NAGGING ME LIKE CRAZY. EVEN WITH OUR CONNECTIONS AND MONEY, WE ONLY MANAGED TO HAVE ONE KID.
YOU'RE LUCKY. MY WIFE AND I COULDN'T BOOK A HATCHERY.
MAYBE THINGS WILL CHANGE IF MY DAUGHTER'S GENERATION WORKS HARD.
WELL, IF YOU THINK ABOUT IT, WE CAN'T BE GRATEFUL ENOUGH FOR THAT WAR.
YEAH.
GEROTERO'S BOY LEFT TO ENLIST IN THE ARMY, AND NEVER CAME BACK.
IT WOULDN'T BE RIGHT IF THE WORLD DIDN'T CHANGE AFTER ALL THAT.
CREAK

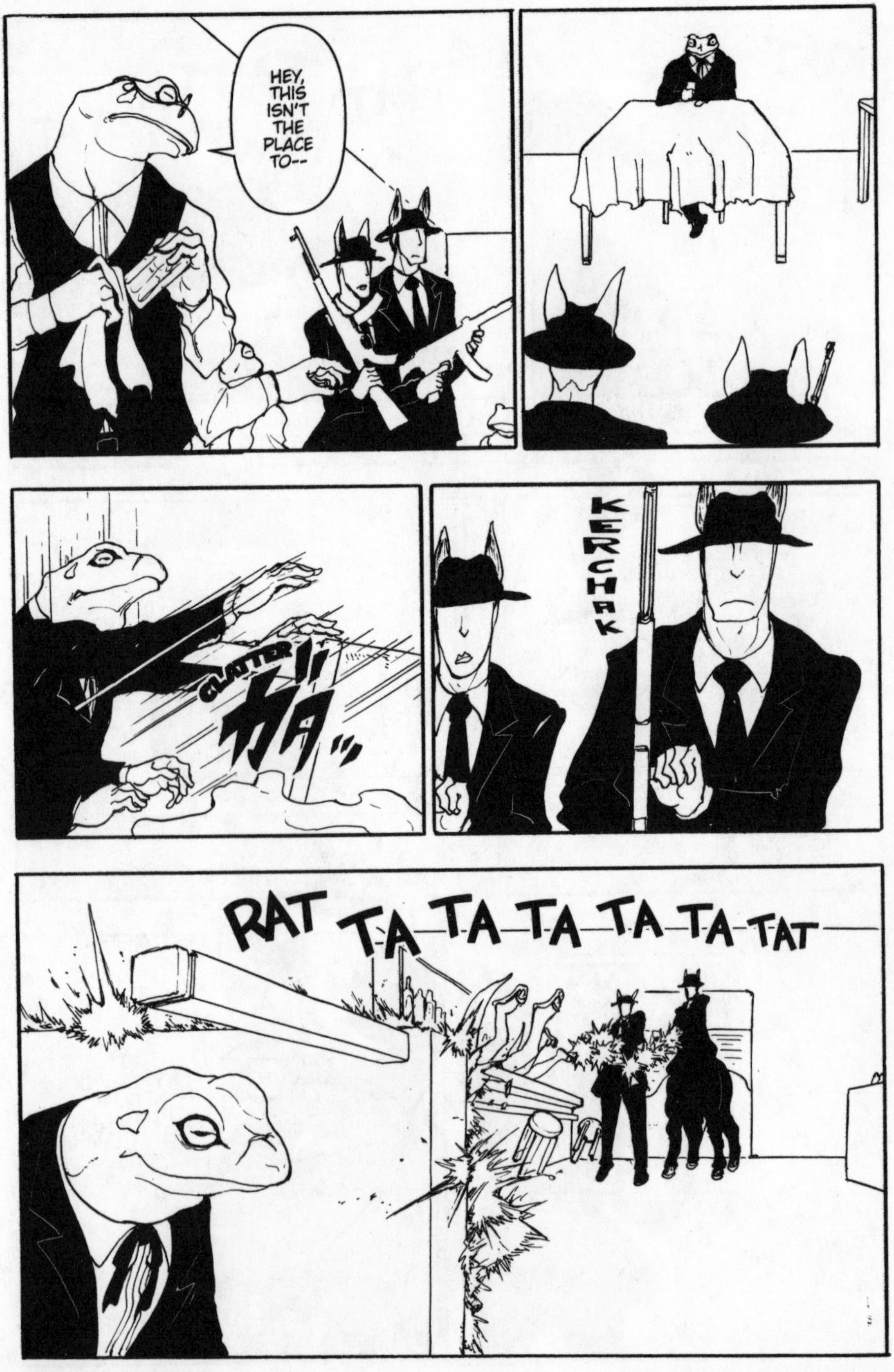
HEY, THIS ISN'T THE PLACE TO--
KERCHAK
CLATTER
カタッ
RAT TA TA TA TA TA TAT

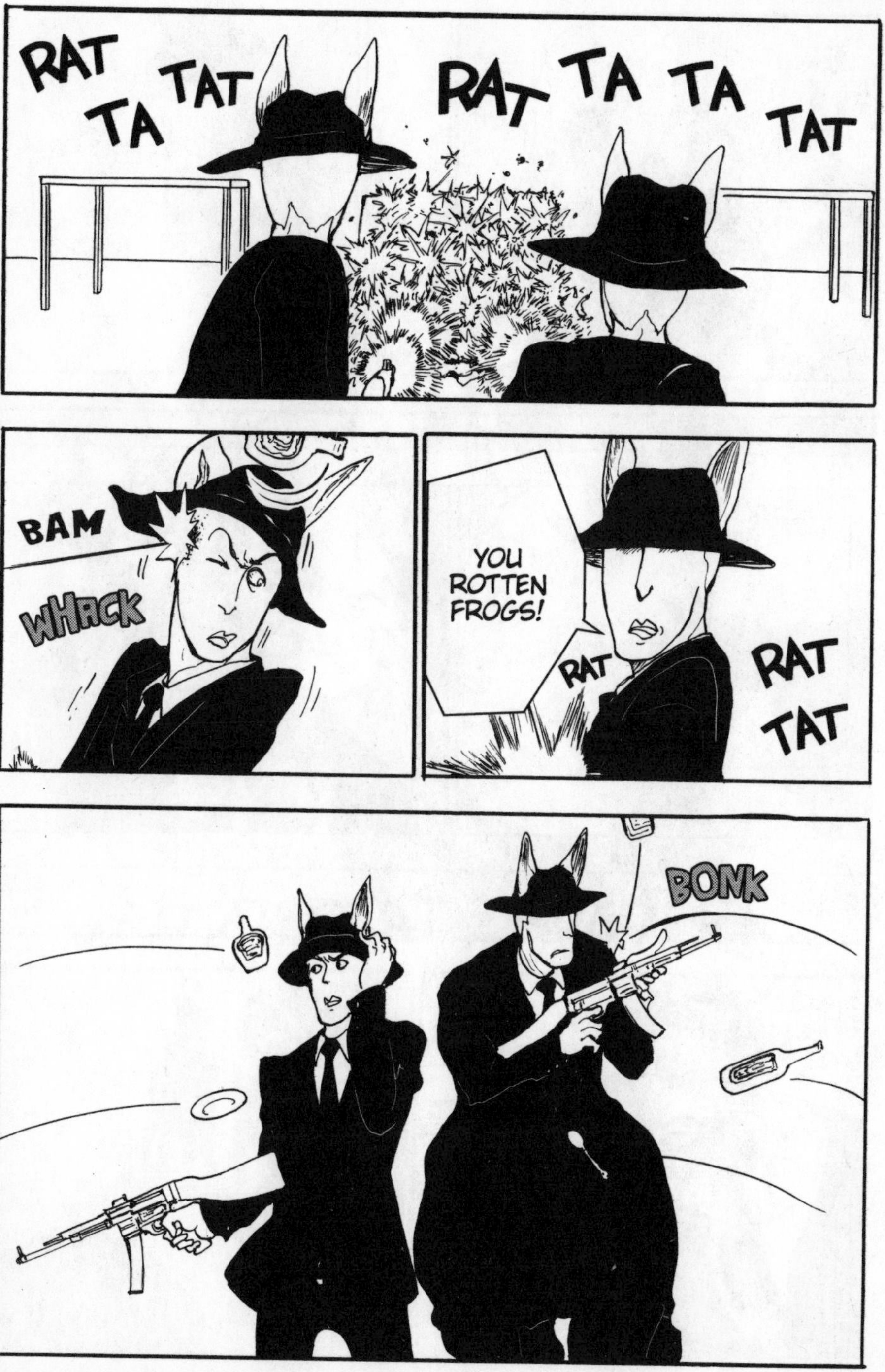
RAT TA TA TAT
RAT TA TAT
YOU ROTTEN FROGS!
RAT
RAT TAT
BAM
WHACK
BONK

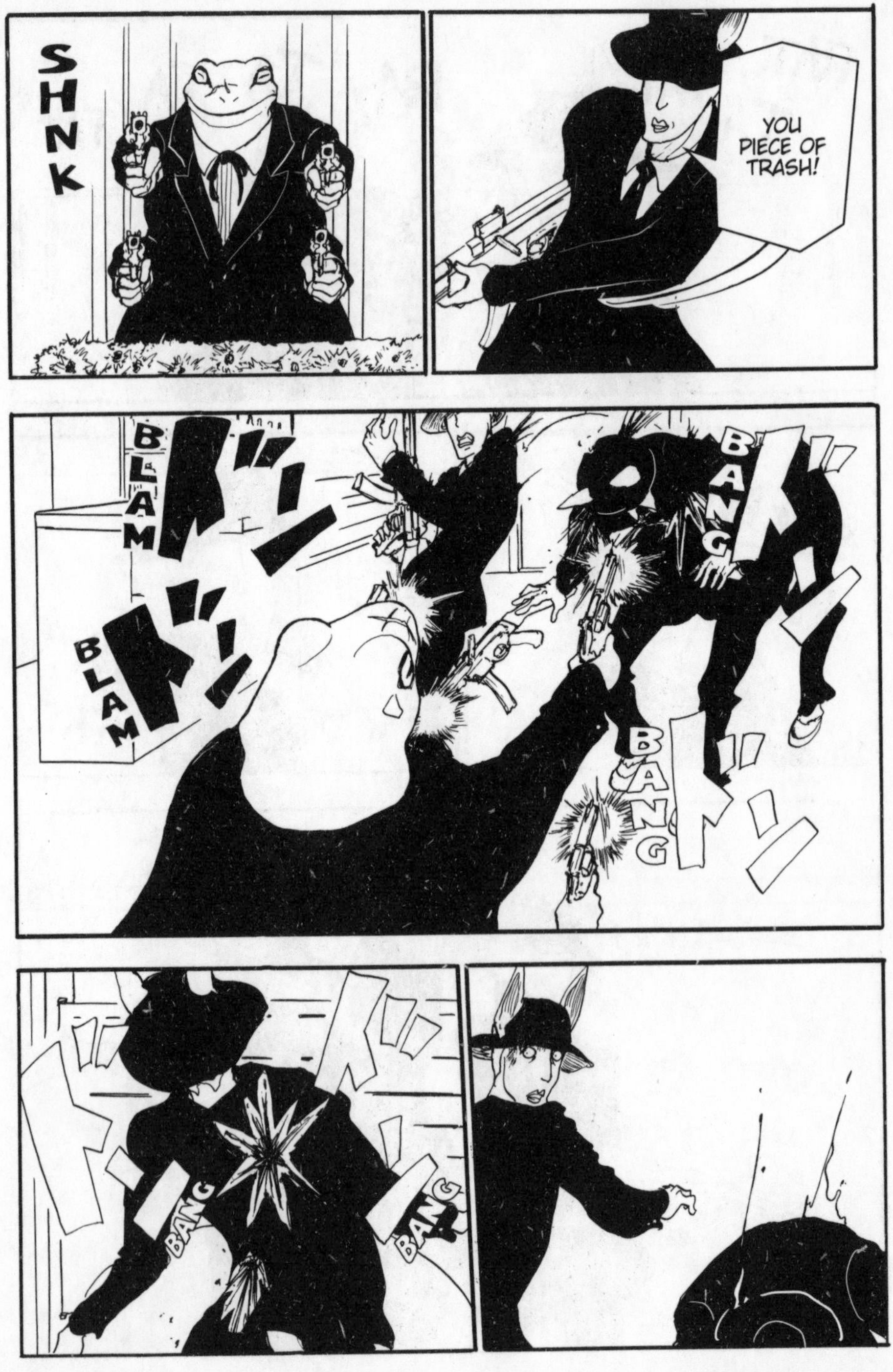
YOU PIECE OF TRASH!
SHNK
BANG
BANG
BLAM
BLAM
BANG
BANG

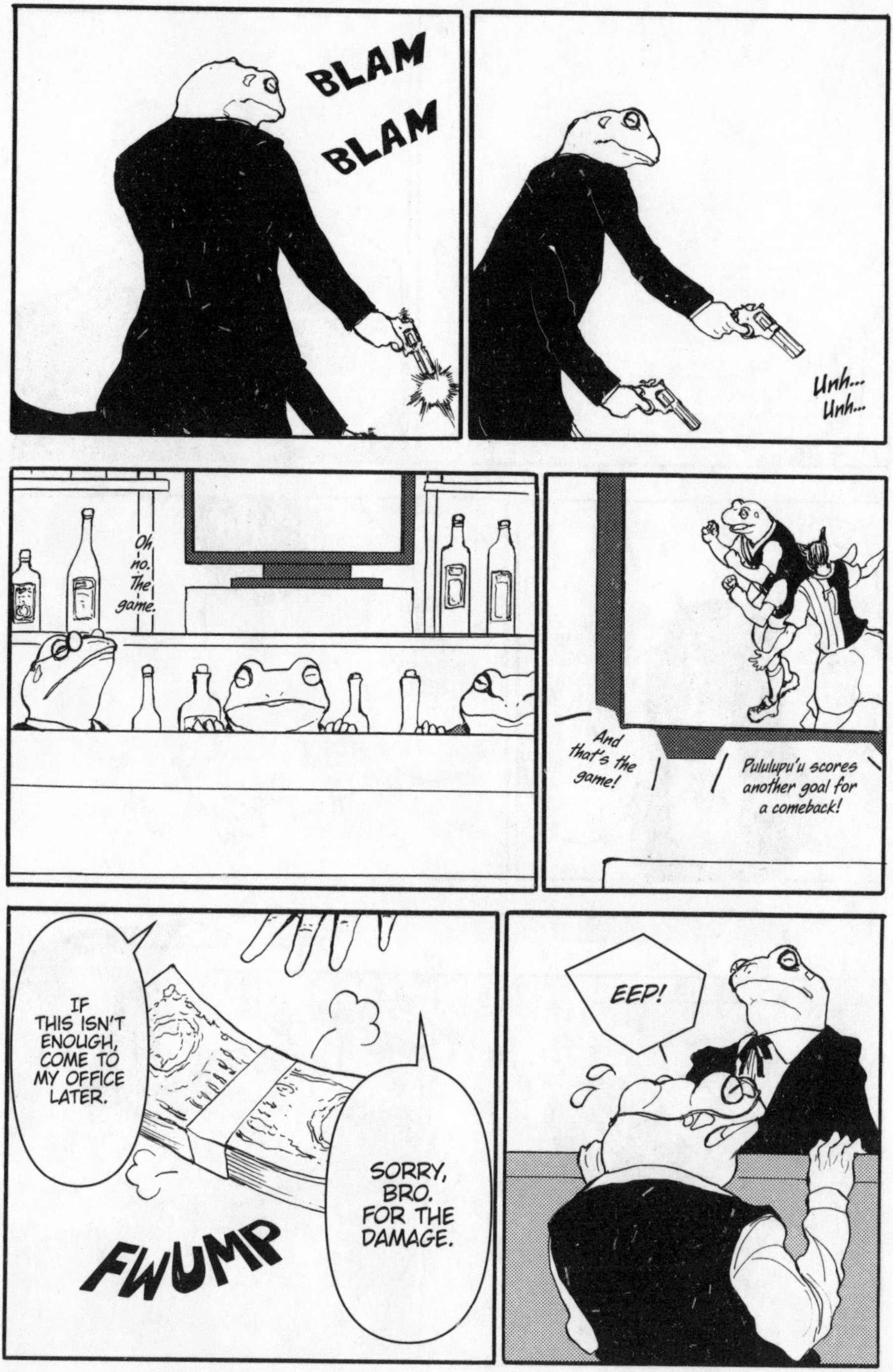

Unh... Unh...
BLAM
BLAM
Pululupu'u scores another goal for a comeback!
And that's the game!
Oh, no. The game.
EEP!
SORRY, BRO. FOR THE DAMAGE.
IF THIS ISN'T ENOUGH, COME TO MY OFFICE LATER.
FWUMP

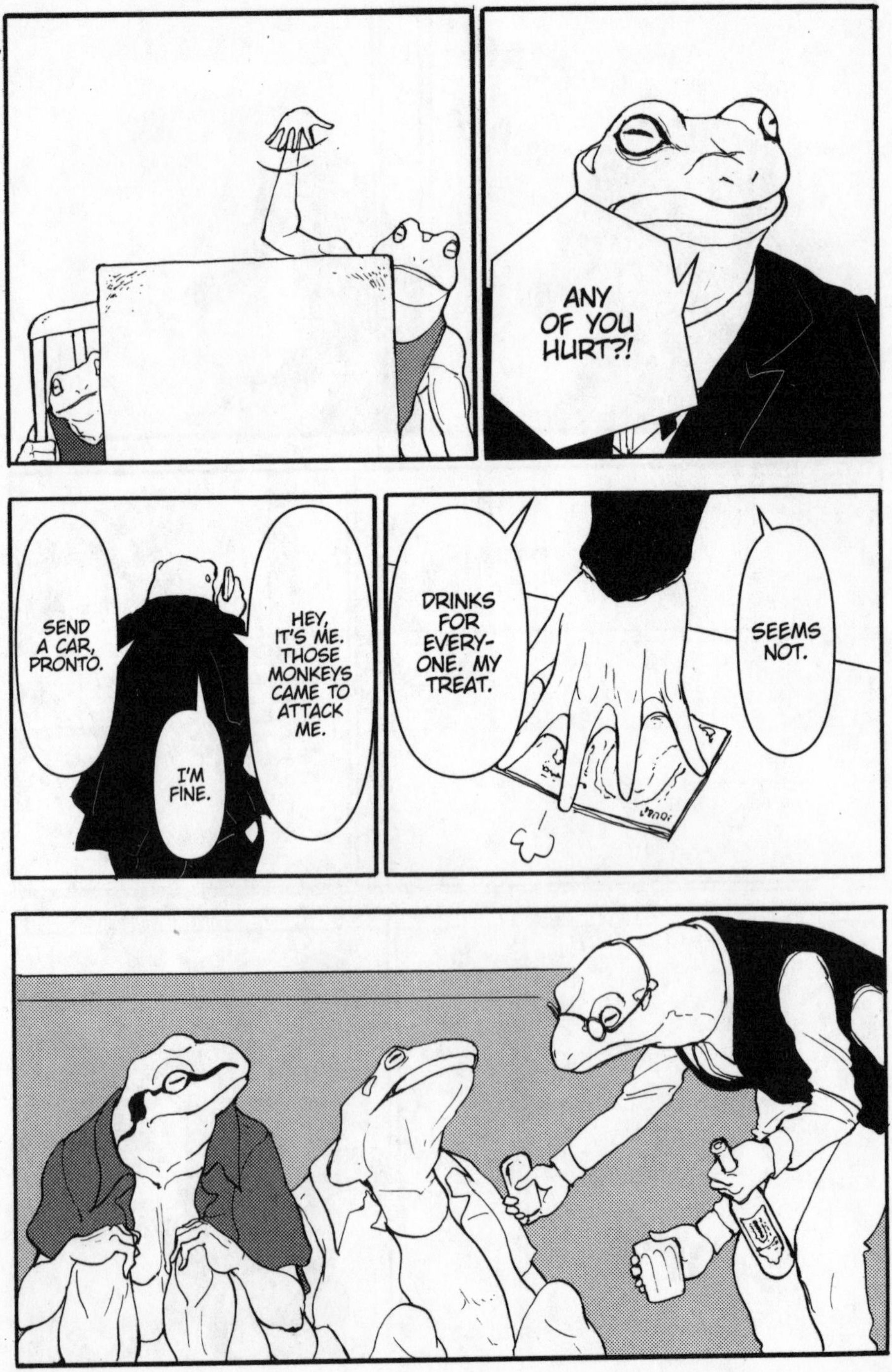

ANY OF YOU HURT?!
SEEMS NOT.
DRINKS FOR EVERY-ONE. MY TREAT.
HEY, IT'S ME. THOSE MONKEYS CAME TO ATTACK ME.
I'M FINE.
SEND A CAR, PRONTO.

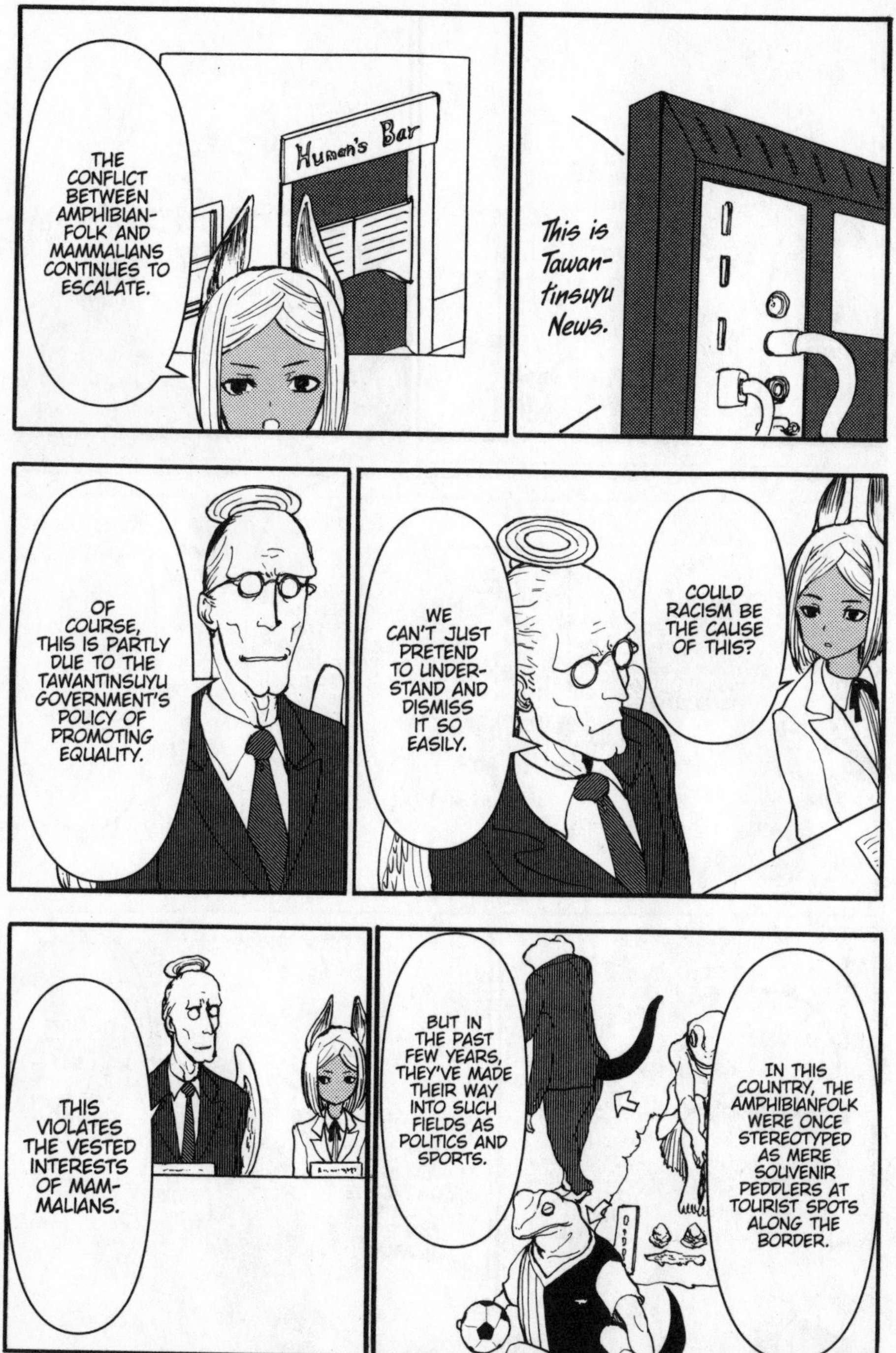
This is Tawantinsuyu News.
Human's Bar
THE CONFLICT BETWEEN AMPHIBIAN-FOLK AND MAMMALIANS CONTINUES TO ESCALATE.
COULD RACISM BE THE CAUSE OF THIS?
WE CAN'T JUST PRETEND TO UNDERSTAND AND DISMISS IT SO EASILY.
OF COURSE, THIS IS PARTLY DUE TO THE TAWANTINSUYU GOVERNMENT'S POLICY OF PROMOTING EQUALITY.
IN THIS COUNTRY, THE AMPHIBIANFOLK WERE ONCE STEREOTYPED AS MERE SOUVENIR PEDDLERS AT TOURIST SPOTS ALONG THE BORDER.
BUT IN THE PAST FEW YEARS, THEY'VE MADE THEIR WAY INTO SUCH FIELDS AS POLITICS AND SPORTS.
THIS VIOLATES THE VESTED INTERESTS OF MAMMALIANS.

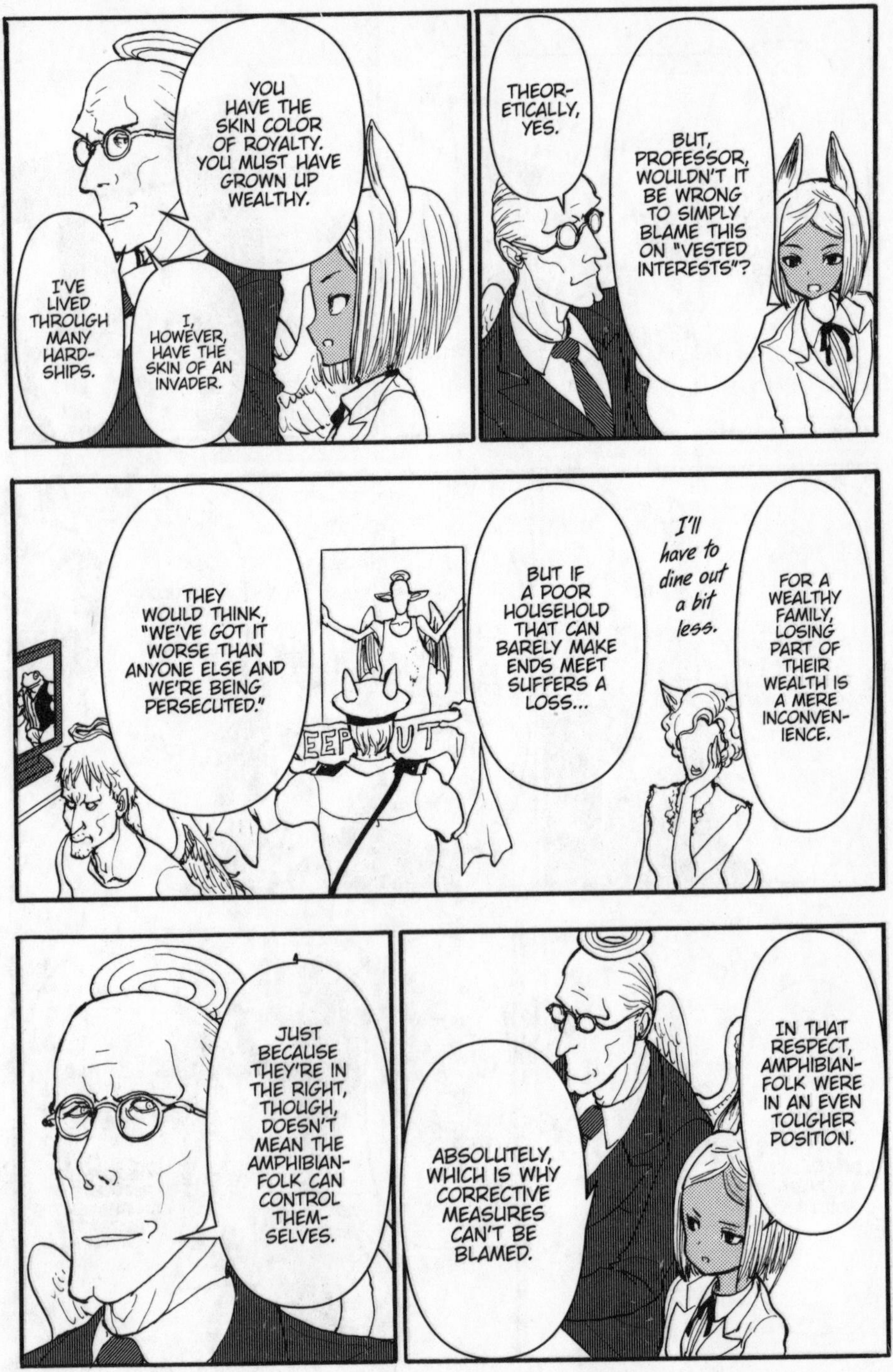
BUT, PROFESSOR, WOULDN'T IT BE WRONG TO SIMPLY BLAME THIS ON "VESTED INTERESTS"?
THEORETICALLY, YES.
YOU HAVE THE SKIN COLOR OF ROYALTY. YOU MUST HAVE GROWN UP WEALTHY.
I, HOWEVER, HAVE THE SKIN OF AN INVADER.
I'VE LIVED THROUGH MANY HARDSHIPS.
FOR A WEALTHY FAMILY, LOSING PART OF THEIR WEALTH IS A MERE INCONVENIENCE.
I'll have to dine out a bit less.
BUT IF A POOR HOUSEHOLD THAT CAN BARELY MAKE ENDS MEET SUFFERS A LOSS...
THEY WOULD THINK, "WE'VE GOT IT WORSE THAN ANYONE ELSE AND WE'RE BEING PERSECUTED."
IN THAT RESPECT, AMPHIBIAN-FOLK WERE IN AN EVEN TOUGHER POSITION.
ABSOLUTELY, WHICH IS WHY CORRECTIVE MEASURES CAN'T BE BLAMED.
JUST BECAUSE THEY'RE IN THE RIGHT, THOUGH, DOESN'T MEAN THE AMPHIBIAN-FOLK CAN CONTROL THEMSELVES.

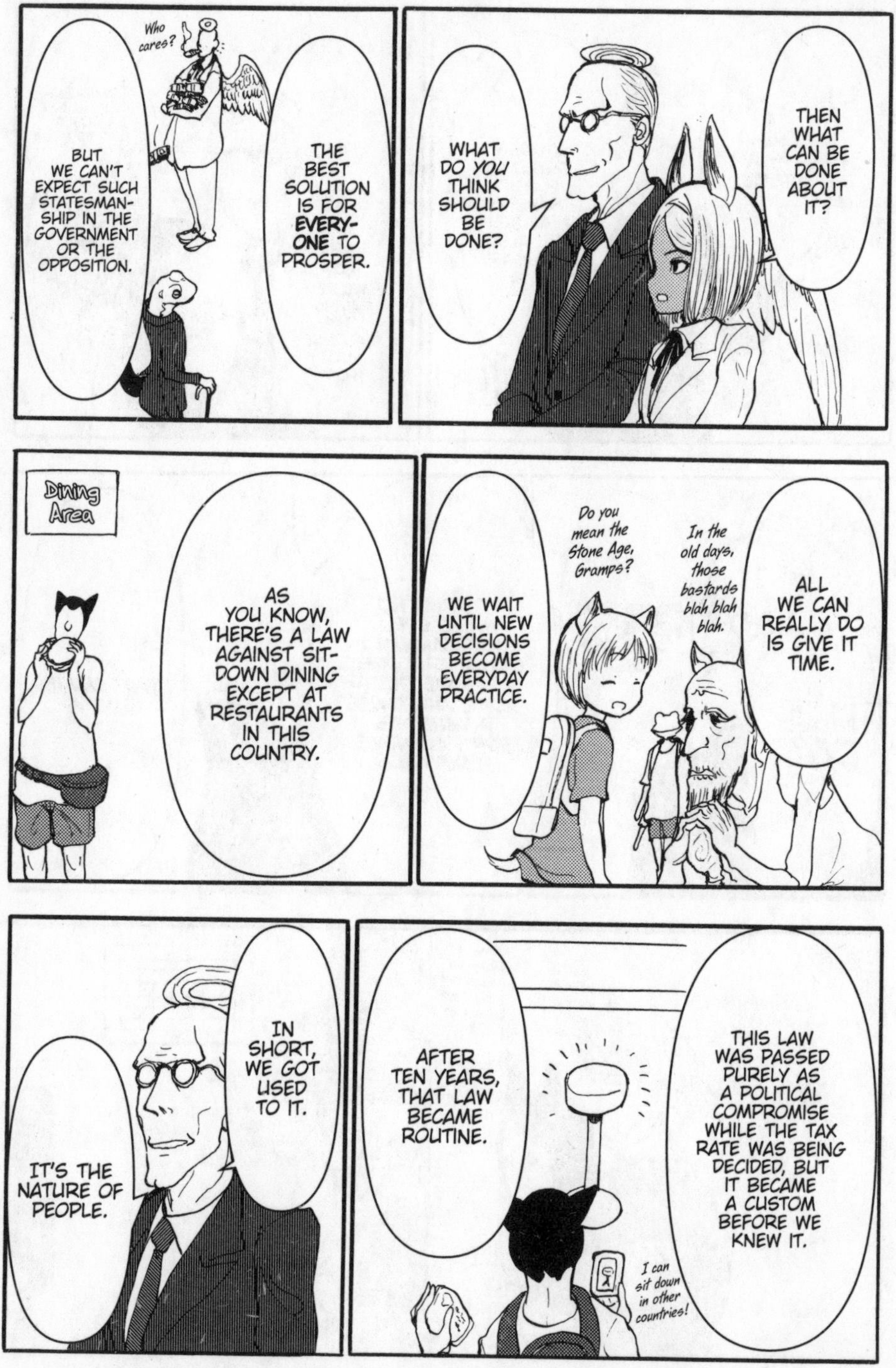
THEN WHAT CAN BE DONE ABOUT IT?
WHAT DO YOU THINK SHOULD BE DONE?
THE BEST SOLUTION IS FOR EVERYONE TO PROSPER.
Who cares?
BUT WE CAN'T EXPECT SUCH STATESMANSHIP IN THE GOVERNMENT OR THE OPPOSITION.
ALL WE CAN REALLY DO IS GIVE IT TIME.
In the old days, those bastards blah blah blah.
Do you mean the Stone Age, Gramps?
WE WAIT UNTIL NEW DECISIONS BECOME EVERYDAY PRACTICE.
Dining Area
AS YOU KNOW, THERE'S A LAW AGAINST SIT-DOWN DINING EXCEPT AT RESTAURANTS IN THIS COUNTRY.
THIS LAW WAS PASSED PURELY AS A POLITICAL COMPROMISE WHILE THE TAX RATE WAS BEING DECIDED, BUT IT BECAME A CUSTOM BEFORE WE KNEW IT.
AFTER TEN YEARS, THAT LAW BECAME ROUTINE.
I can sit down in other countries!
IN SHORT, WE GOT USED TO IT.
IT'S THE NATURE OF PEOPLE.

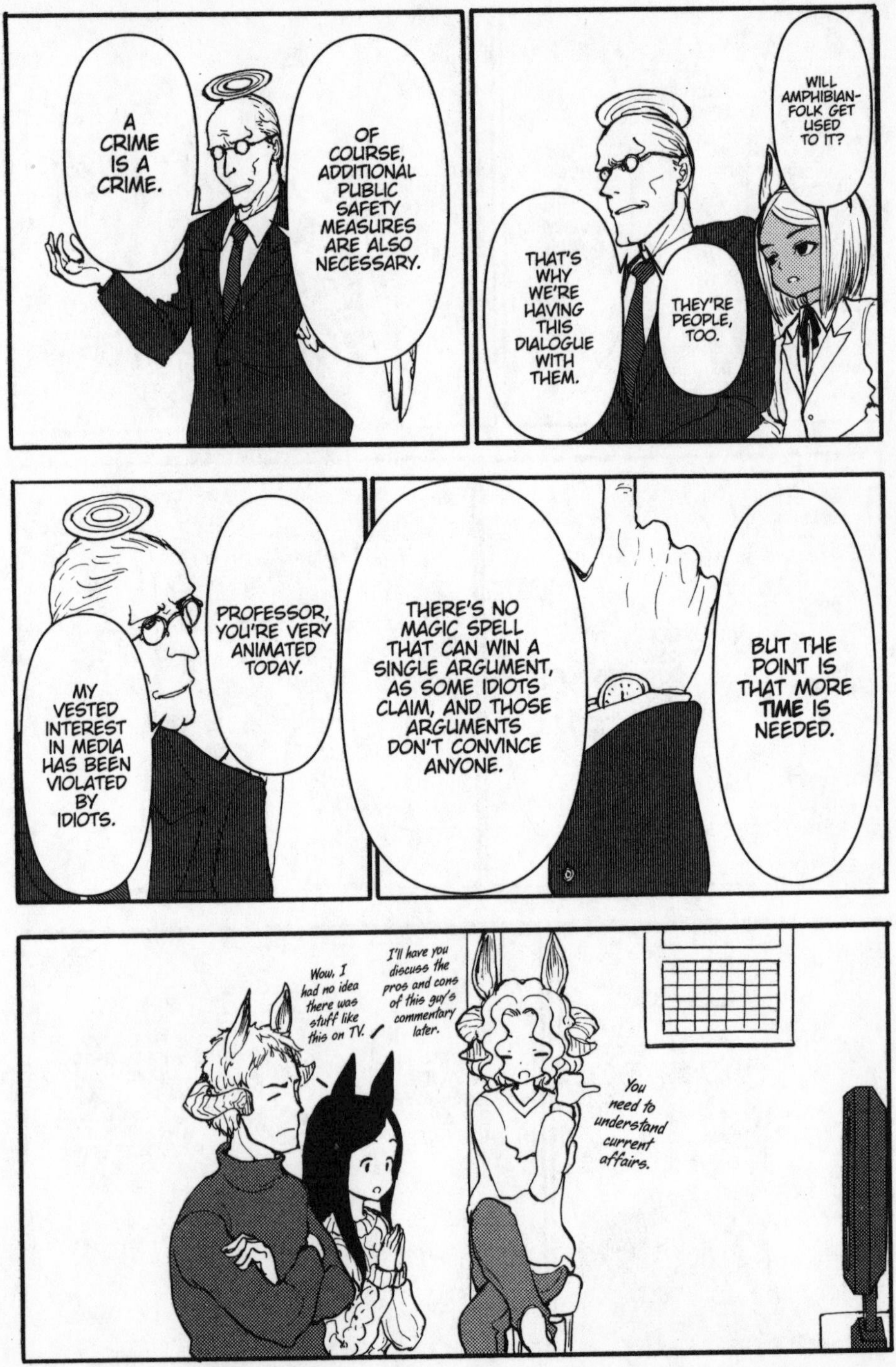
WILL AMPHIBIAN-FOLK GET USED TO IT?
THEY'RE PEOPLE, TOO.
THAT'S WHY WE'RE HAVING THIS DIALOGUE WITH THEM.
OF COURSE, ADDITIONAL PUBLIC SAFETY MEASURES ARE ALSO NECESSARY.
A CRIME IS A CRIME.
BUT THE POINT IS THAT MORE TIME IS NEEDED.
THERE'S NO MAGIC SPELL THAT CAN WIN A SINGLE ARGUMENT, AS SOME IDIOTS CLAIM, AND THOSE ARGUMENTS DON'T CONVINCE ANYONE.
PROFESSOR, YOU'RE VERY ANIMATED TODAY.
MY VESTED INTEREST IN MEDIA HAS BEEN VIOLATED BY IDIOTS.
You need to understand current affairs.
I'll have you discuss the pros and cons of this guy's commentary later.
Wow, I had no idea there was stuff like this on TV.

A Centaur's Life

RELEARNING THE ORIGIN OF MAMMALIAN HUMANS
2. EVOLUTION IS NOT LINEAR

CURRENT TEXTBOOKS GIVE THE IMPRESSION THAT EVOLUTION HAS PROCEEDED IN A STRAIGHT LINE FROM PRIMATES (*AUSTRALOPITHECUS*) TO ARCHAIC HUMANS (*HOMO ERECTUS*), AND THEN TO MODERN HUMANS (*HOMO SAPIENS*) AS THEIR BRAIN SIZES INCREASED AND THEIR BODIES DEVELOPED FROM PRIMATES TO MODERN HUMANS. HOWEVER, THAT DOESN'T APPEAR TO BE TRUE.

THE *HOMO NALEDI* FOSSILS FOUND IN A CAVE IN SOUTH AFRICA IN 2008 SERVE AS AN EXAMPLE. LIKE *AUSTRALOPITHECUS*, THE HUNCHED SHOULDERS AND CURVED UPPER EXTREMITIES IN *HOMO NALEDI*'S UPPER BODY DEMONSTRATED ITS ADAPTATION TO AN ARBOREAL LIFESTYLE. CONVERSELY, ITS LOWER EXTREMITIES WERE LONG AND SLENDER, WITH ARCHED FEET RESEMBLING THE BIPEDAL FORM OF A MODERN HUMAN TO ACCOMMODATE WALKING ON THE GROUND. FURTHERMORE, ITS MIDDLE LIMBS WERE SHORT AND SHOWED SIGNS OF DEGENERATION, AND ITS OVERALL PHYSICAL PROPORTIONS RESEMBLED THAT OF A BIPEDAL MODERN HUMAN. THE DEVELOPMENT OF ITS TEETH AND LOWER JAW BORE AN EVEN CLOSER RESEMBLANCE TO MODERN HUMANS. HOWEVER, ITS BRAIN WAS HALF THE SIZE OF THAT OF *HOMO ERECTUS*, WHICH CHARACTERIZED IT AS A HOMINID OR PRIMATE. THIS MEANS THAT *HOMO NALEDI* HAD A MIX OF PRIMITIVE AND MODERN CHARACTERISTICS.

THE PERIOD IN WHICH *HOMO NALEDI* EXISTED IS STILL UNCERTAIN. THERE IS ALSO THE QUESTION OF WHETHER IT SHOULD BE CLASSIFIED AS A PRIMATE WITH BIPEDALISM WITH A SMALLER BRAIN SIZE AND PRIMITIVE CHARACTERISTICS, OR AS A MODERN SPECIES DUE TO ITS UNIQUE EVOLUTION. IN ANY CASE, THE EVOLUTION OF MAMMALIAN HUMANS DOES NOT APPEAR TO HAVE FOLLOWED A SINGLE LINEAR PATTERN.

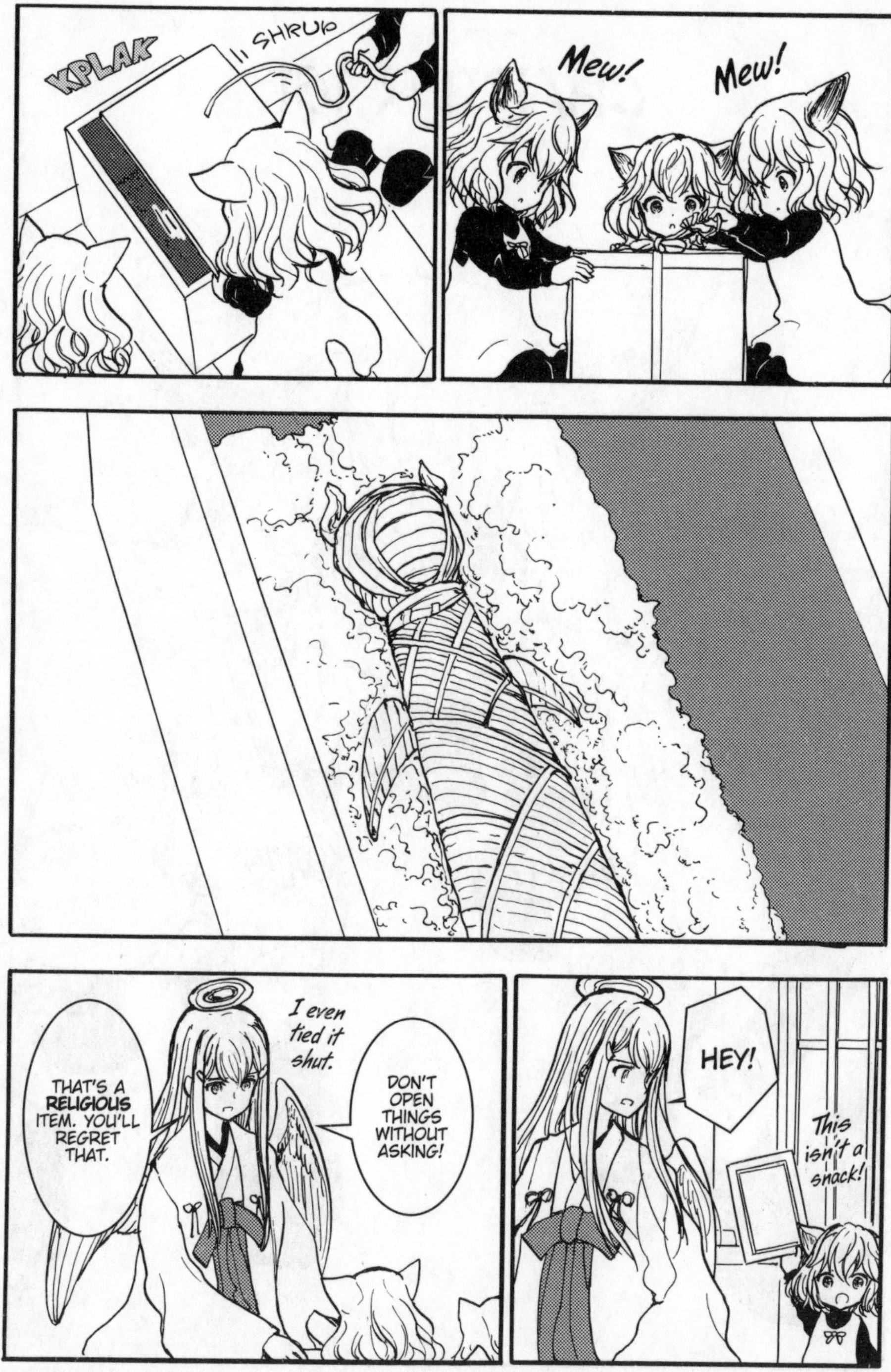

Mew!
Mew!
SHRUP
KPLAK
HEY!
This isn't a snack!
I even tied it shut.
DON'T OPEN THINGS WITHOUT ASKING!
THAT'S A **RELIGIOUS** ITEM. YOU'LL REGRET THAT.

CHAPTER 161

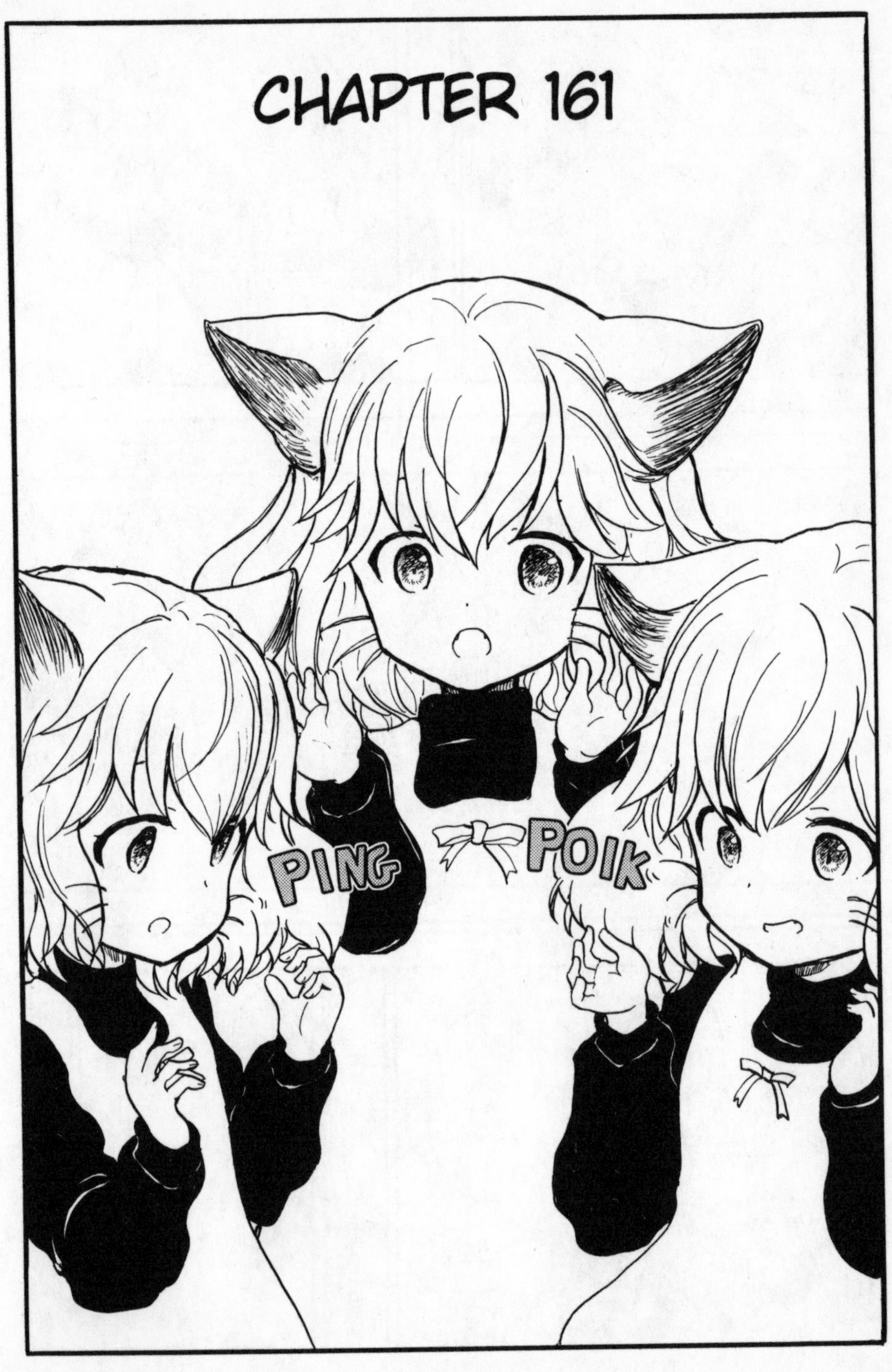
POIK
PING

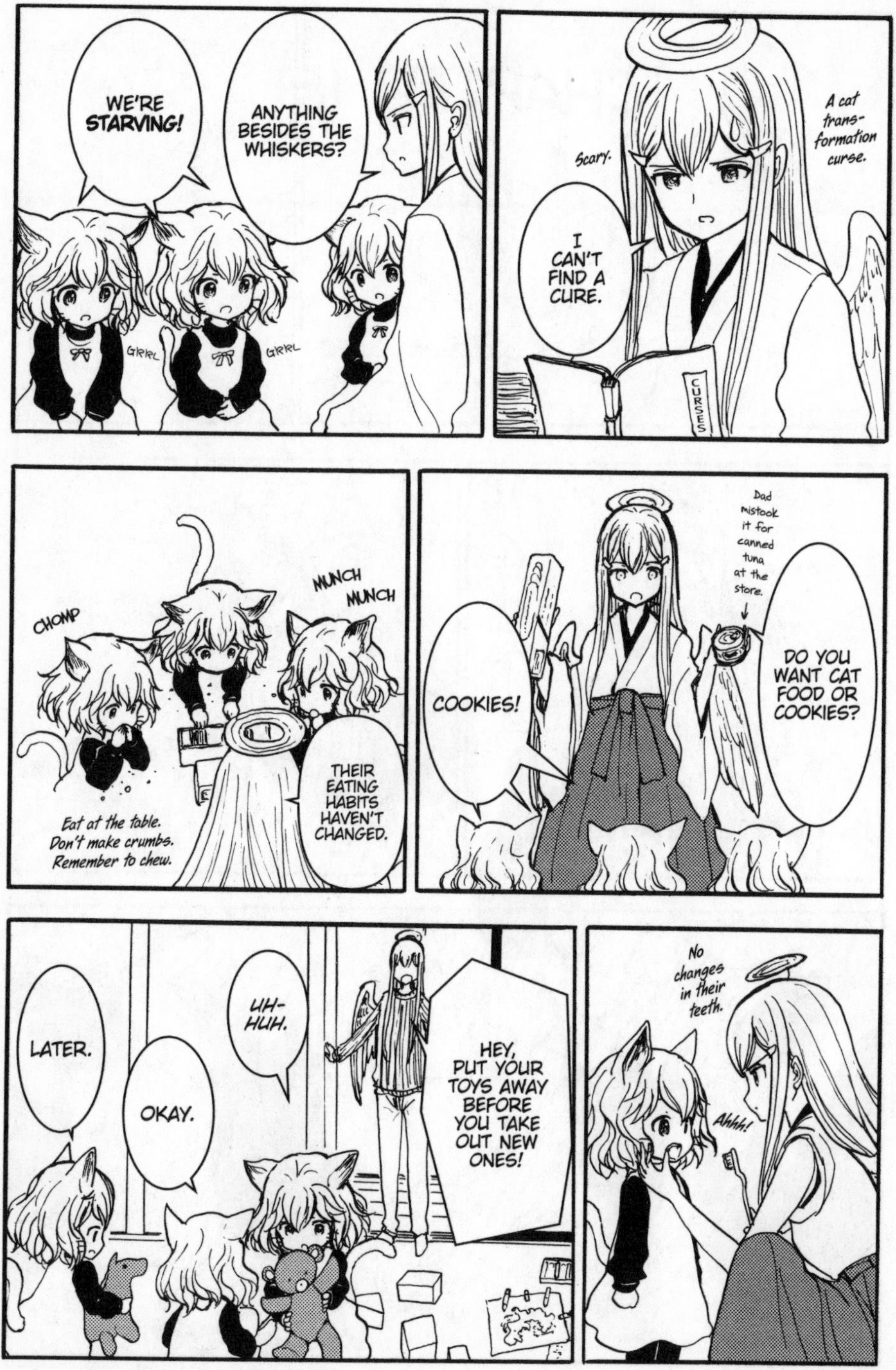
A cat transformation curse.
Scary.
I CAN'T FIND A CURE.
CURSES
ANYTHING BESIDES THE WHISKERS?
WE'RE STARVING!
GRRL
GRRL
Dad mistook it for canned tuna at the store.
DO YOU WANT CAT FOOD OR COOKIES?
COOKIES!
MUNCH
MUNCH
THEIR EATING HABITS HAVEN'T CHANGED.
CHOMP
Eat at the table. Don't make crumbs. Remember to chew.
No changes in their teeth.
Ahhh!
HEY, PUT YOUR TOYS AWAY BEFORE YOU TAKE OUT NEW ONES!
UH-HUH.
OKAY.
LATER.

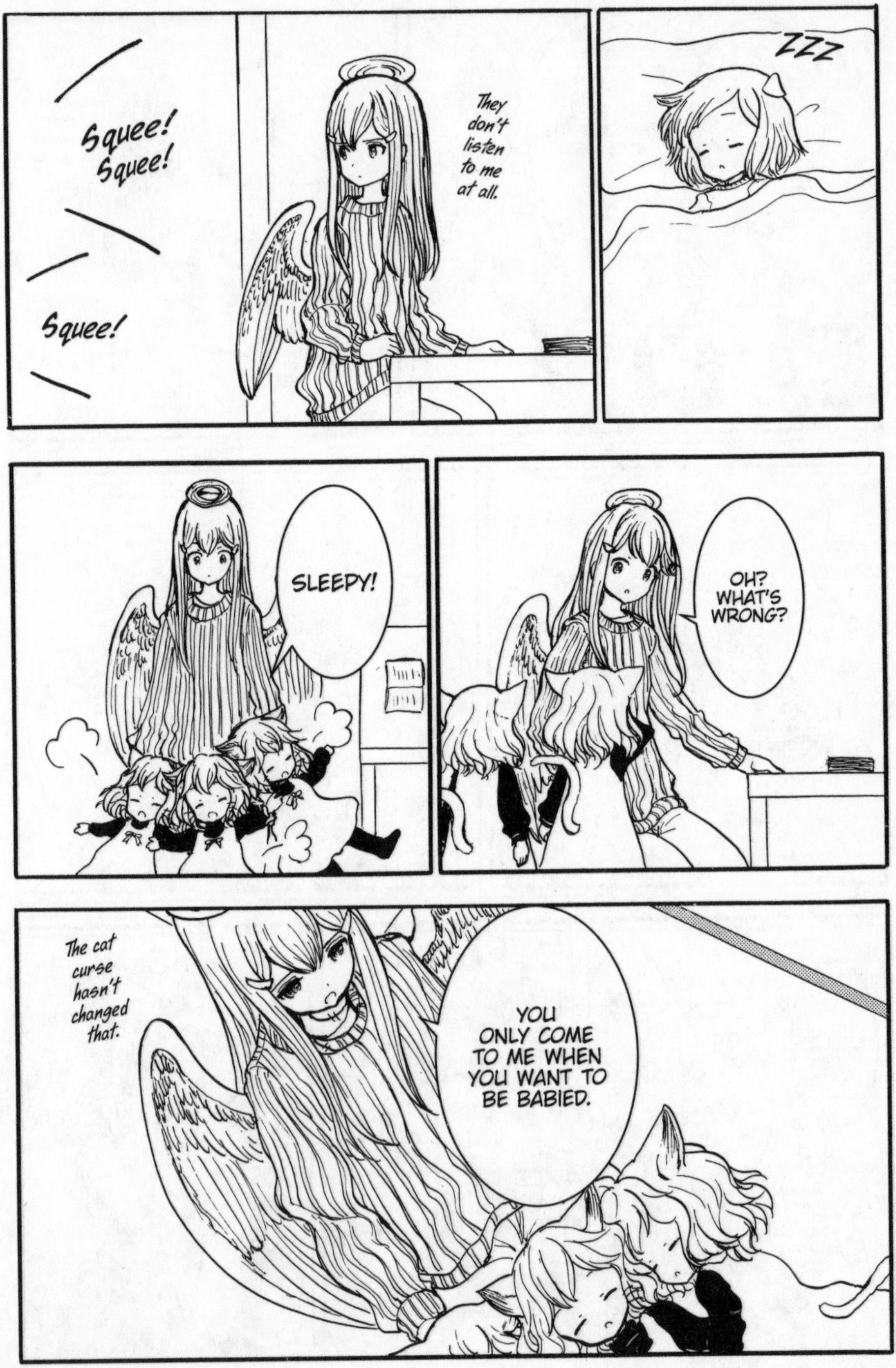
ZZZ
They don't listen to me at all.
Squee! Squee!
Squee!
OH? WHAT'S WRONG?
SLEEPY!
YOU ONLY COME TO ME WHEN YOU WANT TO BE BABIED.
The cat curse hasn't changed that.

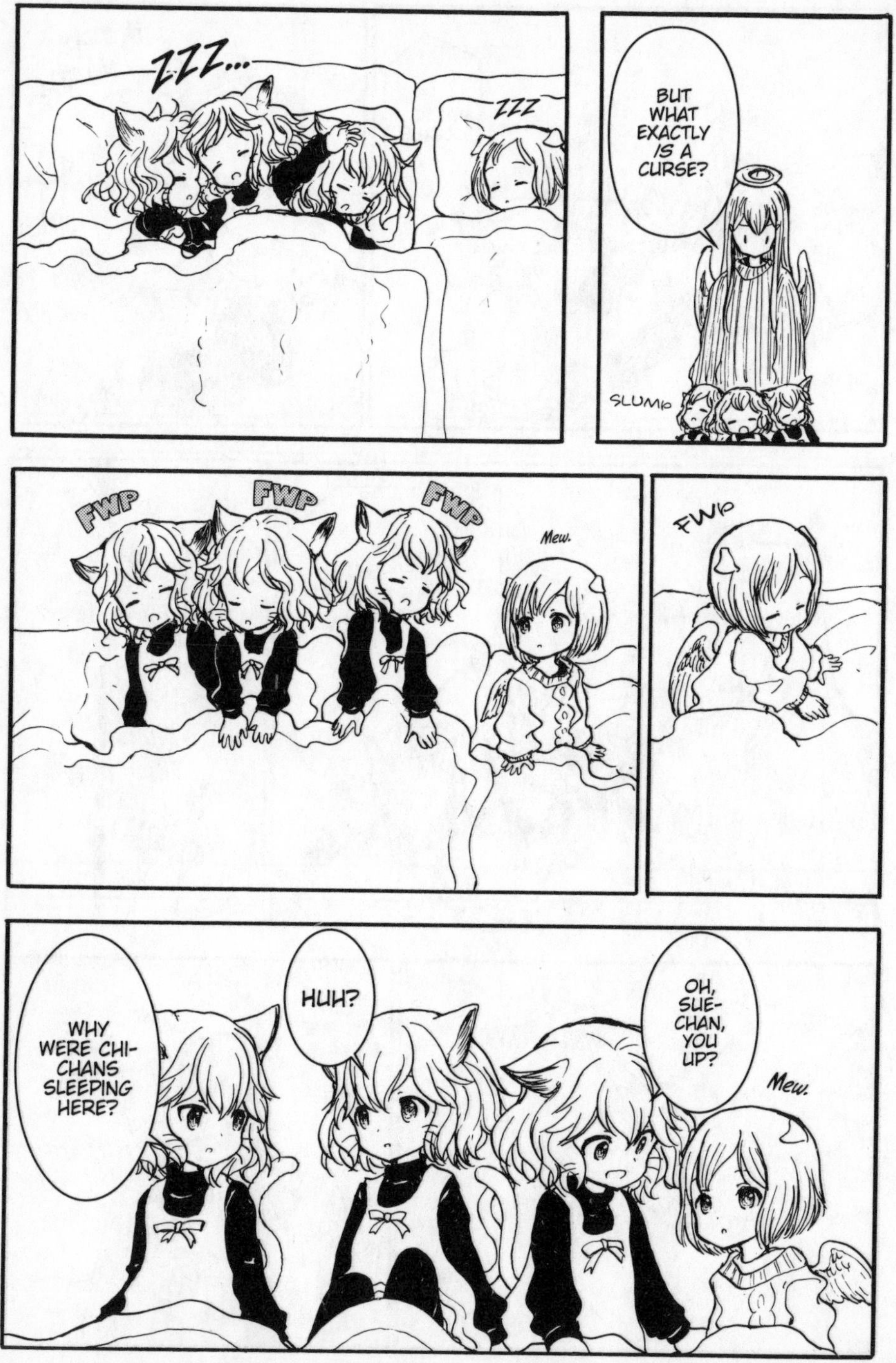
BUT WHAT EXACTLY IS A CURSE?
SLUMP
ZZZ...
ZZZ
FWP
FWP
FWP
FWP
Mew.
OH, SUE-CHAN, YOU UP?
Mew.
HUH?
WHY WERE CHI-CHANS SLEEPING HERE?

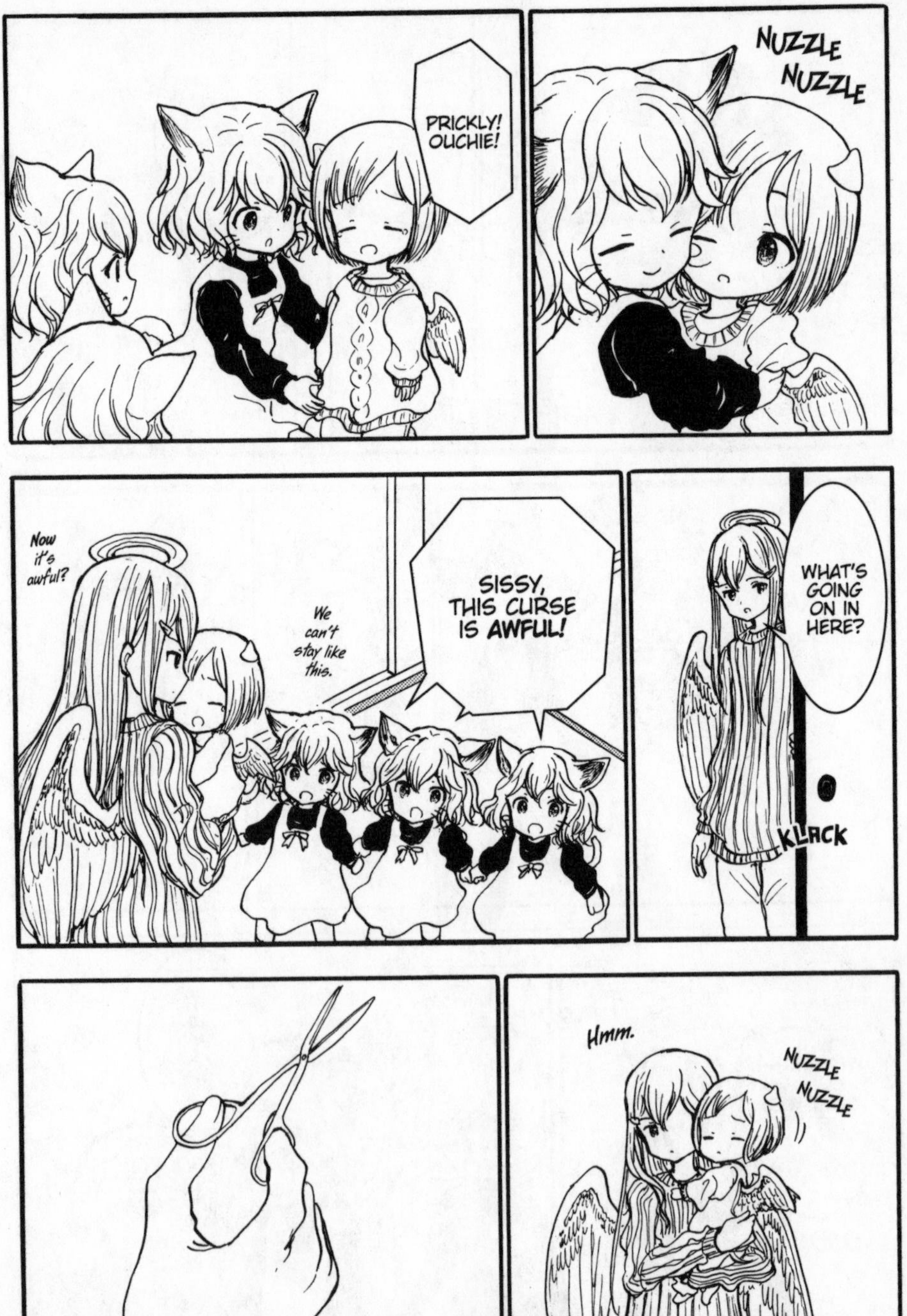
NUZZLE NUZZLE
PRICKLY! OUCHIE!
WHAT'S GOING ON IN HERE?
KLACK
SISSY, THIS CURSE IS AWFUL!
We can't stay like this.
Now it's awful?
NUZZLE NUZZLE
Hmm.

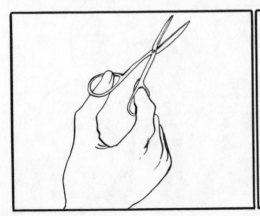

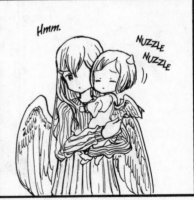

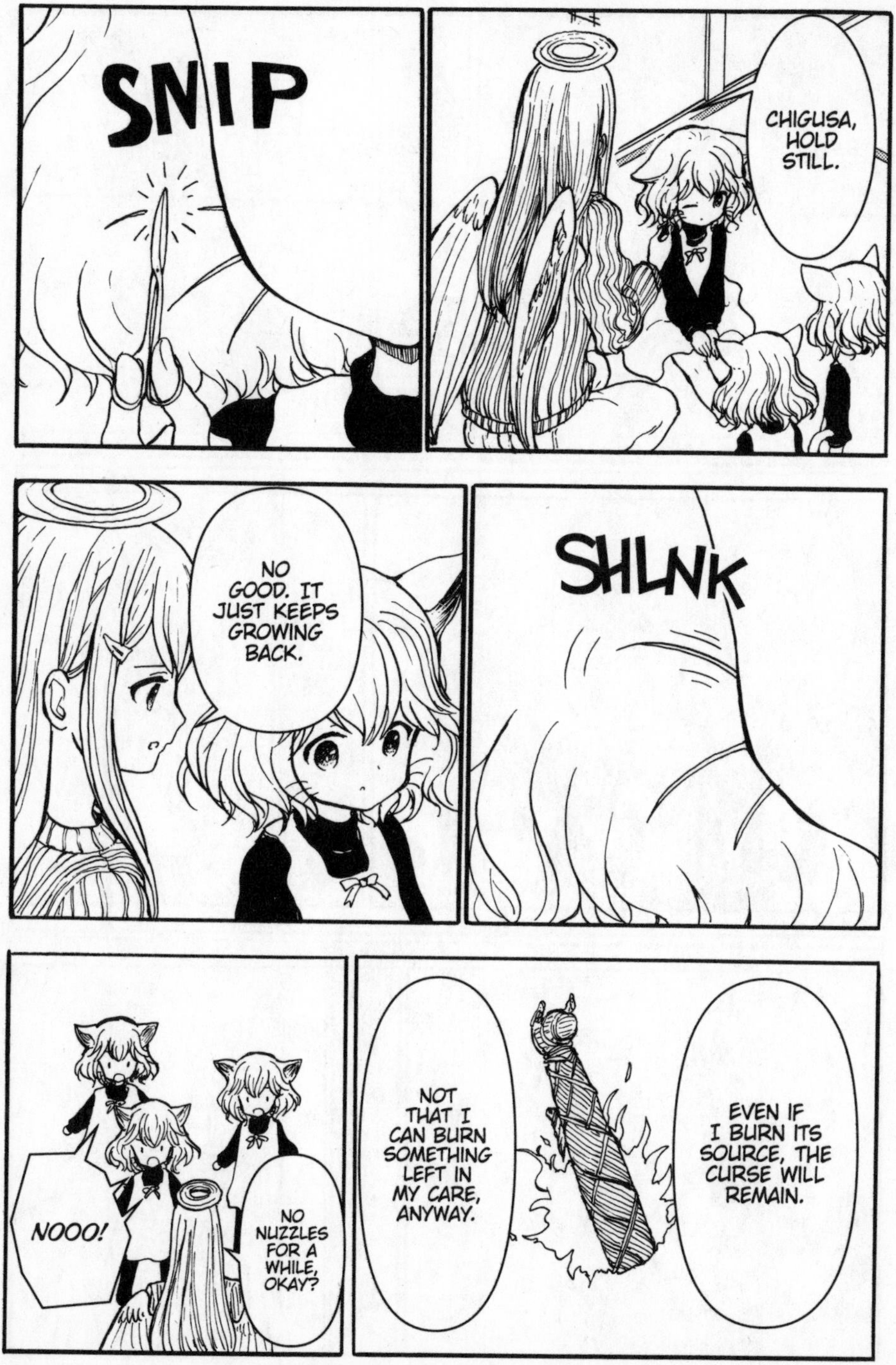
CHIGUSA, HOLD STILL.
SNIP
SHLNK
NO GOOD. IT JUST KEEPS GROWING BACK.
EVEN IF I BURN ITS SOURCE, THE CURSE WILL REMAIN.
NOT THAT I CAN BURN SOMETHING LEFT IN MY CARE, ANYWAY.
NO NUZZLES FOR A WHILE, OKAY?
NOOO!

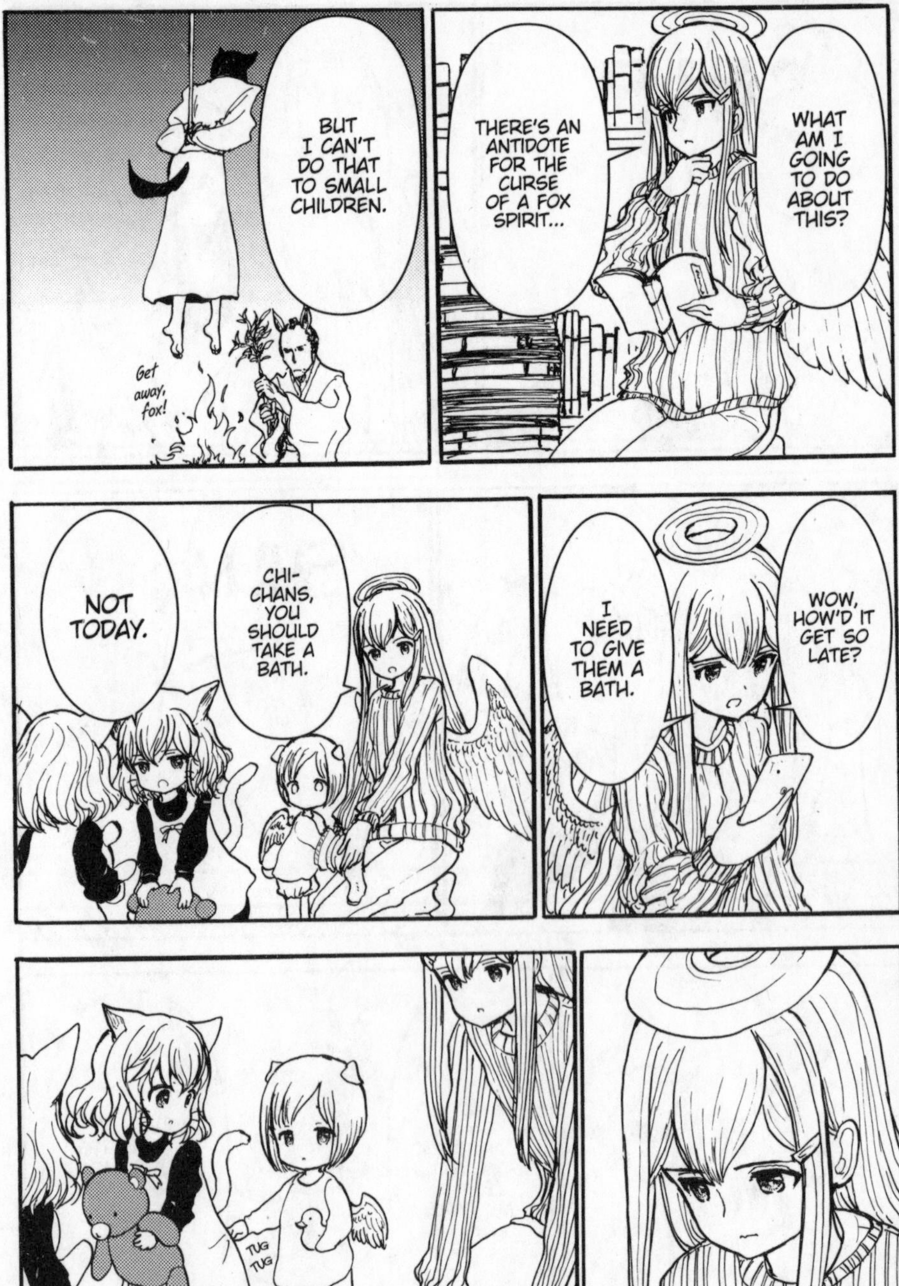
WHAT AM I GOING TO DO ABOUT THIS?
THERE'S AN ANTIDOTE FOR THE CURSE OF A FOX SPIRIT...
BUT I CAN'T DO THAT TO SMALL CHILDREN.
Get away, fox!
WOW, HOW'D IT GET SO LATE?
I NEED TO GIVE THEM A BATH.
CHI-CHANS, YOU SHOULD TAKE A BATH.
NOT TODAY.
TUG TUG

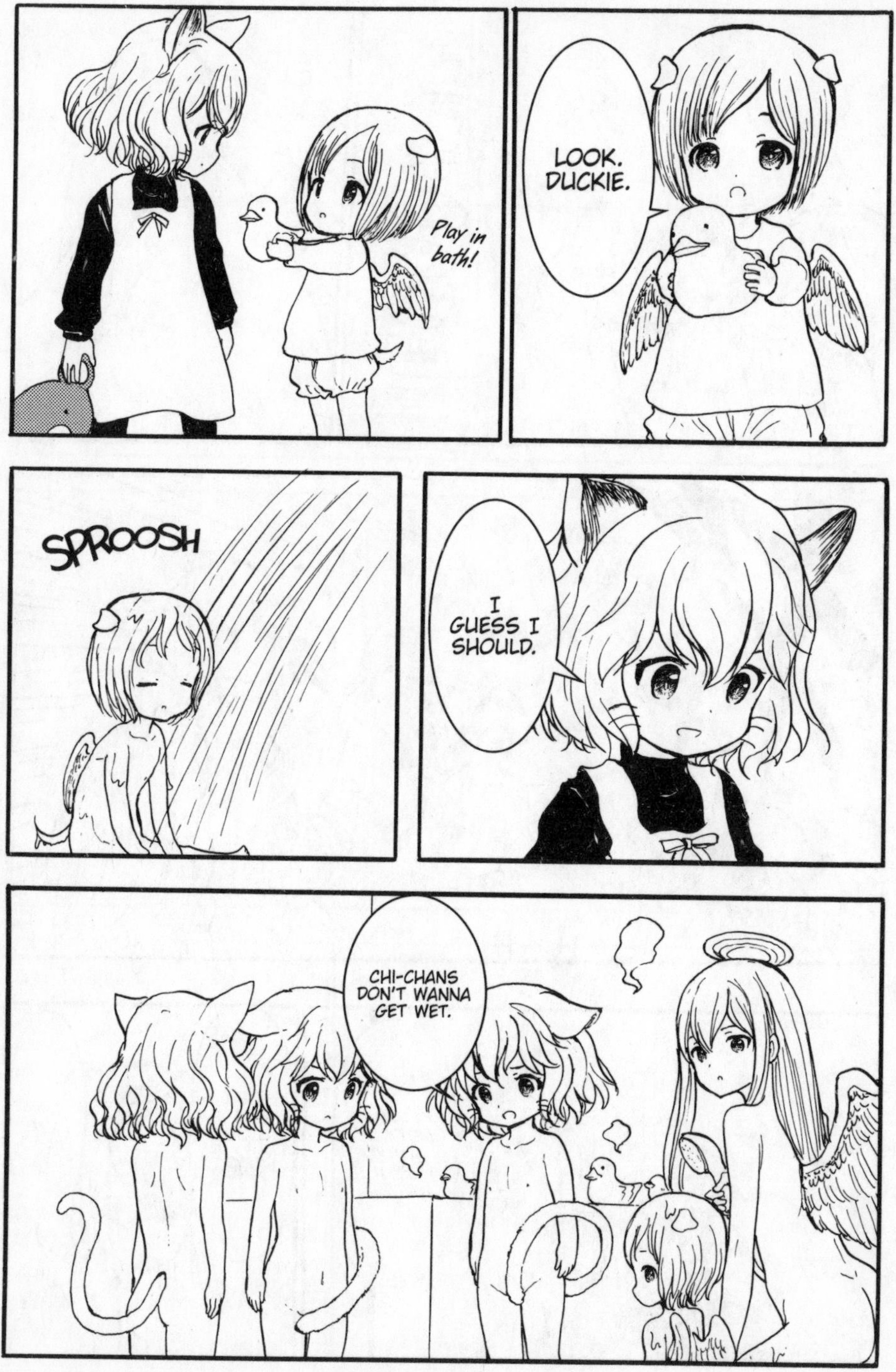
LOOK. DUCKIE.
Play in bath!
I GUESS I SHOULD.
SPROOSH
CHI-CHANS DON'T WANNA GET WET.

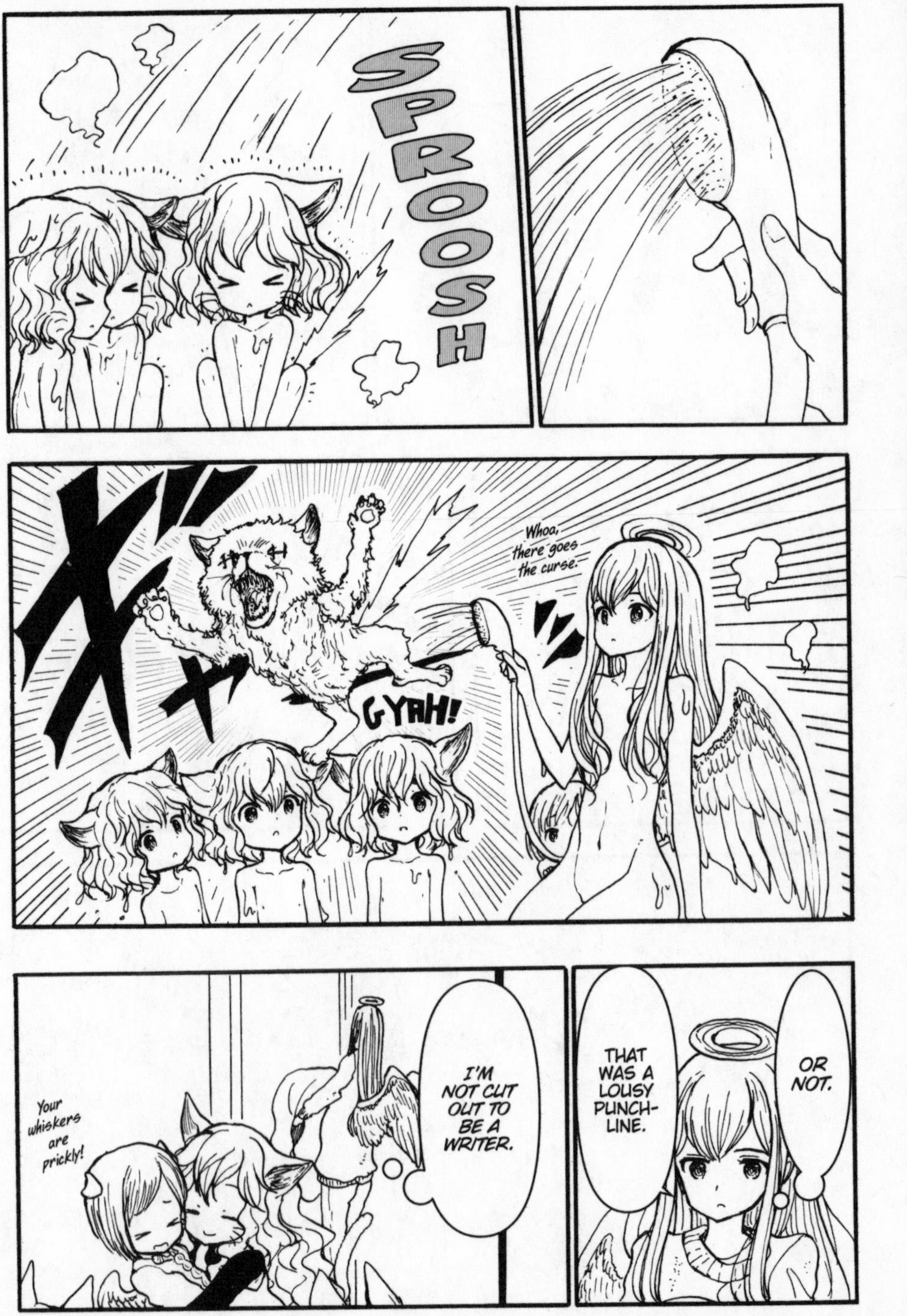
SPROOSH
GYAH!
Whoa, there goes the curse.
OR NOT.
THAT WAS A LOUSY PUNCHLINE.
I'M NOT CUT OUT TO BE A WRITER.
Your whiskers are prickly!

A Centaur's Life

RELEARNING THE ORIGIN OF MAMMALIAN HUMANS
3. RETHINKING THE ORIGINS OF FULLY BIPEDAL
AND FULLY QUADRUPEDAL ANIMALS

THE DISCOVERY OF *HOMO NALEDI* URGED RETHINKING OF
THE EVOLUTION OF THE FUNCTIONALITY OF SIX LIMBS.

THE MIDDLE LIMBS OF PRIMATES LIKE *AUSTRALOPITHECUS*,
AS WELL AS THOSE OF ARCHAIC HUMANS LIKE *HOMO ERECTUS*,
WERE USED TO HELP THEM MOVE THROUGH THEIR ENVIRONMENTS.
THIS INTERIM STATE SEEMED TO SUGGEST THAT THEY RAPIDLY EVOLVED
INTO ARCHAIC HUMANS (NEANDERTHALS AND *HOMO HEIDELBERGENSIS*)
AND MODERN SPECIES, SUCH AS FULLY BIPEDAL OR QUADRUPEDAL
HUMANS. AS A SIDE NOTE, IT HAS BECOME EVIDENT THAT SUBSPECIATION
OCCURRED FROM A BIPEDAL FORM IN MERFOLK. HOWEVER, ASSUMING
THAT *HOMO NALEDI* APPEARED IN THE SAME PERIOD AS *AUSTRALOPITHECUS*
OR *HOMO ERECTUS*, THEIR FOSSILS INDICATE THAT MAMMALIAN HUMANS
BEGAN TO ATTAIN FULL BIPEDAL STATES MUCH EARLIER THAN PREVIOUSLY
THOUGHT. IT ALSO SUGGESTS THAT *HOMO NALEDI* WAS AN ANCESTOR OF
MODERN HUMANS, AND THAT THE QUADRUPEDAL FORM OF MODERN HUMANS
ORIGINATED FROM A BIPEDAL FORM. OTHER EXAMPLES OF THIS CAN BE FOUND
AS WELL. DINOSAURS WERE BIPEDAL, AND HEXAPEDAL SPECIES
APPEARED TO REVERT TO THEIR ANCESTRAL FORMS.

IN ANY CASE, THIS THEORY REMAINS UNPROVEN. PERHAPS NEW
INFORMATION CAN BE FOUND THROUGH FURTHER RESEARCH.

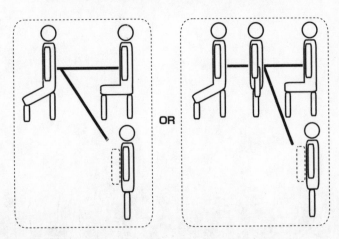

OR

CHAPTER 162

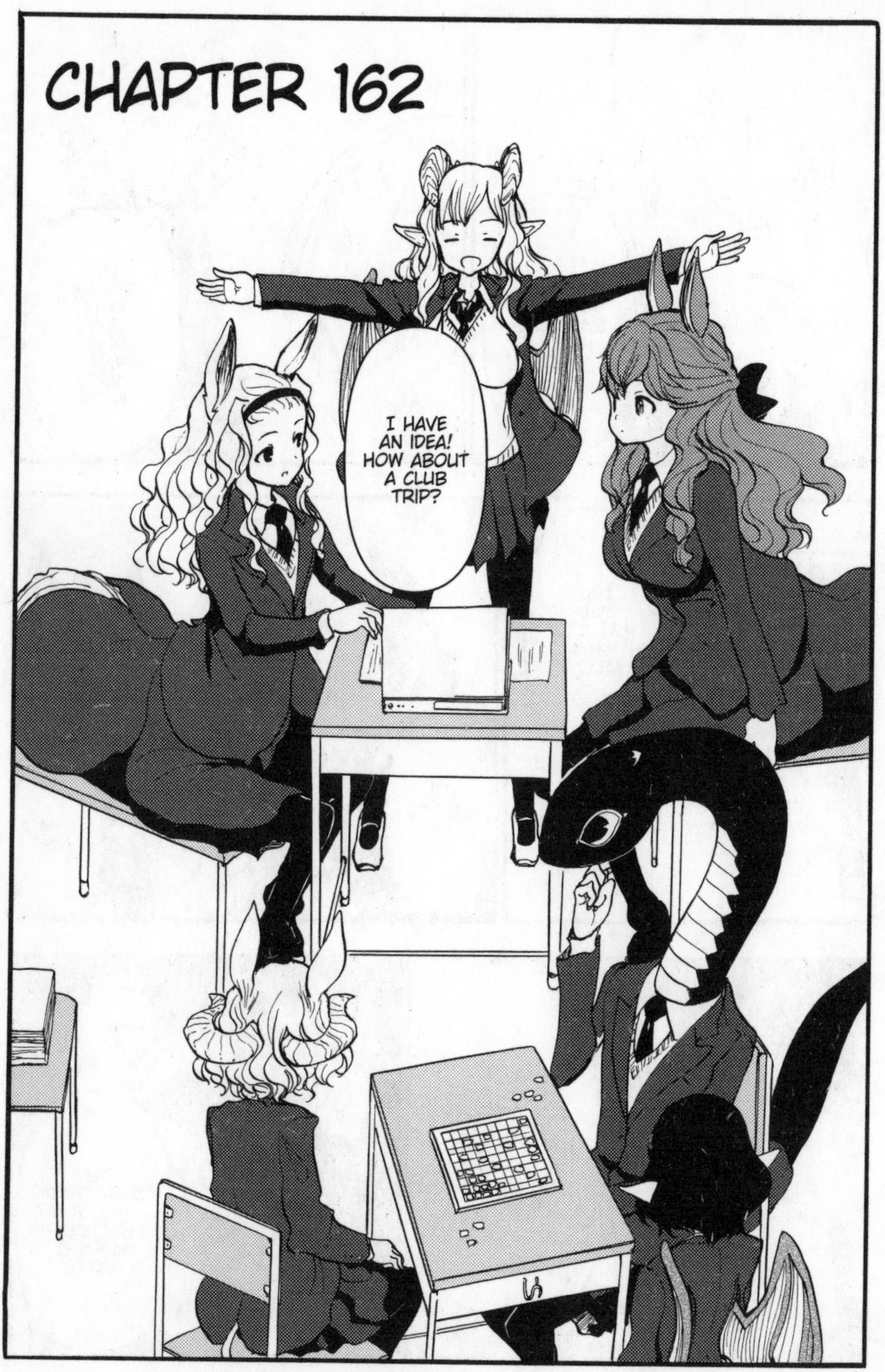
I HAVE AN IDEA! HOW ABOUT A CLUB TRIP?

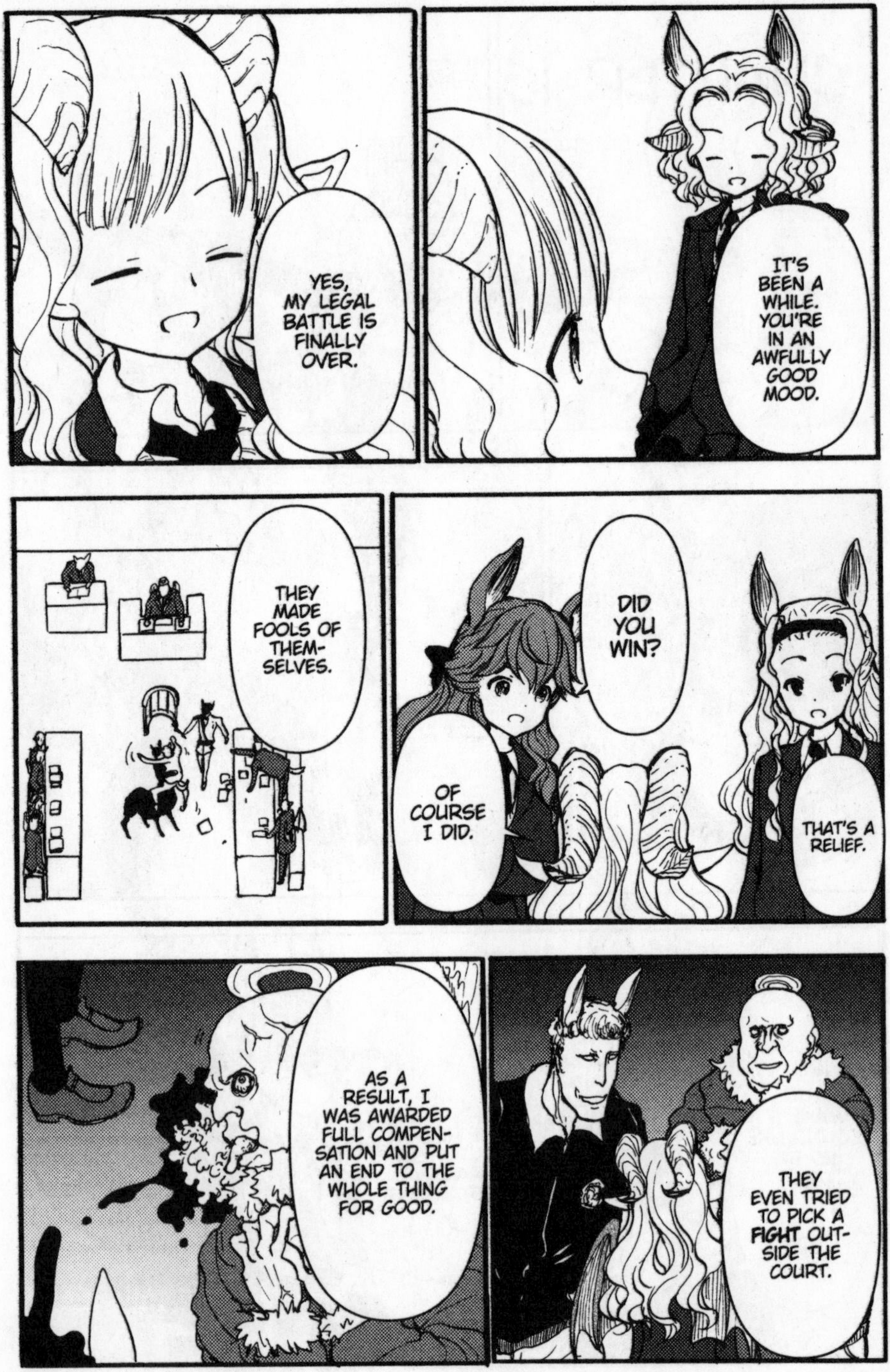
IT'S BEEN A WHILE. YOU'RE IN AN AWFULLY GOOD MOOD.
YES, MY LEGAL BATTLE IS FINALLY OVER.
DID YOU WIN?
OF COURSE I DID.
THAT'S A RELIEF.
THEY MADE FOOLS OF THEM-SELVES.
THEY EVEN TRIED TO PICK A FIGHT OUT-SIDE THE COURT.
AS A RESULT, I WAS AWARDED FULL COMPEN-SATION AND PUT AN END TO THE WHOLE THING FOR GOOD.

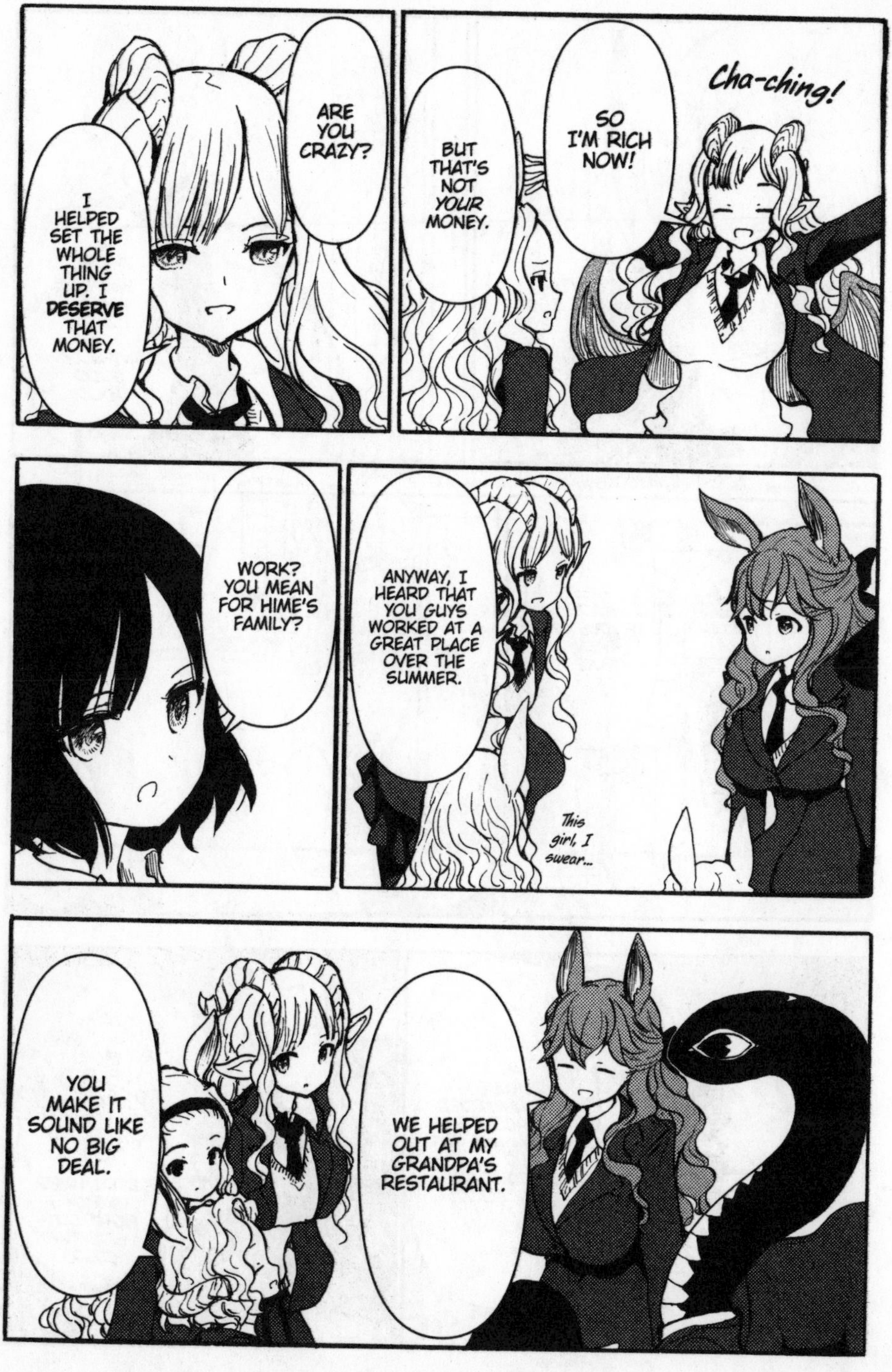
Cha-ching!
SO I'M RICH NOW!
BUT THAT'S NOT YOUR MONEY.
ARE YOU CRAZY?
I HELPED SET THE WHOLE THING UP. I DESERVE THAT MONEY.
ANYWAY, I HEARD THAT YOU GUYS WORKED AT A GREAT PLACE OVER THE SUMMER.
This girl, I swear...
WORK? YOU MEAN FOR HIME'S FAMILY?
WE HELPED OUT AT MY GRANDPA'S RESTAURANT.
YOU MAKE IT SOUND LIKE NO BIG DEAL.

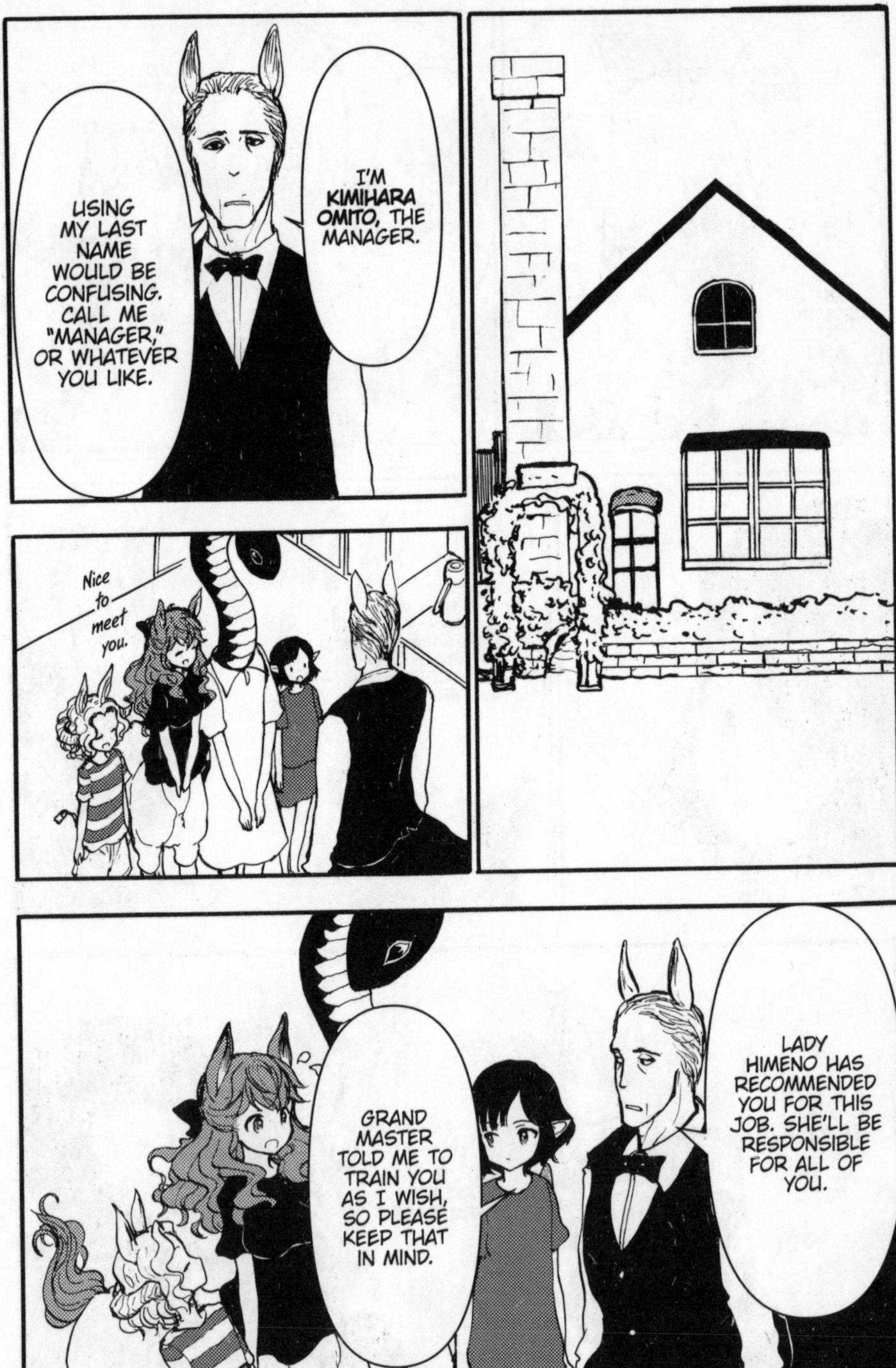
I'M KIMIHARA OMITO, THE MANAGER.
USING MY LAST NAME WOULD BE CONFUSING. CALL ME "MANAGER," OR WHATEVER YOU LIKE.
Nice to meet you.
LADY HIMENO HAS RECOMMENDED YOU FOR THIS JOB. SHE'LL BE RESPONSIBLE FOR ALL OF YOU.
GRAND MASTER TOLD ME TO TRAIN YOU AS I WISH, SO PLEASE KEEP THAT IN MIND.

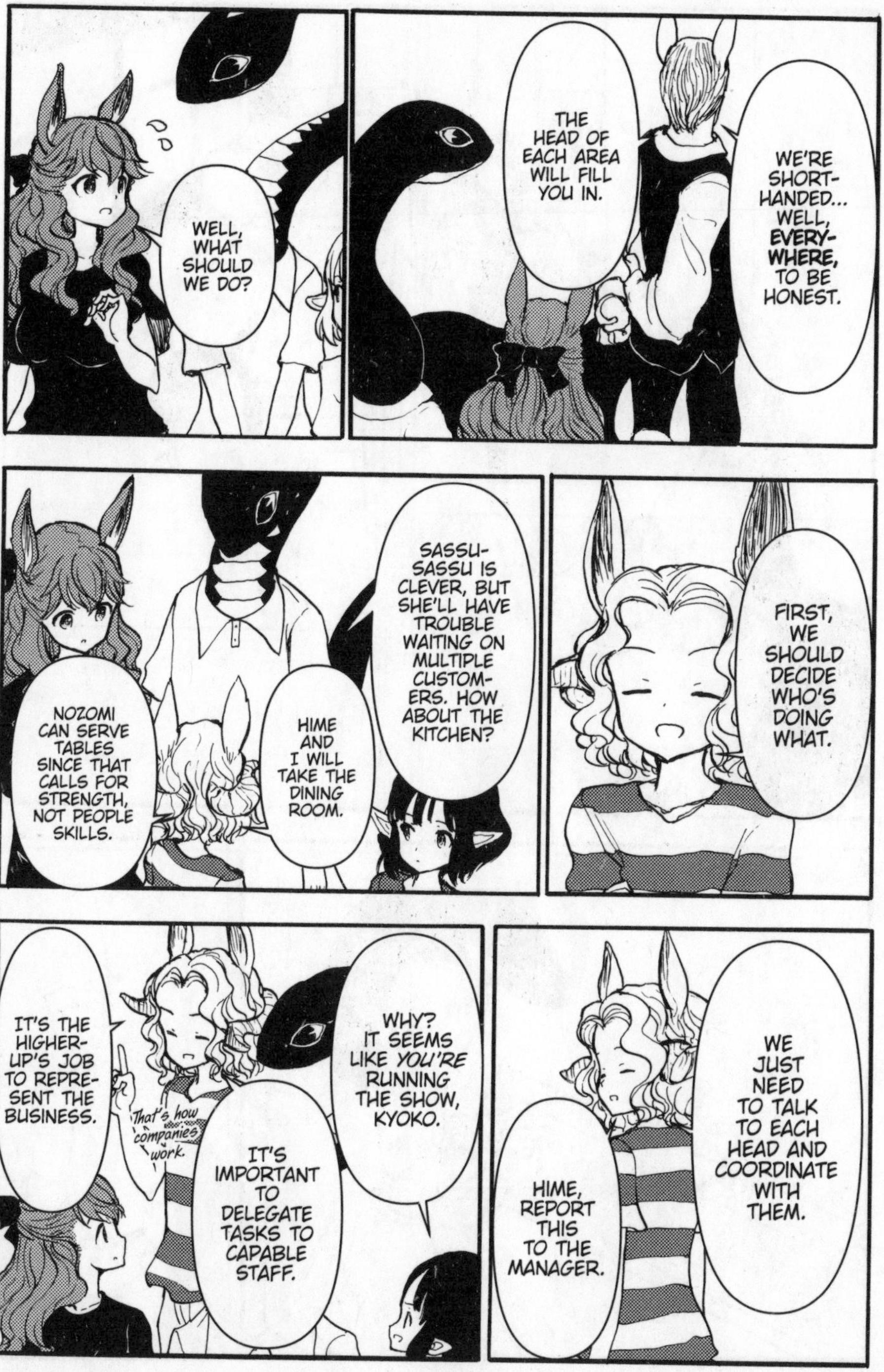
WE'RE SHORT-HANDED... WELL, **EVERYWHERE,** TO BE HONEST.
THE HEAD OF EACH AREA WILL FILL YOU IN.
WELL, WHAT SHOULD WE DO?
FIRST, WE SHOULD DECIDE WHO'S DOING WHAT.
SASSU-SASSU IS CLEVER, BUT SHE'LL HAVE TROUBLE WAITING ON MULTIPLE CUSTOMERS. HOW ABOUT THE KITCHEN?
HIME AND I WILL TAKE THE DINING ROOM.
NOZOMI CAN SERVE TABLES SINCE THAT CALLS FOR STRENGTH, NOT PEOPLE SKILLS.
WE JUST NEED TO TALK TO EACH HEAD AND COORDINATE WITH THEM.
HIME, REPORT THIS TO THE MANAGER.
WHY? IT SEEMS LIKE *YOU'RE* RUNNING THE SHOW, KYOKO.
IT'S THE HIGHER-UP'S JOB TO REPRESENT THE BUSINESS.
That's how companies work.
IT'S IMPORTANT TO DELEGATE TASKS TO CAPABLE STAFF.

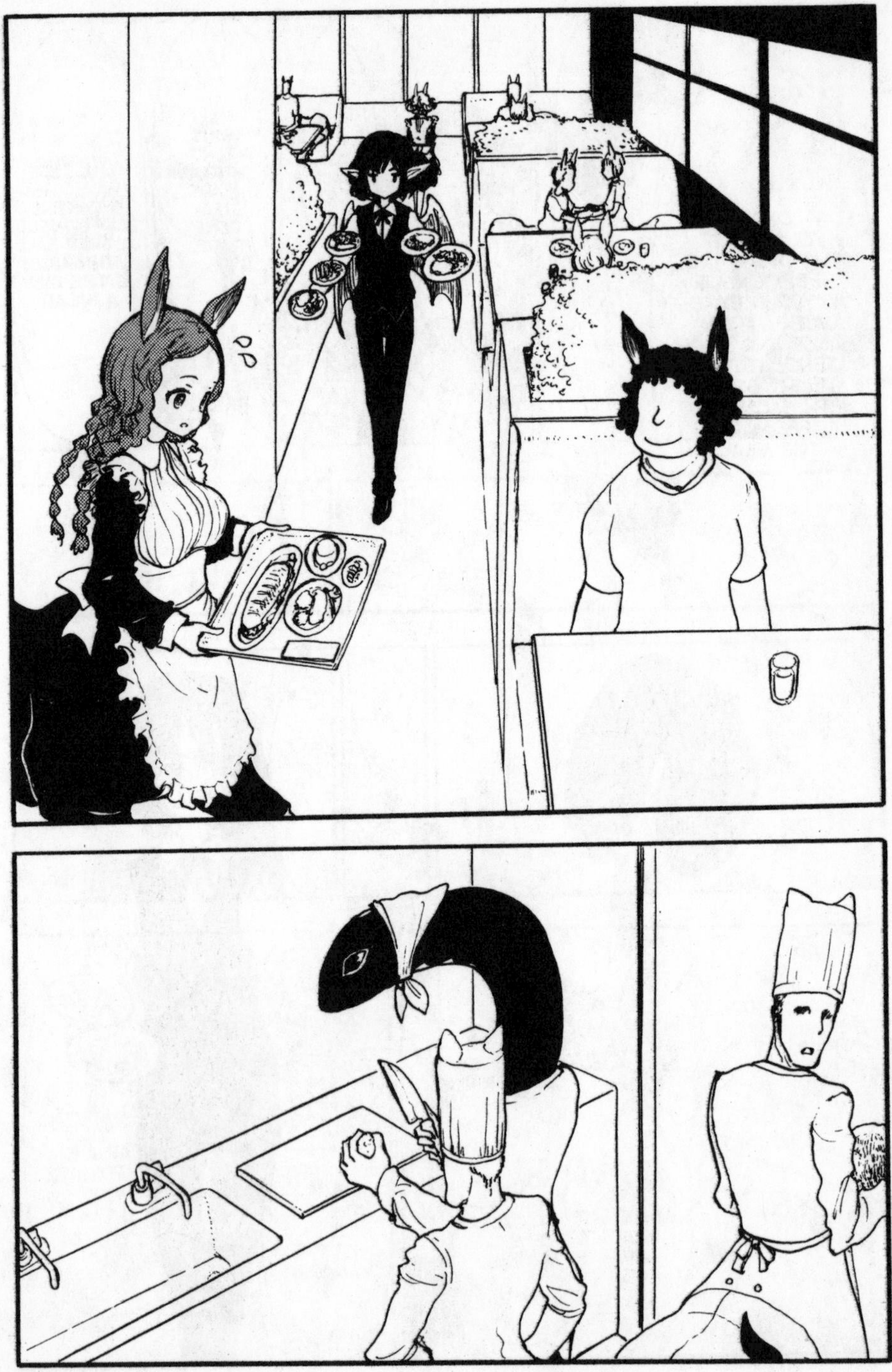

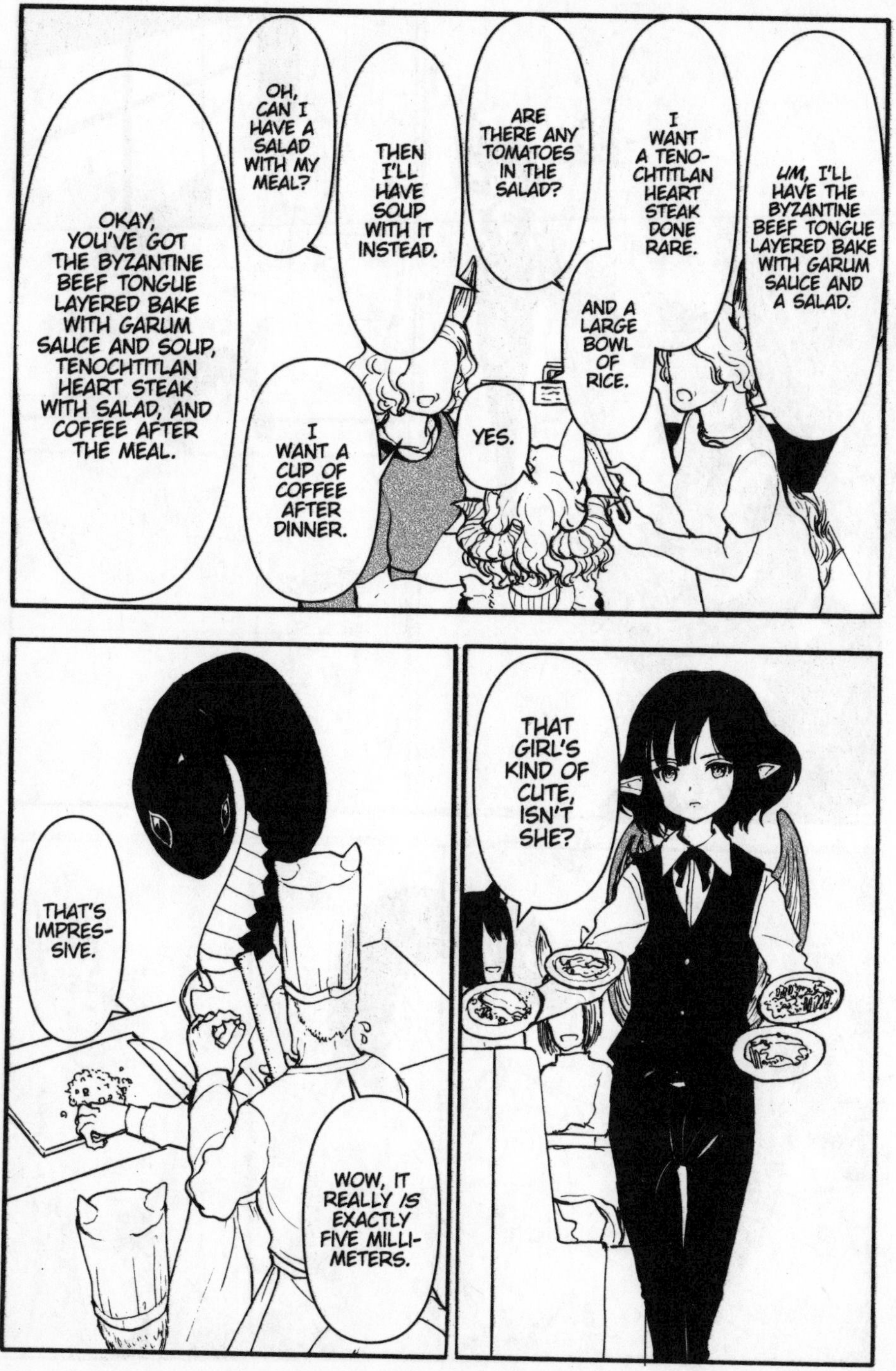
UM, I'LL HAVE THE BYZANTINE BEEF TONGUE LAYERED BAKE WITH GARUM SAUCE AND A SALAD.
I WANT A TENO-CHTITLAN HEART STEAK DONE RARE.
AND A LARGE BOWL OF RICE.
ARE THERE ANY TOMATOES IN THE SALAD?
YES.
THEN I'LL HAVE SOUP WITH IT INSTEAD.
OH, CAN I HAVE A SALAD WITH MY MEAL?
I WANT A CUP OF COFFEE AFTER DINNER.
OKAY, YOU'VE GOT THE BYZANTINE BEEF TONGUE LAYERED BAKE WITH GARUM SAUCE AND SOUP, TENOCHTITLAN HEART STEAK WITH SALAD, AND COFFEE AFTER THE MEAL.
THAT GIRL'S KIND OF CUTE, ISN'T SHE?
THAT'S IMPRES-SIVE.
WOW, IT REALLY *IS* EXACTLY FIVE MILLI-METERS.

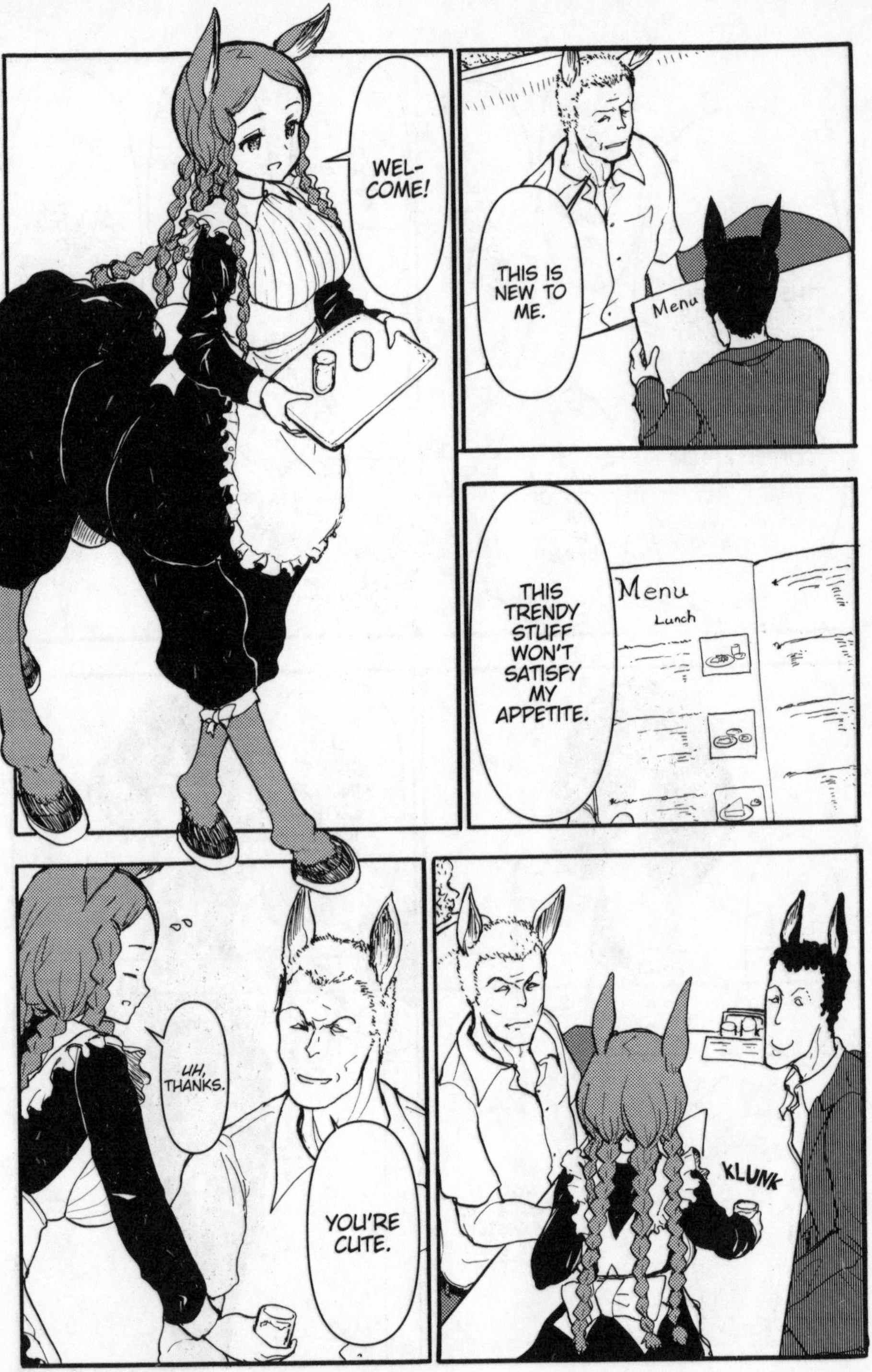
THIS IS NEW TO ME.
Menu
Menu
Lunch
THIS TRENDY STUFF WON'T SATISFY MY APPETITE.
WEL-COME!
KLUNK
YOU'RE CUTE.
UH, THANKS.

WHSH

SHWIP

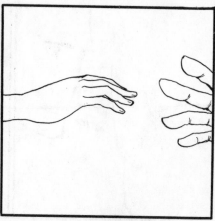

LOOK WHAT YOU DID!

OH, MAN.

SST

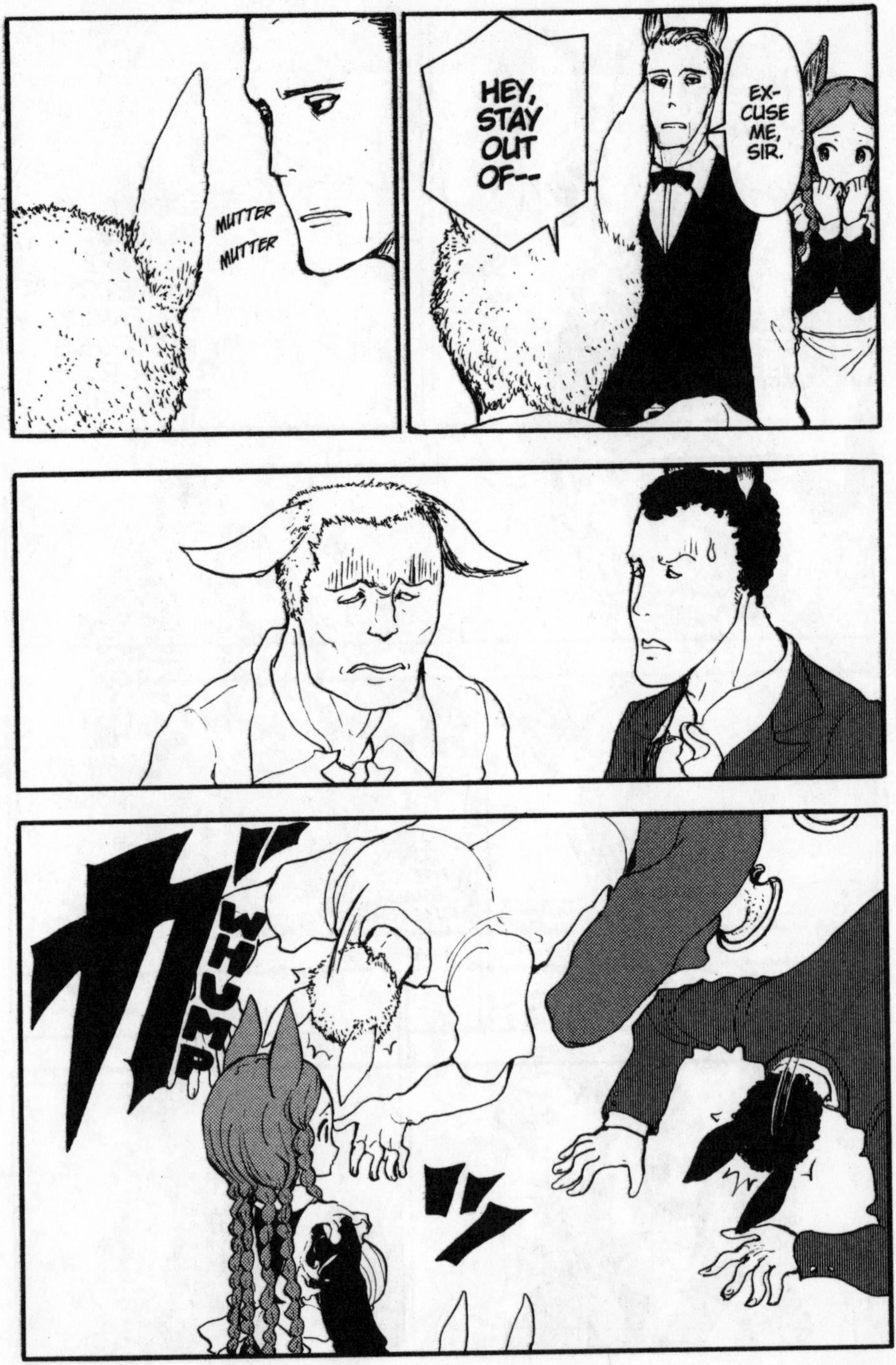
EX-CUSE ME, SIR.
HEY, STAY OUT OF--
MUTTER MUTTER
WHUMP

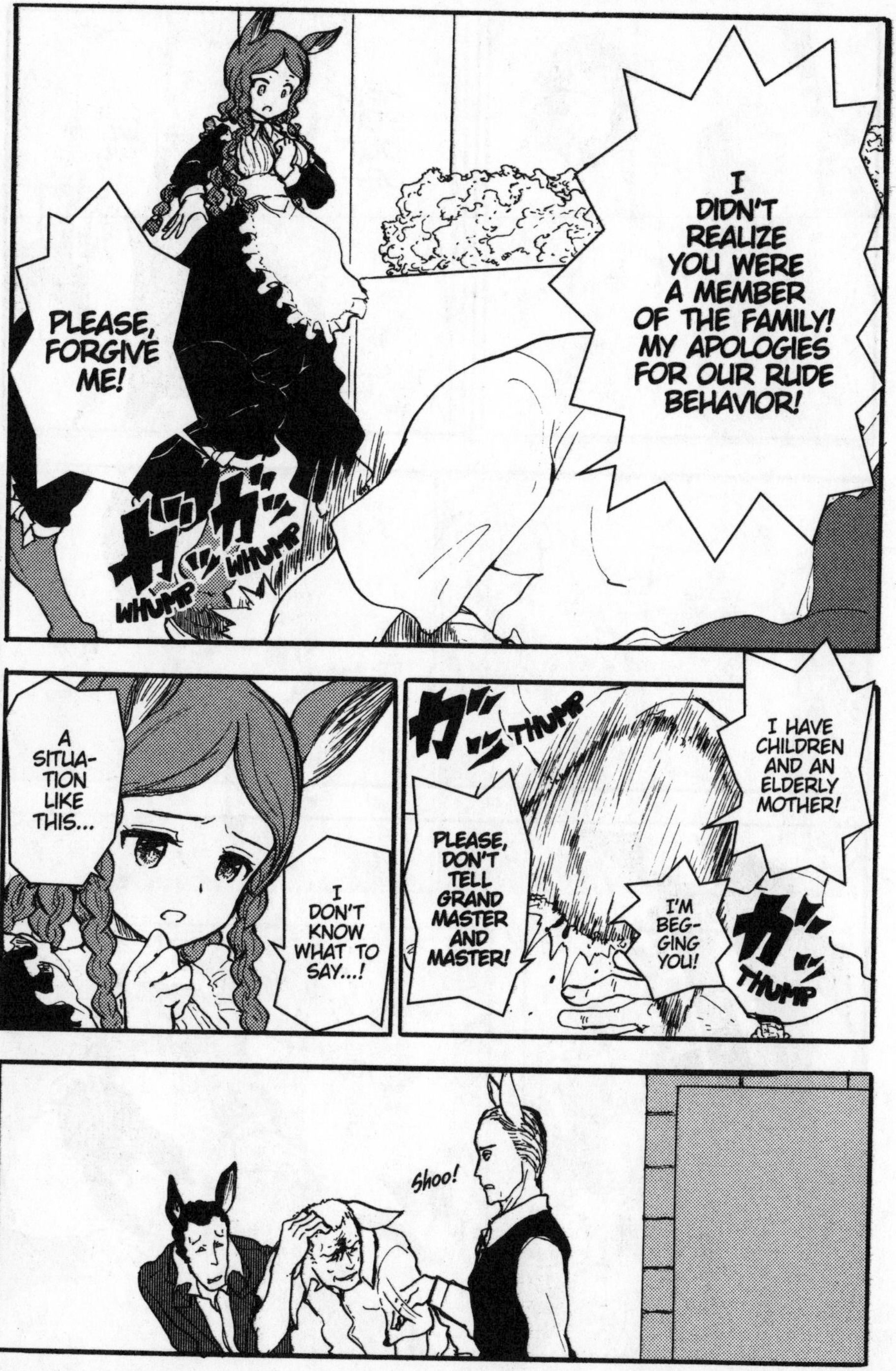
I DIDN'T REALIZE YOU WERE A MEMBER OF THE FAMILY! MY APOLOGIES FOR OUR RUDE BEHAVIOR!
PLEASE, FORGIVE ME!
WHUMP
WHUMP
I HAVE CHILDREN AND AN ELDERLY MOTHER!
THUMP
PLEASE, DON'T TELL GRAND MASTER AND MASTER!
I'M BEG-GING YOU!
THUMP
A SITUA-TION LIKE THIS...
I DON'T KNOW WHAT TO SAY...!
Shoo!

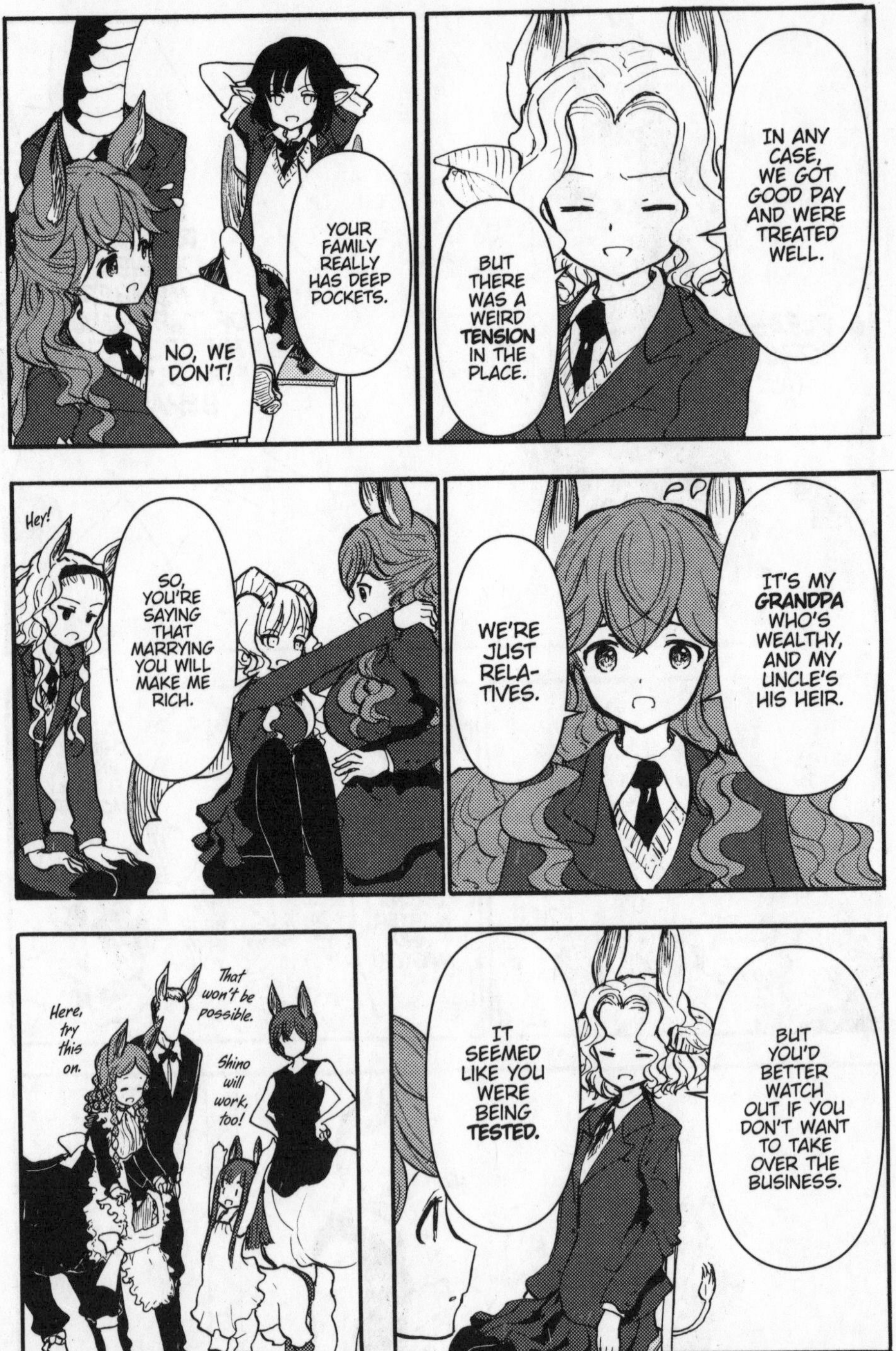
IN ANY CASE, WE GOT GOOD PAY AND WERE TREATED WELL.
BUT THERE WAS A WEIRD **TENSION** IN THE PLACE.
YOUR FAMILY REALLY HAS DEEP POCKETS.
NO, WE DON'T!
IT'S MY **GRANDPA** WHO'S WEALTHY, AND MY UNCLE'S HIS HEIR.
WE'RE JUST RELA-TIVES.
SO, YOU'RE SAYING THAT MARRYING YOU WILL MAKE ME RICH.
Hey!
BUT YOU'D BETTER WATCH OUT IF YOU DON'T WANT TO TAKE OVER THE BUSINESS.
IT SEEMED LIKE YOU WERE BEING **TESTED**.
That won't be possible.
Here, try this on.
Shino will work, too!

A Centaur's Life

RELEARNING THE ORIGIN OF MAMMALIAN HUMANS
4. HOW MAMMALIAN HUMANS CAME ABOUT

THE MODEL OF THE ARCHAIC HUMAN, *HOMO ERECTUS*, WILL CHANGE AS FURTHER RESEARCH IS DONE ON ITS TIME PERIOD AND HABITAT. BACK WHEN IT WAS CALLED *PITHECANTROPES ERECTUS*, IT WAS THE PERFECT IMAGE OF A PRIMATE AND WAS DEPICTED AS PITHECOID WITH A TILTED UPPER BODY. HOWEVER, IN MANY REPRODUCTIONS, IT APPEARS MUCH LIKE A MEMBER OF *HOMO* WITH A SLENDER BODY. JAVA MAN IS CURRENTLY REGARDED AS A SUBSPECIES OF *HOMO ERECTUS*, BUT ITS TEETH AND JAW GREW SMALLER, AND ITS FOREHEAD AND BRAIN GREW LARGER OVER TIME. ALTHOUGH THIS TREND WAS SEEN IN ARCHAIC HUMANS FROM OTHER PARTS OF THE WORLD, SOME SPECIES HAVE DEVELOPED SIGNIFICANTLY SMALLER BODIES AND BRAINS LIKE *HOMO FLORESIENSIS*, WHICH BRANCHED OFF FROM JAVA MAN AND MIGRATED TO AN ISLAND.

IN ANY CASE, IT SEEMS THAT AN UPRIGHT BODY WAS WHAT MADE MAMMALIAN HUMANS UNIQUE. IT WAS ONCE THOUGHT THAT THIS WAS ACCOMPLISHED BY ITS INCREASING BRAIN SIZE, WHICH IS WHY IT WAS DEPICTED WITH A LARGE HEAD AND TILTED UPPER BODY. HOWEVER, *HOMO FLORESIENSIS*, WHICH BECAME DWARFED PER THE ISLAND RULE, ULTIMATELY KEPT THE UPRIGHT BODY BUT LACKED A LARGE BRAIN.

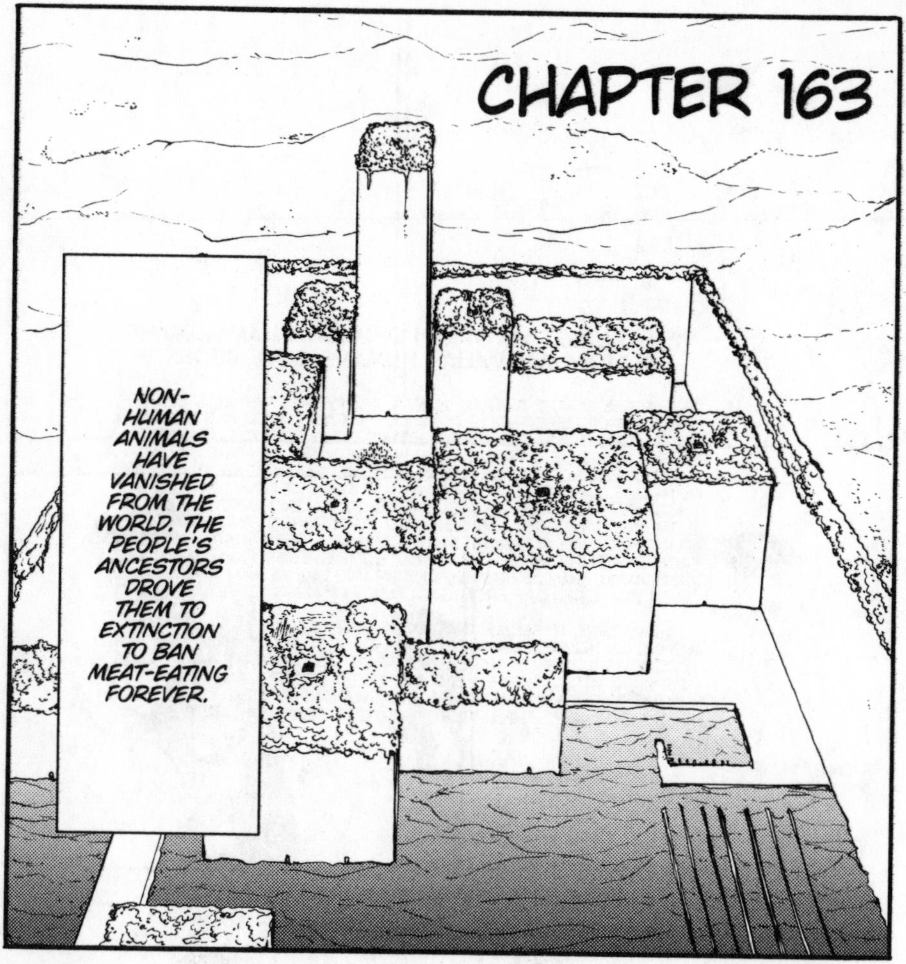
CHAPTER 163
NON-HUMAN ANIMALS HAVE VANISHED FROM THE WORLD. THE PEOPLE'S ANCESTORS DROVE THEM TO EXTINCTION TO BAN MEAT-EATING FOREVER.
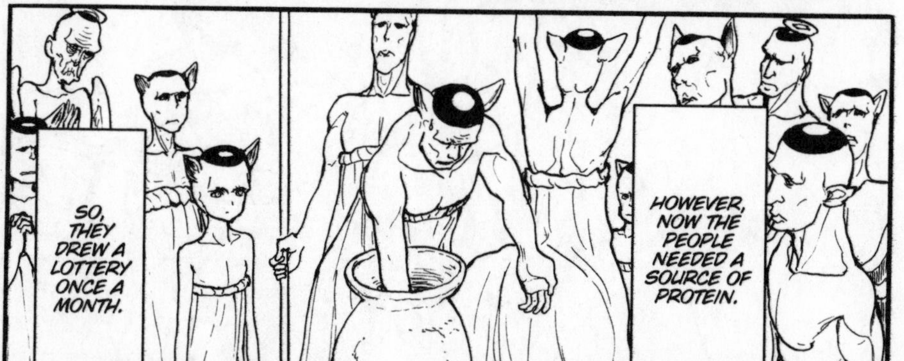
HOWEVER, NOW THE PEOPLE NEEDED A SOURCE OF PROTEIN.
SO, THEY DREW A LOTTERY ONCE A MONTH.

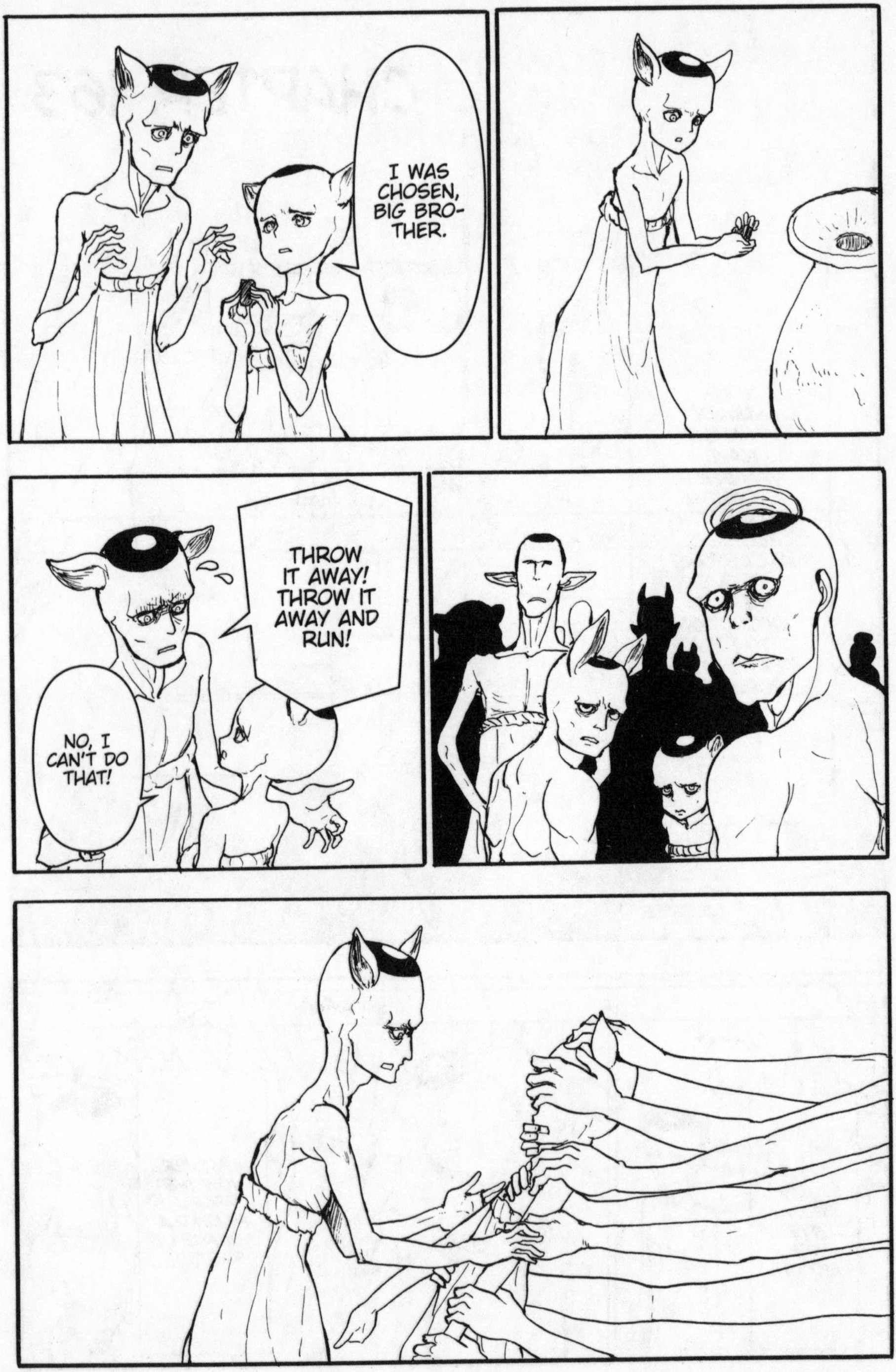
I WAS CHOSEN, BIG BROTHER.
THROW IT AWAY! THROW IT AWAY AND RUN!
NO, I CAN'T DO THAT!

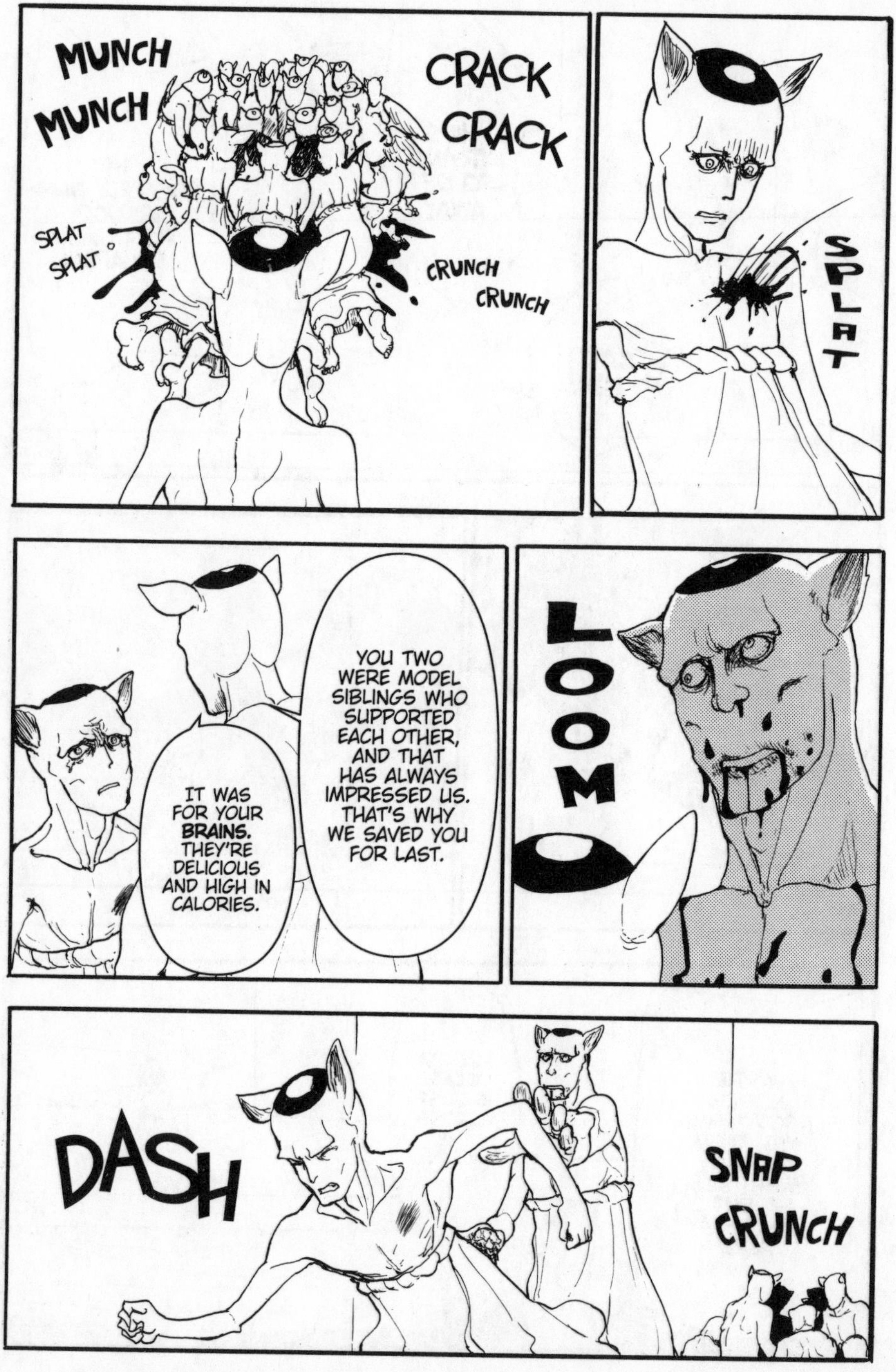

SPLAT
CRACK CRACK
MUNCH MUNCH
CRUNCH CRUNCH
SPLAT SPLAT
LOOOOM
YOU TWO WERE MODEL SIBLINGS WHO SUPPORTED EACH OTHER, AND THAT HAS ALWAYS IMPRESSED US. THAT'S WHY WE SAVED YOU FOR LAST.
IT WAS FOR YOUR **BRAINS.** THEY'RE DELICIOUS AND HIGH IN CALORIES.
SNAP CRUNCH
DASH

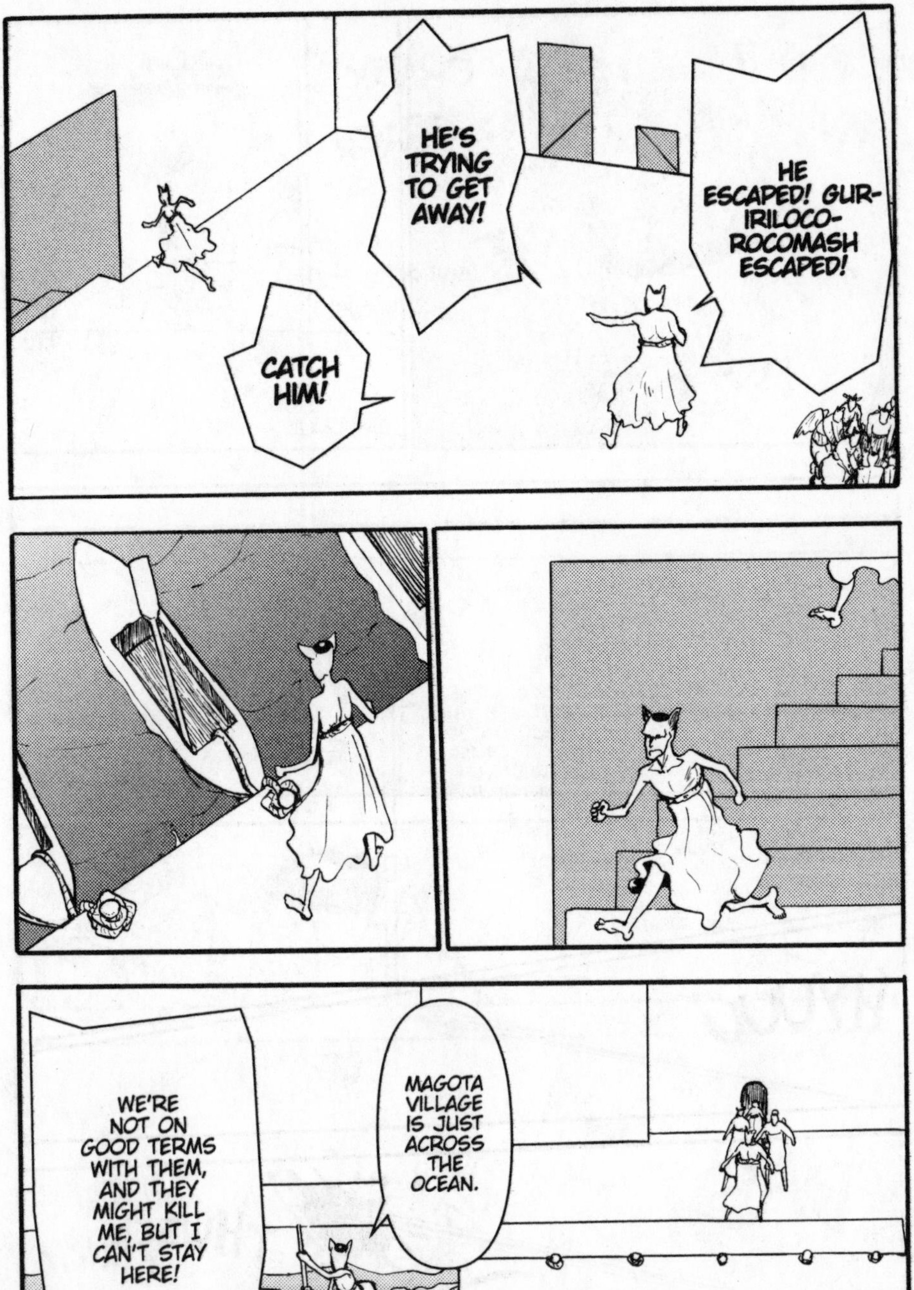
HE ESCAPED! GUR-IRILOCO-ROCOMASH ESCAPED!
HE'S TRYING TO GET AWAY!
CATCH HIM!
MAGOTA VILLAGE IS JUST ACROSS THE OCEAN.
WE'RE NOT ON GOOD TERMS WITH THEM, AND THEY MIGHT KILL ME, BUT I CAN'T STAY HERE!

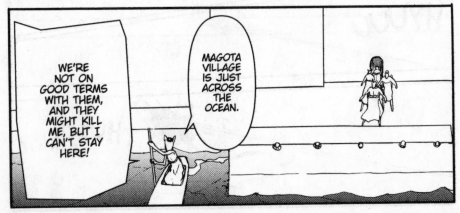

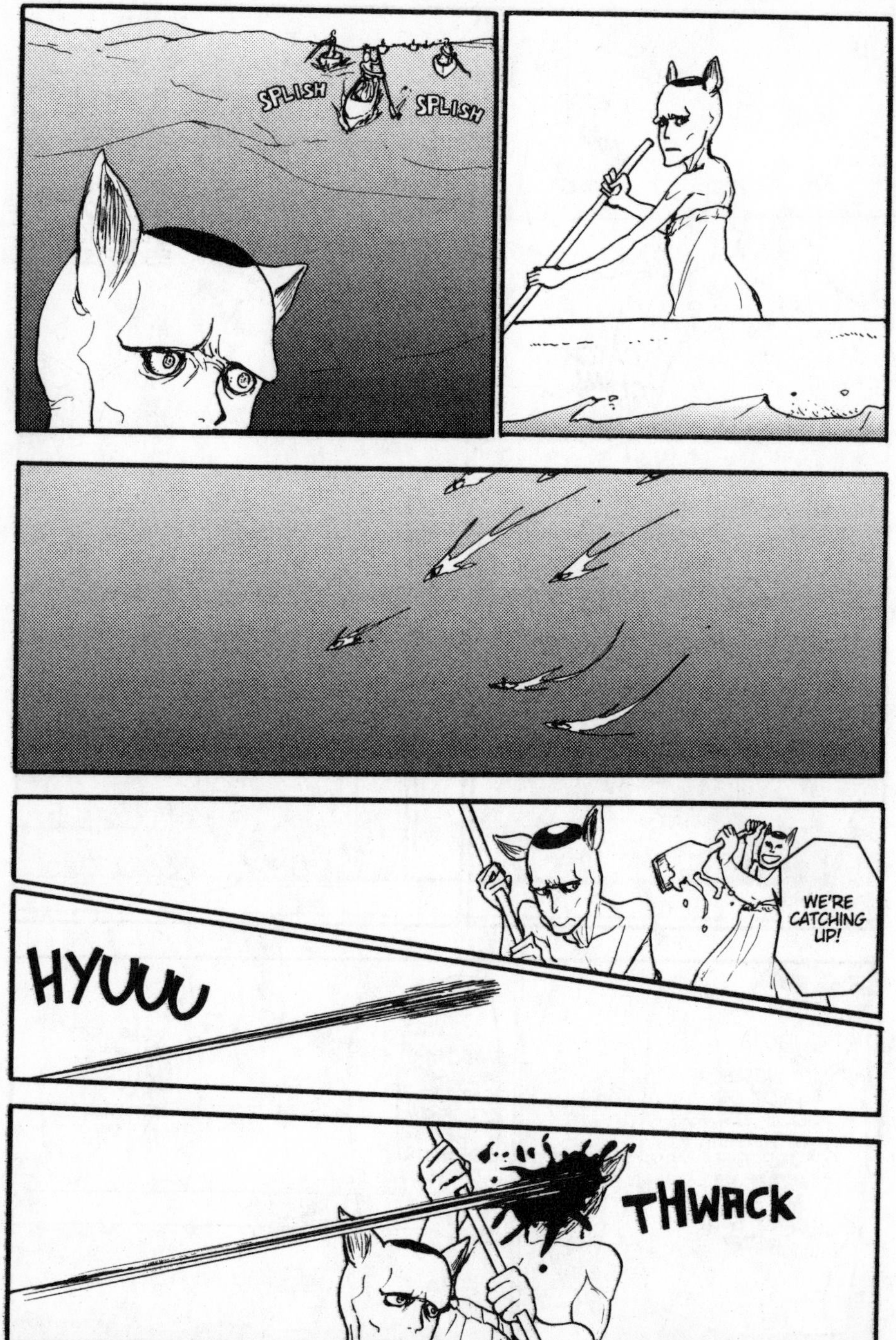
SPLISH
SPLISH
WE'RE CATCHING UP!
HYUUU
THWACK

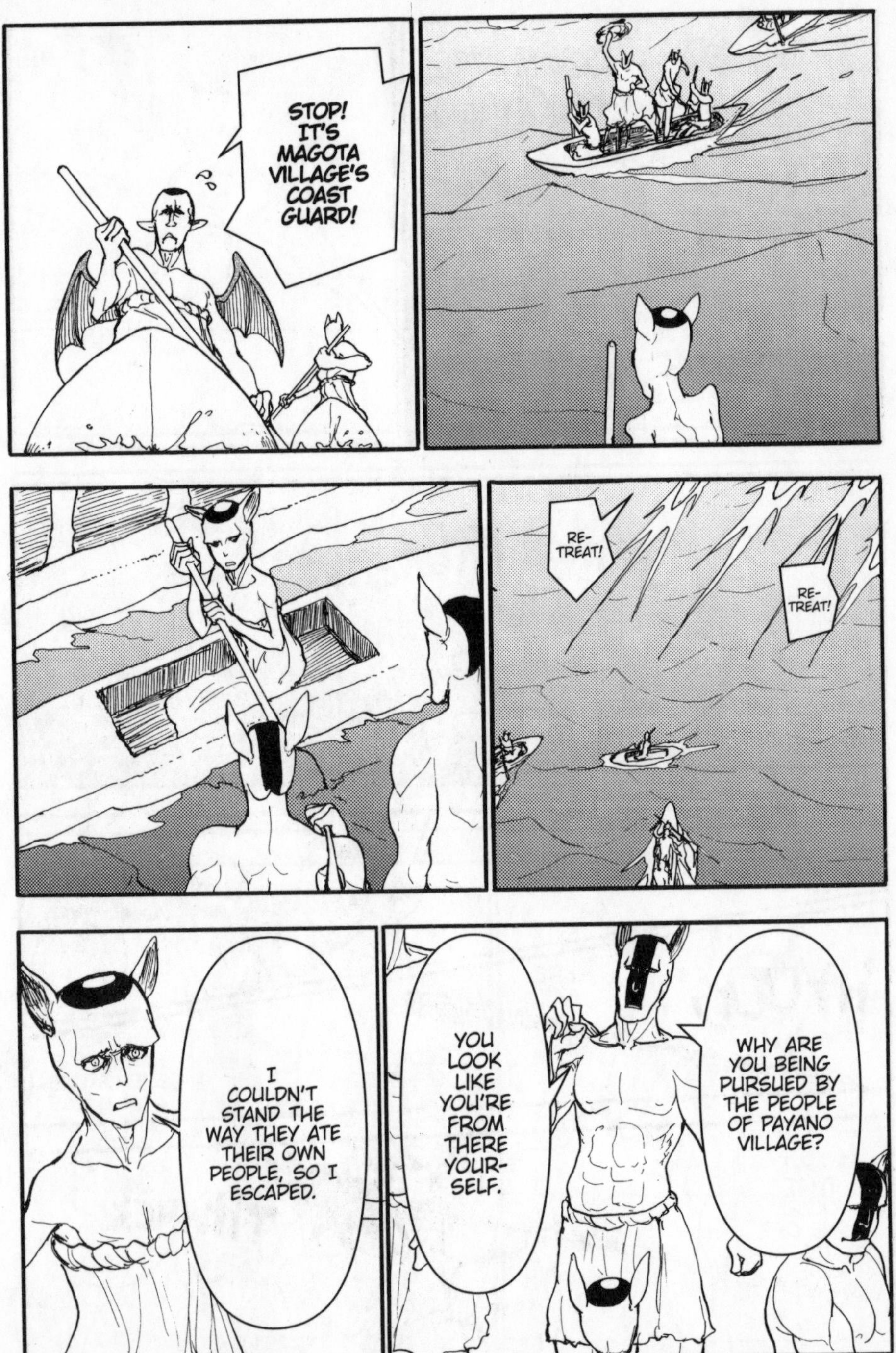
STOP! IT'S MAGOTA VILLAGE'S COAST GUARD!
RE-TREAT!
RE-TREAT!
WHY ARE YOU BEING PURSUED BY THE PEOPLE OF PAYANO VILLAGE?
YOU LOOK LIKE YOU'RE FROM THERE YOURSELF.
I COULDN'T STAND THE WAY THEY ATE THEIR OWN PEOPLE, SO I ESCAPED.

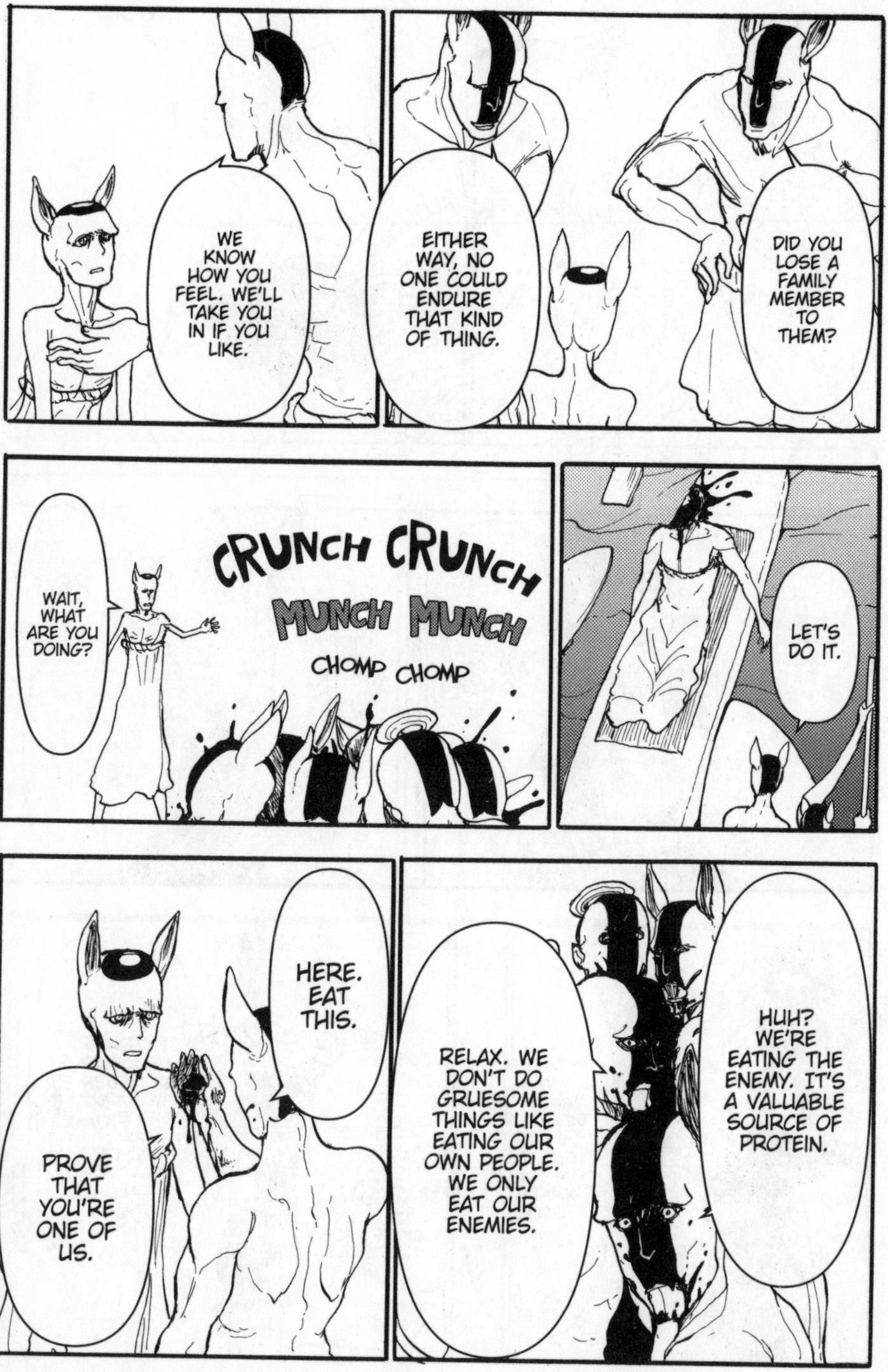
DID YOU LOSE A FAMILY MEMBER TO THEM?
EITHER WAY, NO ONE COULD ENDURE THAT KIND OF THING.
WE KNOW HOW YOU FEEL. WE'LL TAKE YOU IN IF YOU LIKE.
LET'S DO IT.
CRUNCH CRUNCH
MUNCH MUNCH
CHOMP CHOMP
WAIT, WHAT ARE YOU DOING?
HUH? WE'RE EATING THE ENEMY. IT'S A VALUABLE SOURCE OF PROTEIN.
RELAX. WE DON'T DO GRUESOME THINGS LIKE EATING OUR OWN PEOPLE. WE ONLY EAT OUR ENEMIES.
HERE. EAT THIS.
PROVE THAT YOU'RE ONE OF US.

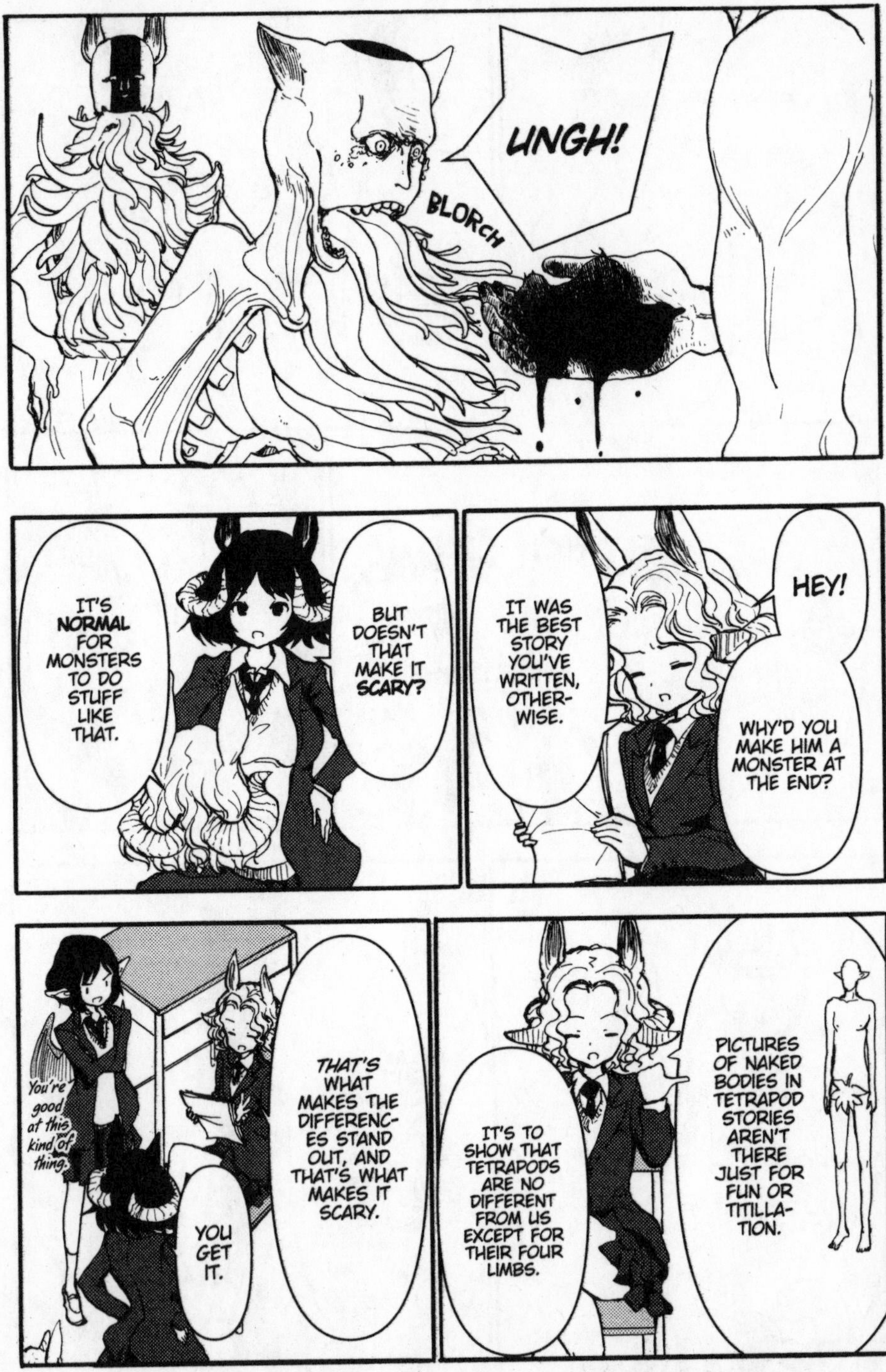
UNGH!
BLORCH
HEY!
WHY'D YOU MAKE HIM A MONSTER AT THE END?
IT WAS THE BEST STORY YOU'VE WRITTEN, OTHERWISE.
BUT DOESN'T THAT MAKE IT SCARY?
IT'S NORMAL FOR MONSTERS TO DO STUFF LIKE THAT.
PICTURES OF NAKED BODIES IN TETRAPOD STORIES AREN'T THERE JUST FOR FUN OR TITILLATION.
IT'S TO SHOW THAT TETRAPODS ARE NO DIFFERENT FROM US EXCEPT FOR THEIR FOUR LIMBS.
THAT'S WHAT MAKES THE DIFFERENCES STAND OUT, AND THAT'S WHAT MAKES IT SCARY.
YOU GET IT.
You're good at this kind of thing.

A Centaur's Life

RELEARNING THE ORIGIN OF MAMMALIAN HUMANS
5. DIVERSITY OF MAMMALIAN HUMANS THAT ONCE EXISTED

THE PHYSIOLOGICAL CHANGES IN JAVA MAN WERE ADDRESSED EARLIER, BUT THE DECREASE IN ITS JAW AND TEETH SIZES AND THE INCREASE IN ITS BRAIN SIZE OVER TIME WERE ALSO SEEN IN *HOMO ERECTUS* FROM OTHER PARTS OF THE WORLD. THIS RAISES SOME QUESTIONS: DID ANY OTHER SPECIES--COMPARABLE TO ARCHAIC HUMANS, NEANDERTHALS, OR MODERN HUMANS--EVER EXIST? IS IT POSSIBLE THAT MODERN HUMANS COULD HAVE BEEN BORN SEPARATELY IN EACH ETHNIC GROUP AND MERGED LATER? THIS THEORY IS CALLED MULTIREGIONAL EVOLUTION, BUT IT HAS BEEN DISPROVEN. JAVA MAN APPARENTLY HAD SIMILAR TRAITS TO *HOMO ERECTUS* FROM OTHER PARTS OF THE WORLD WHEN IT FIRST CAME TO ITS OWN HABITAT. HOWEVER, AS IT BECAME GEOGRAPHICALLY ISOLATED FROM OTHER POPULATIONS AND EVOLVED, IT ACQUIRED CHARACTERISTICS THAT DIDN'T EXIST IN ARCHAIC HUMANS, NEANDERTHALS, OR MODERN HUMANS FROM OTHER AREAS. SOME EXAMPLES INCLUDE LACKING THE STRAIGHT SUPERIOR BORDER OF THE PETROUS PART OF THE TEMPORAL BONE, LIKE THAT OF ARCHAIC OR MODERN HUMANS; AND ITS MIDDLE CRANIAL BASE BEING EXTREMELY ELONGATED. CONSIDERING THE LACK OF EXISTENCE OF ANY MEMBERS OF GENUS *HOMO* THAT INHERITED SUCH TRAITS, JAVA MAN MUST HAVE PERISHED WITHOUT LEAVING ANY DESCENDANTS.

IT WOULD BE CORRECT TO ASSUME THAT THE THEORY OF MULTIREGIONAL EVOLUTION IS ERRONEOUS AND THAT MODERN HUMANS WERE BORN IN ONE PLACE AND SPREAD THROUGHOUT THE WORLD. MODERN HUMANS INHERIT CHARACTERISTICS WITHOUT ANY ASSOCIATION TO OTHER SPECIES, WHICH DIFFERENTIATES THEM FROM OTHER HUMAN FOSSILS.

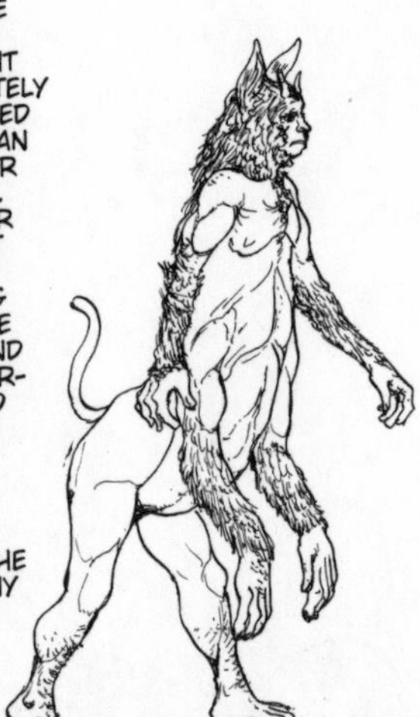

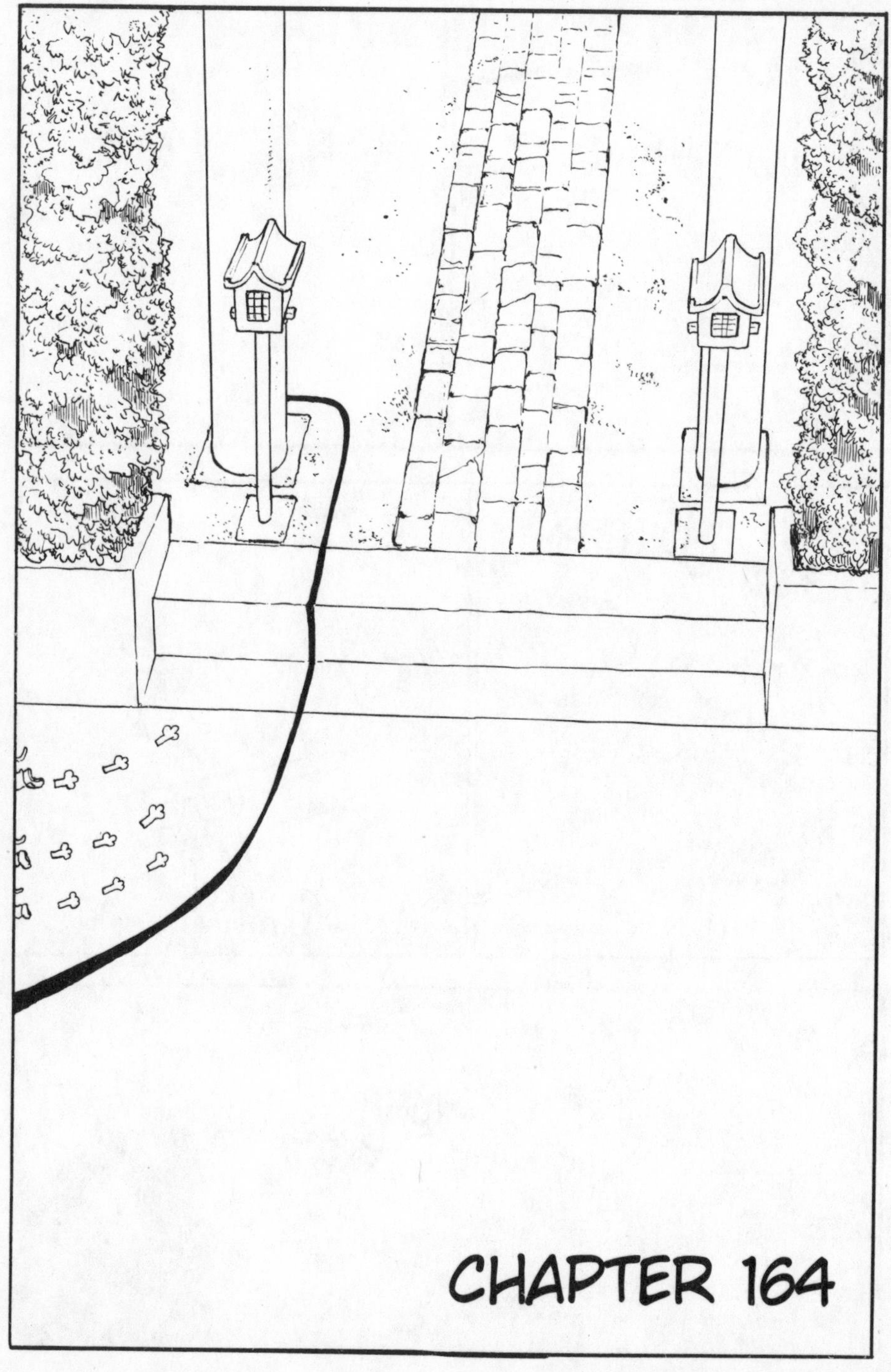
CHAPTER 164

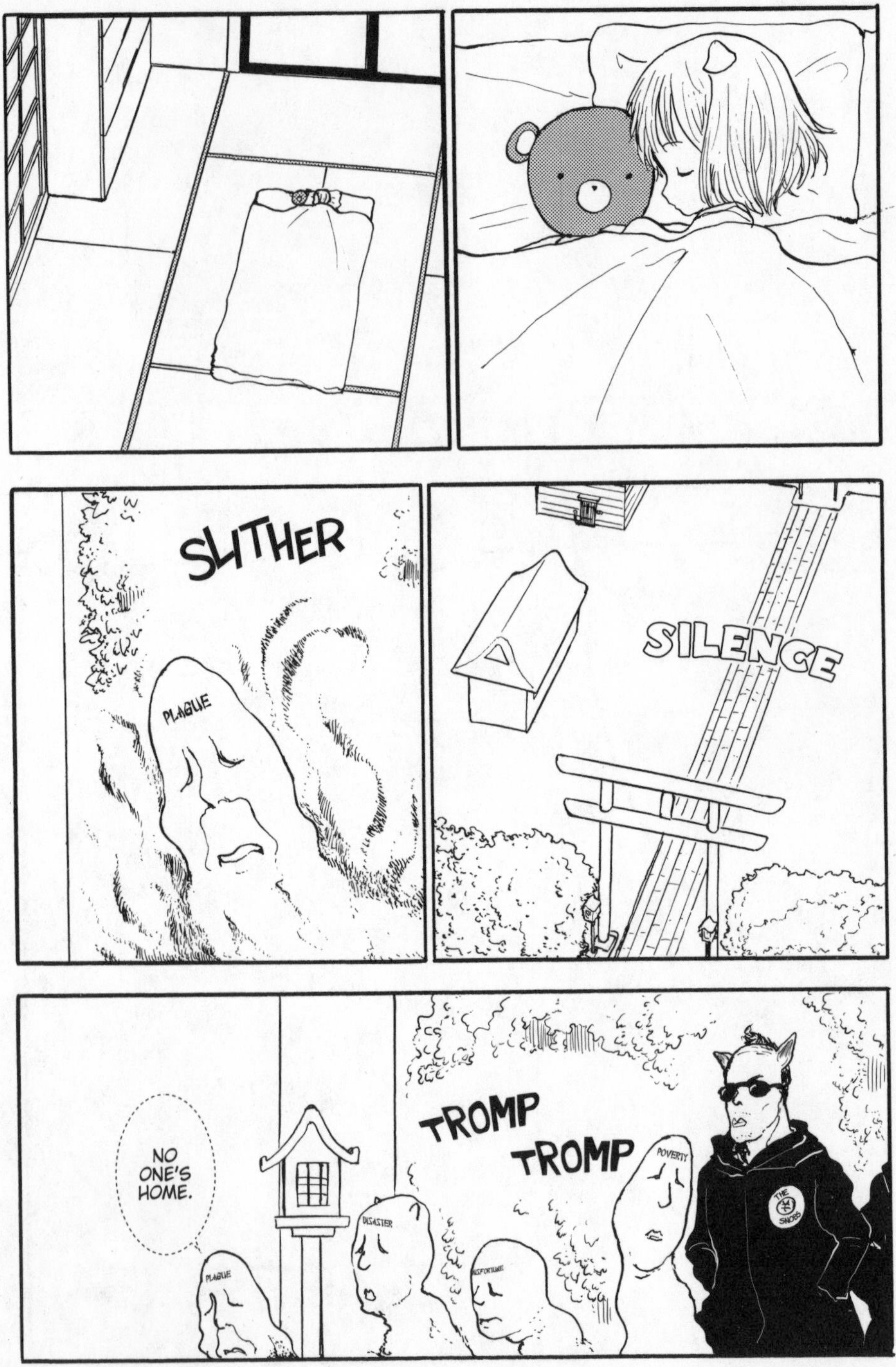
SILENCE
SLITHER
PLAGUE
TROMP
TROMP
POVERTY
THE
SNOBS
MISFORTUNE
DISASTER
NO ONE'S HOME.
PLAGUE

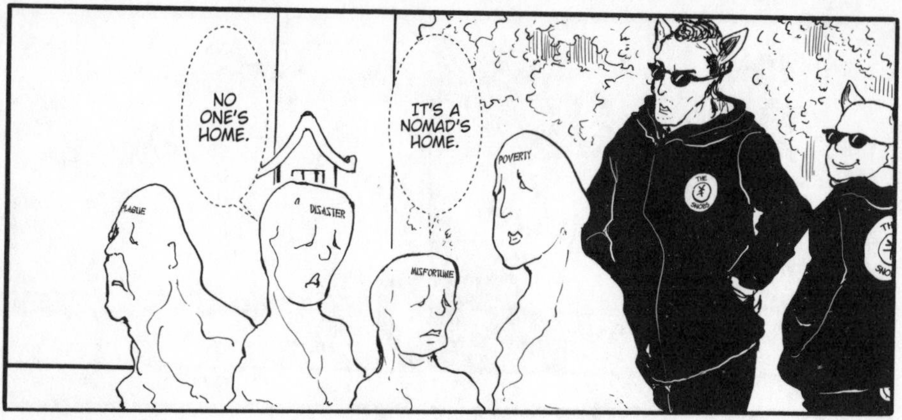
THE SNOBS
POVERTY
IT'S A NOMAD'S HOME.
DISASTER
NO ONE'S HOME.
MISFORTUNE
PLAGUE

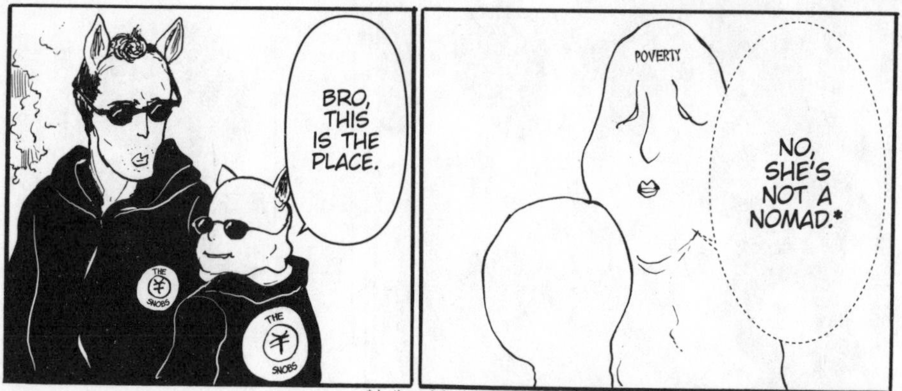
NO, SHE'S NOT A NOMAD.*
POVERTY
BRO, THIS IS THE PLACE.
THE SNOBS

* In the original Japanese, this dialogue is a play on rusu, which means "absent" or "away," and is also a variant on the abbreviation for "Russia" (RUS).

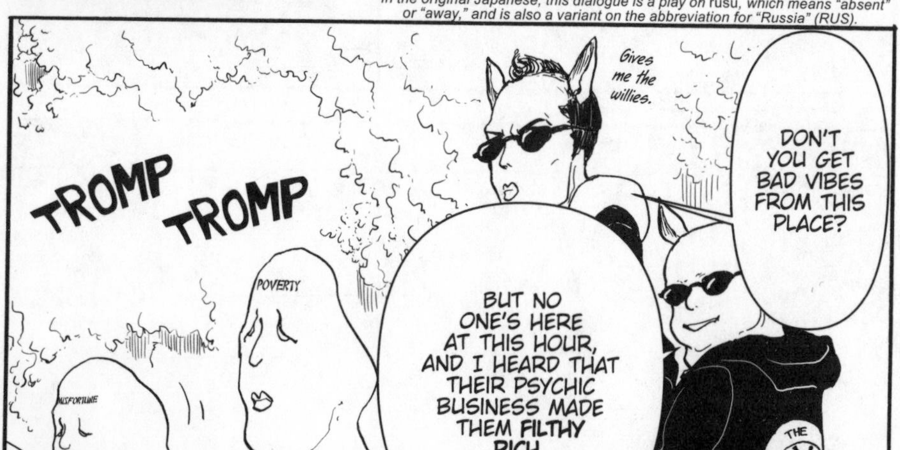
DON'T YOU GET BAD VIBES FROM THIS PLACE?
Gives me the willies.
THE SNOBS
BUT NO ONE'S HERE AT THIS HOUR, AND I HEARD THAT THEIR PSYCHIC BUSINESS MADE THEM FILTHY RICH.
POVERTY
TROMP TROMP
MISFORTUNE

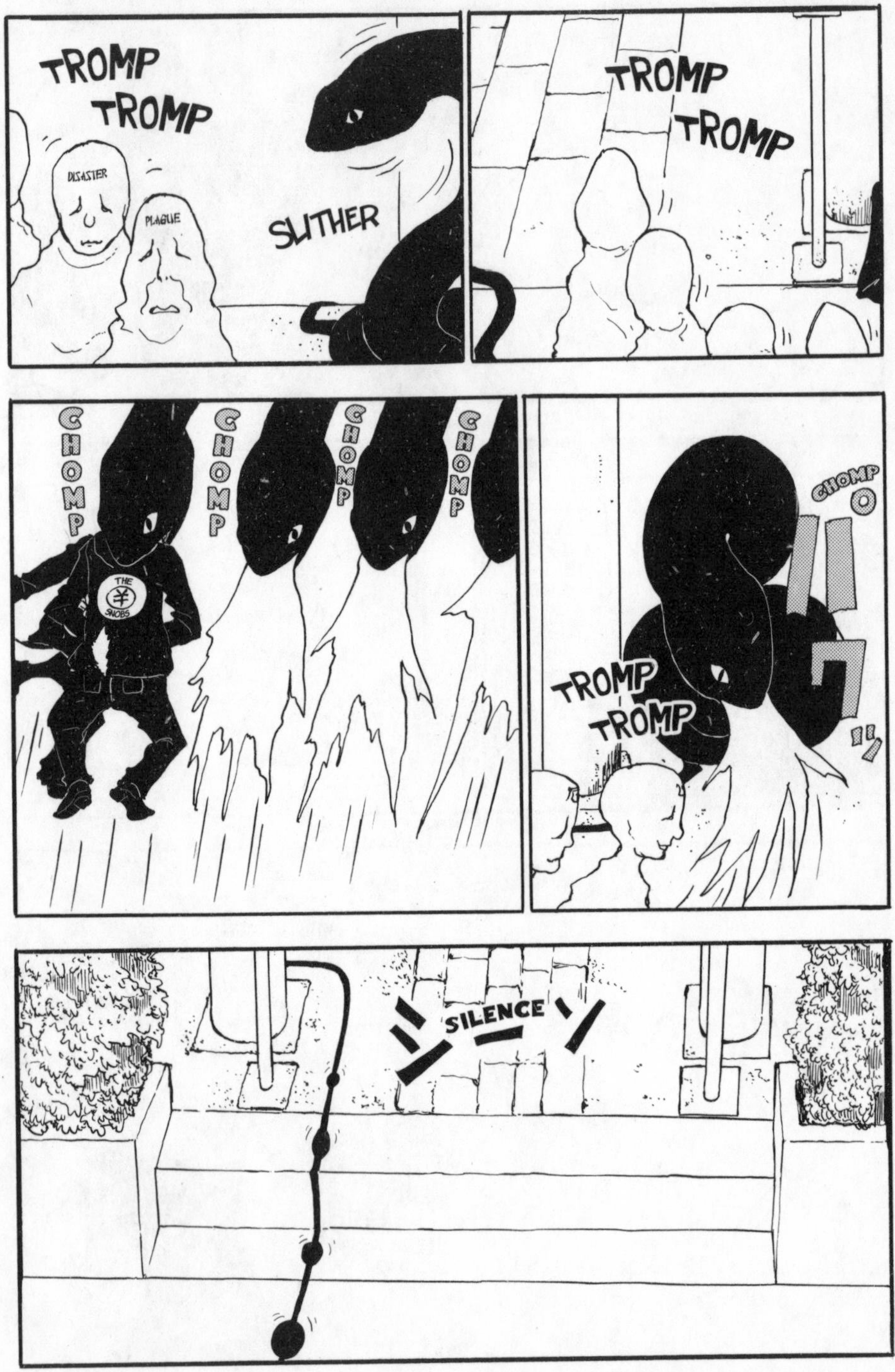
TROMP
TROMP
TROMP
TROMP
DISASTER
PLAGUE
SLITHER
CHOMP
TROMP
TROMP
CHOMP
CHOMP
CHOMP
CHOMP
THE
SNOBS
SILENCE

Mew.

SISSY.

FLAP   FLAP

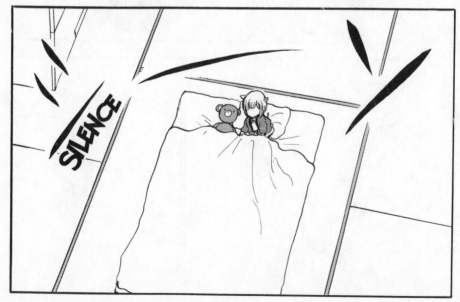

SILENCE

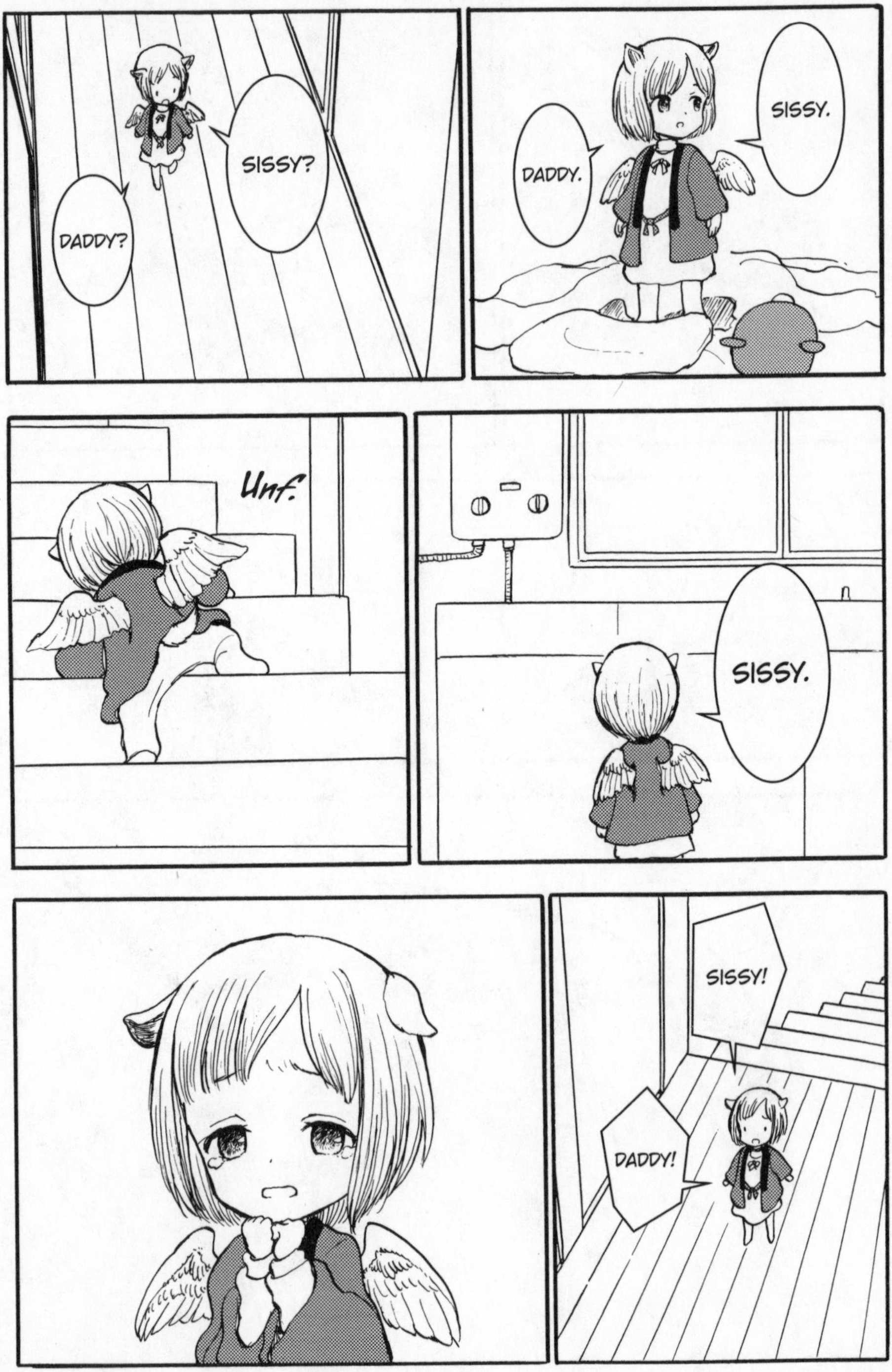
SISSY.
DADDY.
SISSY?
DADDY?
SISSY.
Unf.
SISSY!
DADDY!

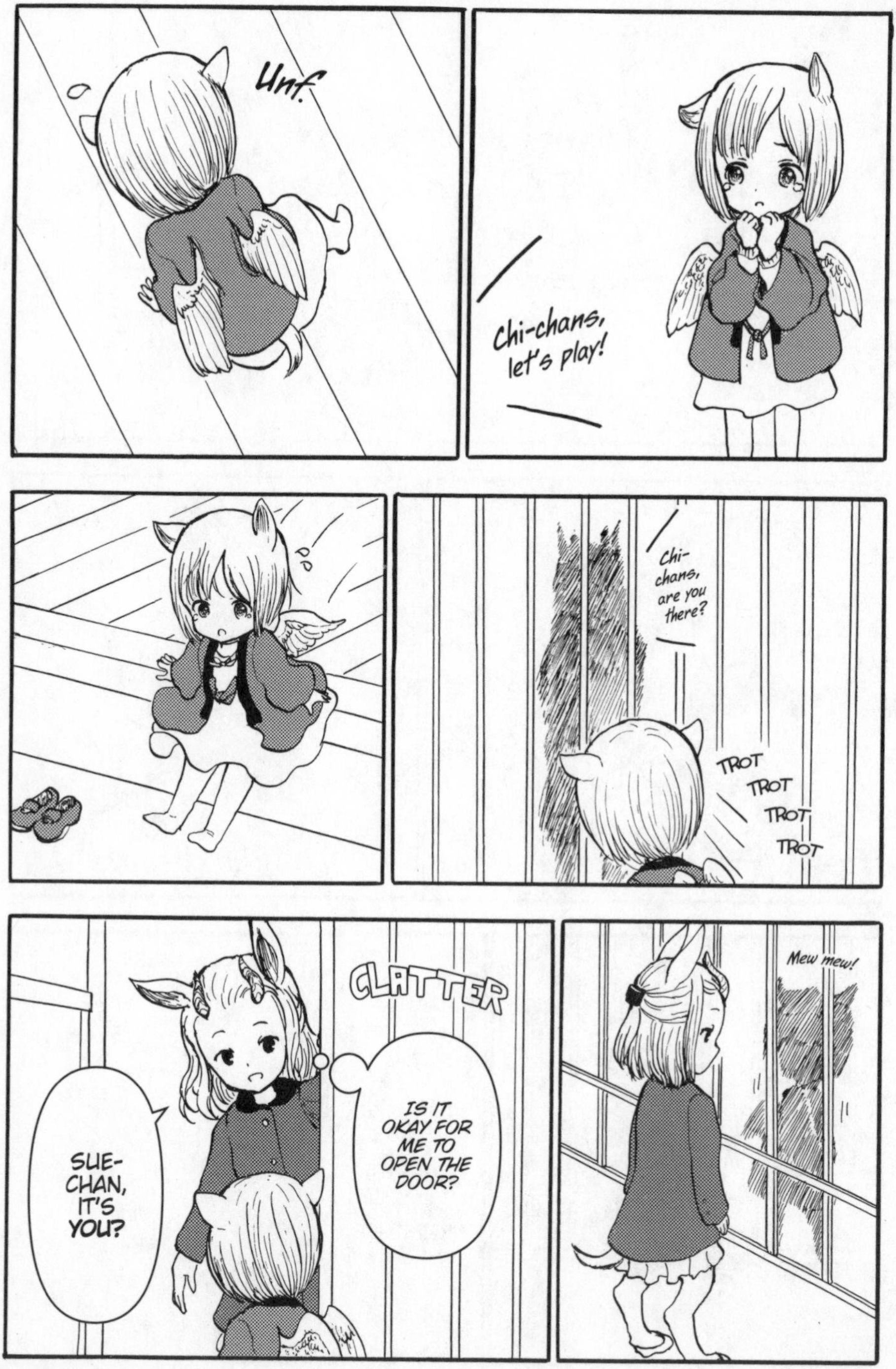
Chi-chans, let's play!
Unf.
Chi-chans, are you there?
TROT TROT TROT TROT
Mew mew!
CLATTER
IS IT OKAY FOR ME TO OPEN THE DOOR?
SUE-CHAN, IT'S YOU?

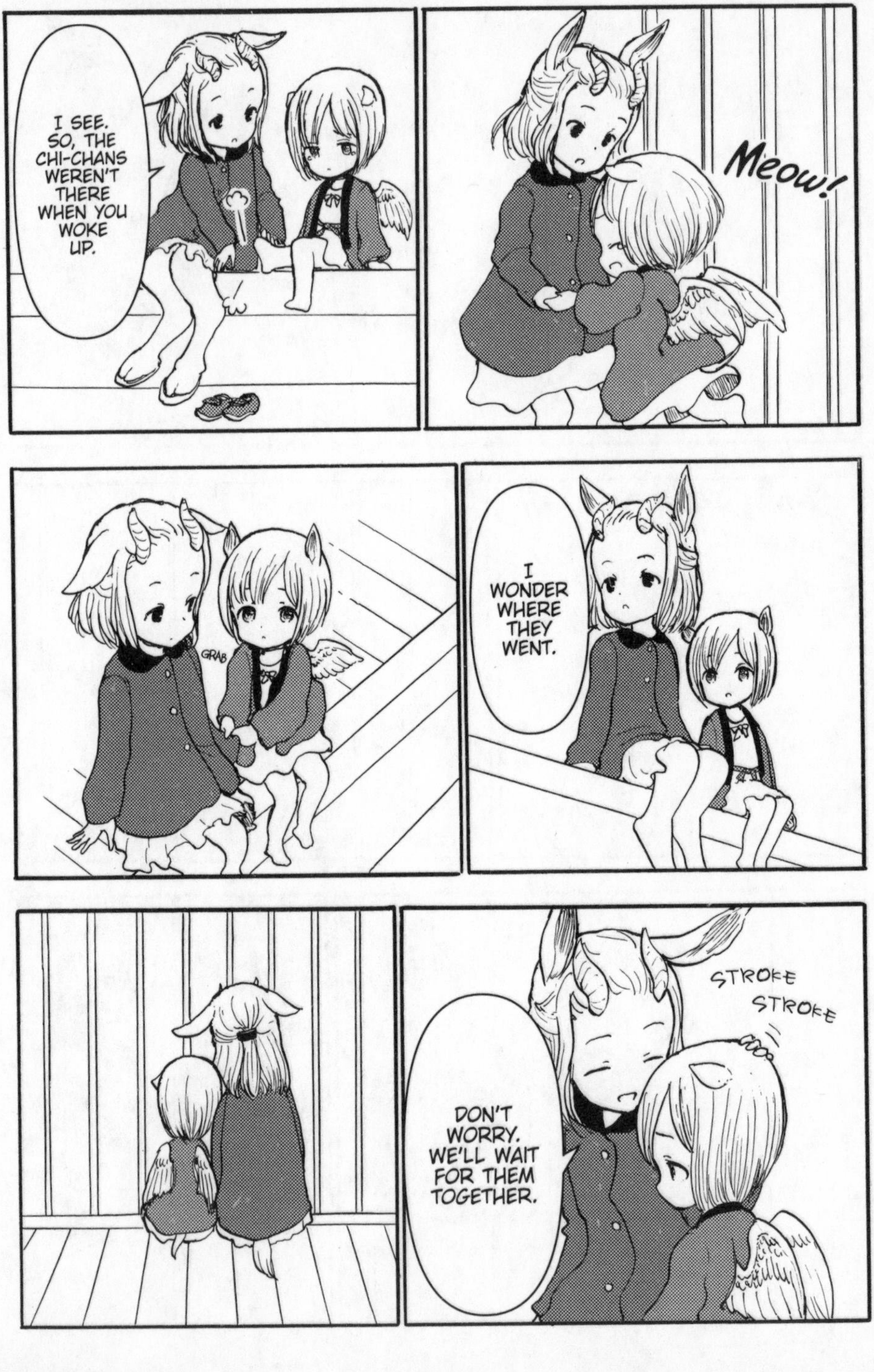
Meow!
I SEE. SO, THE CHI-CHANS WEREN'T THERE WHEN YOU WOKE UP.
I WONDER WHERE THEY WENT.
GRAB
STROKE STROKE
DON'T WORRY. WE'LL WAIT FOR THEM TOGETHER.

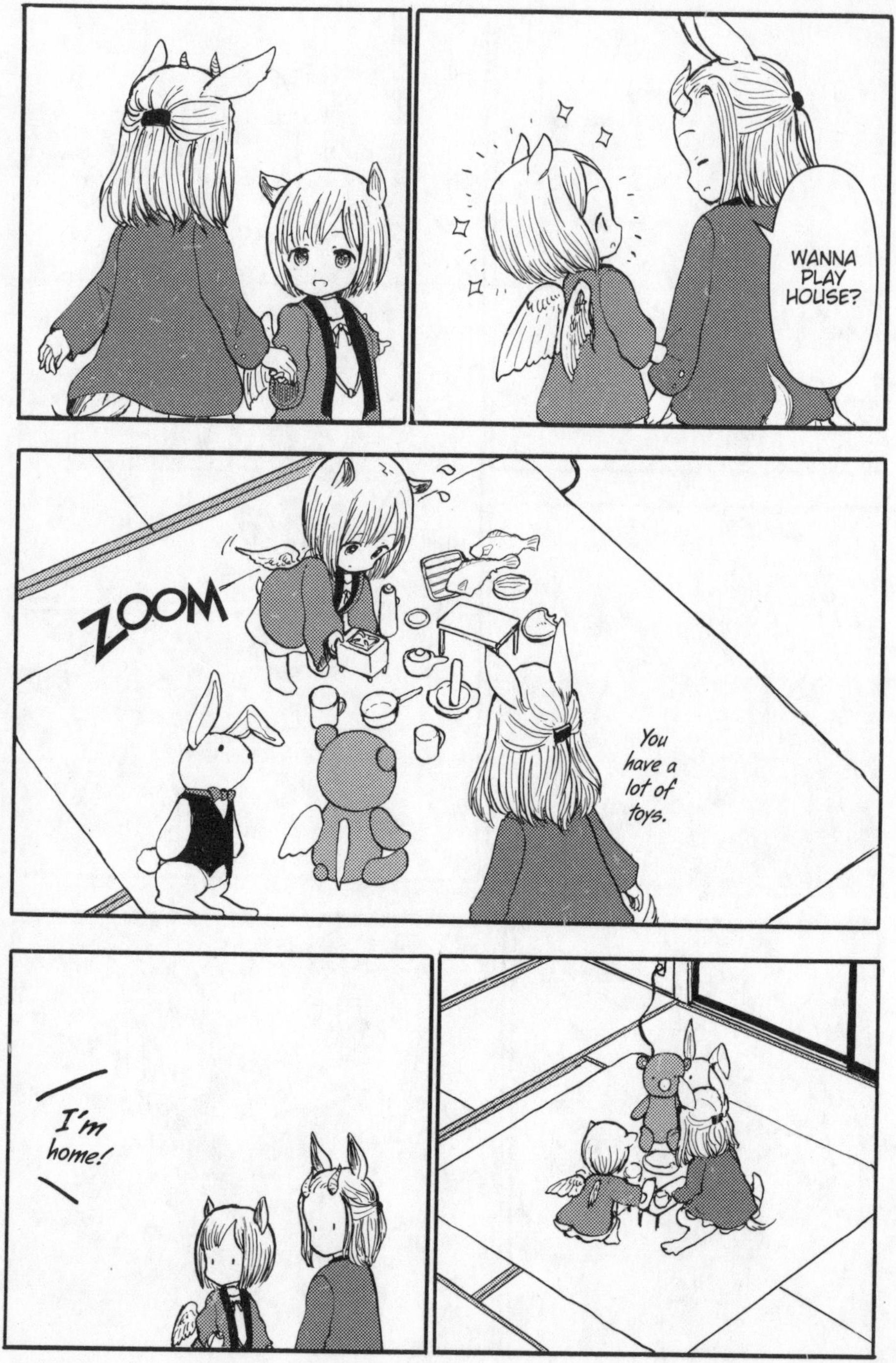
WANNA PLAY HOUSE?
ZOOM
You have a lot of toys.
I'm home!

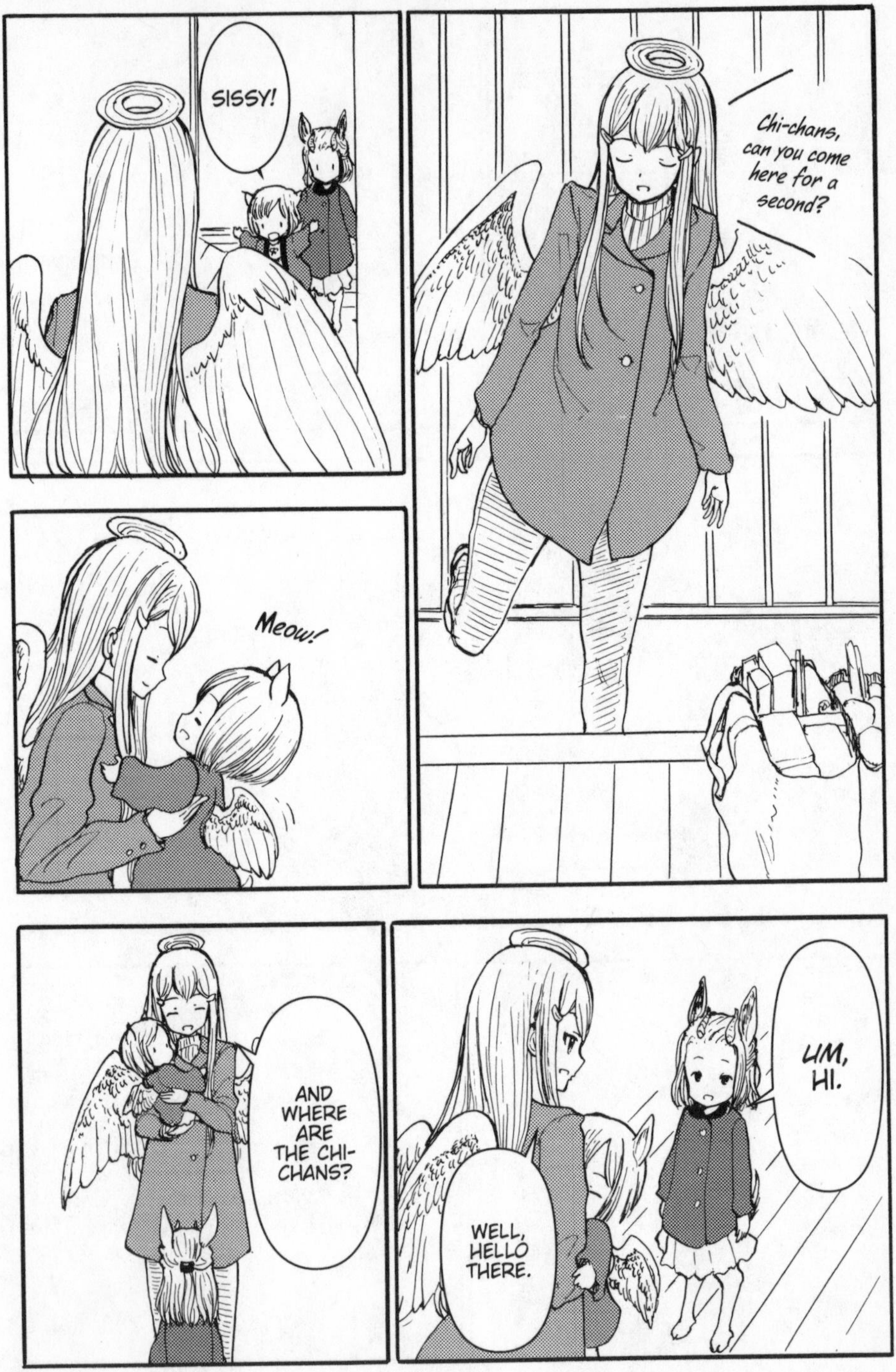
Chi-chans, can you come here for a second?
SISSY!
Meow!
UM, HI.
WELL, HELLO THERE.
AND WHERE ARE THE CHI-CHANS?

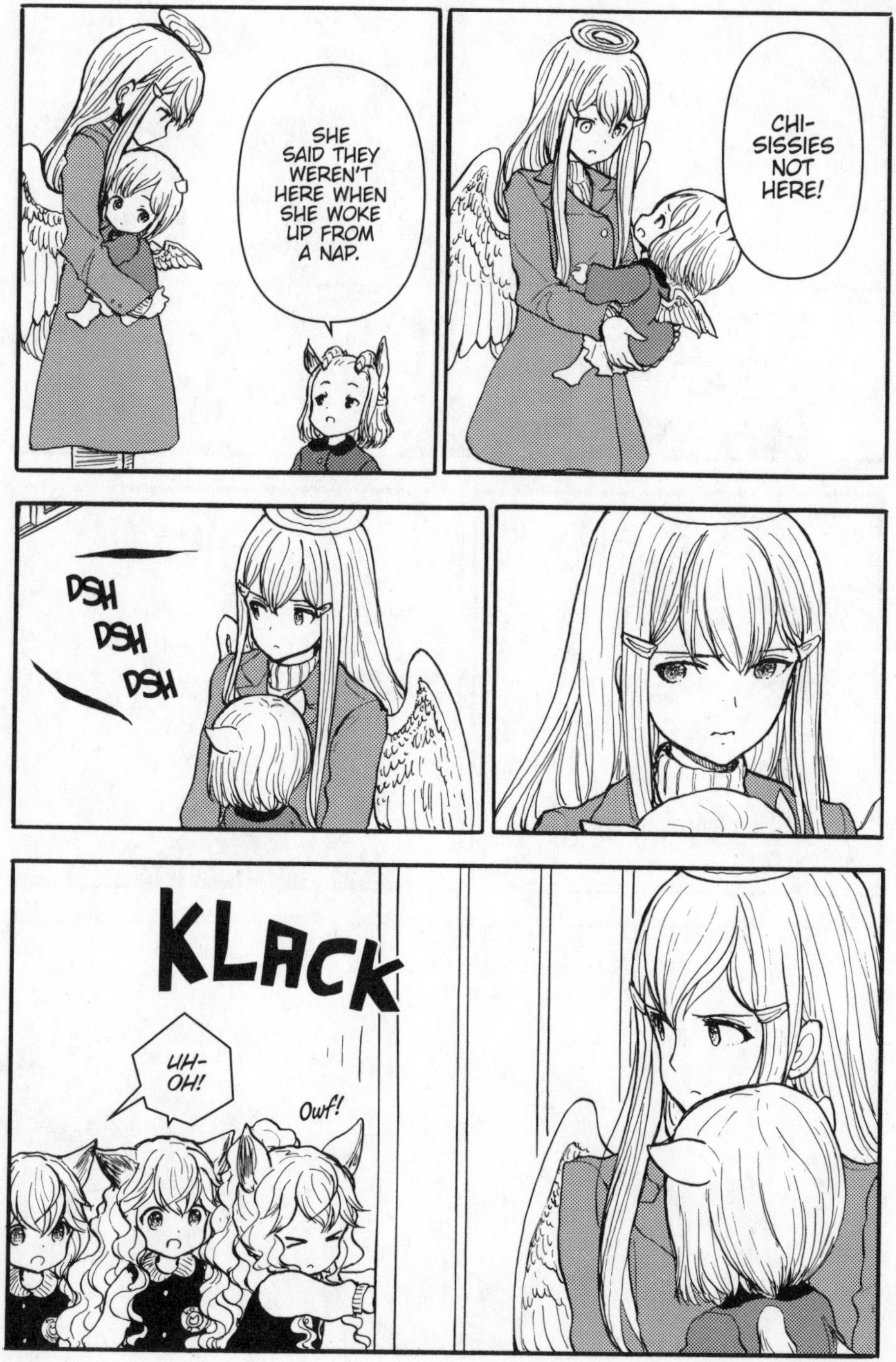
CHI-SISSIES NOT HERE!
SHE SAID THEY WEREN'T HERE WHEN SHE WOKE UP FROM A NAP.
DSH DSH DSH
KLACK
UH-OH!
Owf!

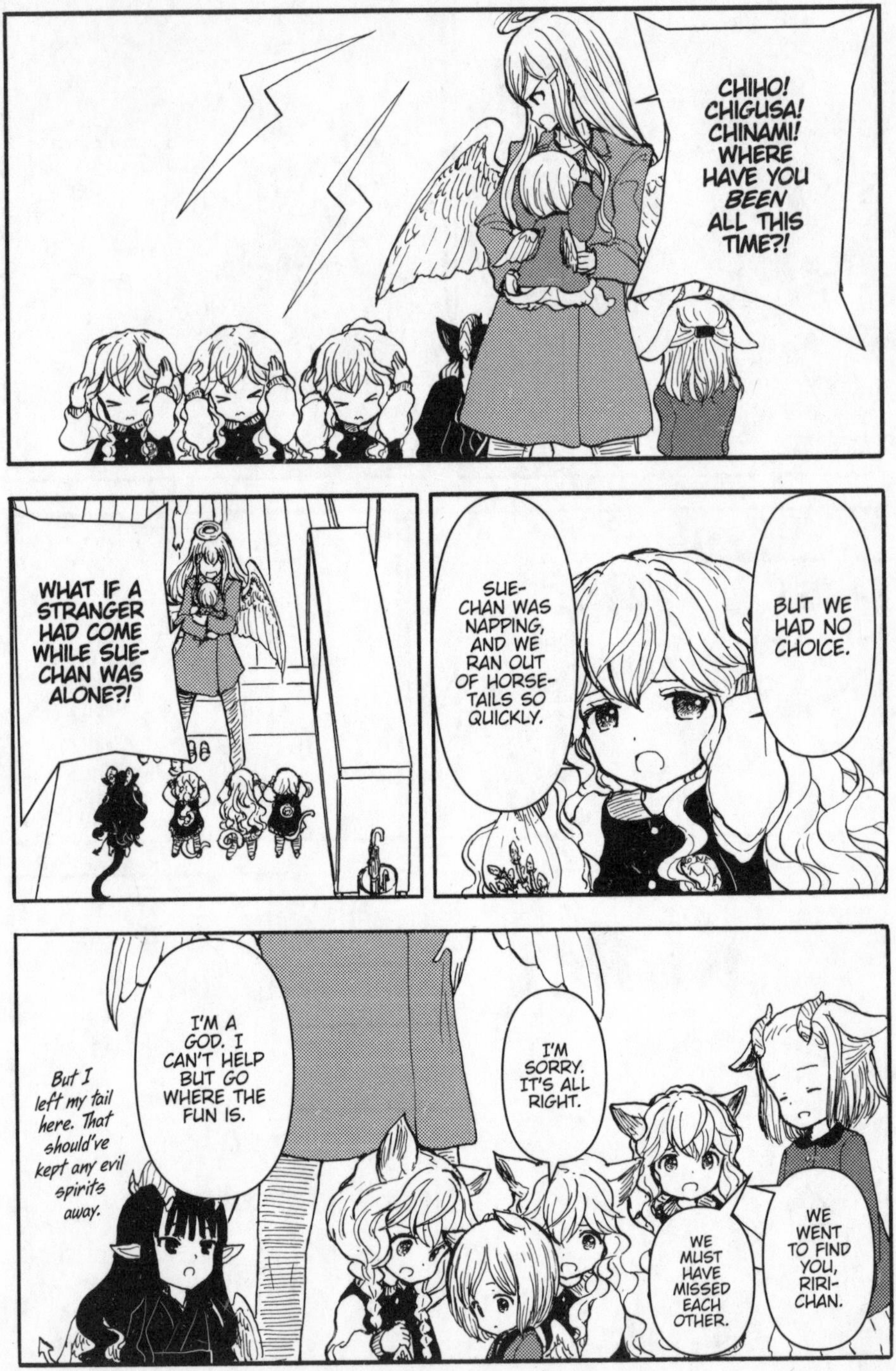

CHIHO! CHIGUSA! CHINAMI! WHERE HAVE YOU BEEN ALL THIS TIME?!
BUT WE HAD NO CHOICE.
SUE-CHAN WAS NAPPING, AND WE RAN OUT OF HORSE-TAILS SO QUICKLY.
WHAT IF A STRANGER HAD COME WHILE SUE-CHAN WAS ALONE?!
WE WENT TO FIND YOU, RIRI-CHAN.
WE MUST HAVE MISSED EACH OTHER.
I'M SORRY. IT'S ALL RIGHT.
I'M A GOD. I CAN'T HELP BUT GO WHERE THE FUN IS.
But I left my tail here. That should've kept any evil spirits away.

A Centaur's Life

RELEARNING THE ORIGIN OF MAMMALIAN HUMANS
6. MAMMALIAN HUMANS THAT LIVED DURING THE TIME OF MODERN HUMANS

MODERN HUMANS, *HOMO SAPIENS*, ARE CURRENTLY THE ONLY MEMBERS OF GENUS *HOMO* THAT EXIST, WHICH MEANS THERE ARE NO OTHER MAMMALIAN HUMANS. HOWEVER, THIS WASN'T TRUE IN THE PAST. *HOMO FLORESIENSIS*, MENTIONED EARLIER, LIVED AROUND 50,000 YEARS AGO. PENGHU MAN, FOUND AT THE BOTTOM OF THE PESCADORES CHANNEL, IS A SPECIES OF THE GENUS *HOMO*, BUT IT IS POSSIBLE THAT IT LIVED MUCH MORE RECENTLY THAN 190,000 YEARS AGO. THAT WAS WHEN ARCHAIC HUMANS, NEANDERTHALS, AND MAMMALIAN HUMANS CONNECTED TO MODERN HUMANS WERE BELIEVED TO HAVE APPEARED. IT WAS ALSO WHEN A SPECIES OF ARCHAIC HUMANS KNOWN AS THE DENISOVANS ARE THOUGHT TO HAVE LIVED. THE BOTTOM LINE IS THAT SEVERAL SPECIES OF MAMMALIAN HUMANS LIVED ON EARTH AT THE TIME THAT MODERN HUMANS EVOLVED.

THIS RAISES SEVERAL QUESTIONS. WHY DOES ONLY ONE SPECIES OF MODERN HUMANS EXIST? WHY ARE THEY SUPERIOR TO OTHER PRIMITIVE SPECIES? IS IT RIGHT TO THINK OF THE DECREASING TEETH AND JAW SIZE AND INCREASING BRAIN SIZE AS EVOLUTION? IT SOUNDS PLAUSIBLE. BUT WOULDN'T CHILDREN WHO EXCELLED AT PHYSICAL STRENGTH OR SPEED HAVE BEEN DEEMED MORE IMPORTANT THAN CHILDREN WHO EXCELLED AT INTELLECTUAL TASKS?

AS TEETH AND JAWS GROW SMALLER, BRAIN SIZE INCREASES. THESE ARE INDICATIONS OF SPECIALIZATION RATHER THAN SUPERIORITY. A DECREASE IN SIZE OF THE TEETH AND JAWS RESULTS IN POORER CHEWING ABILITY, BUT A LARGER BRAIN DEMANDS THE CONSTANT INTAKE OF CALORIES. MODERN HUMANS ARE EXTREMELY SPECIALIZED ANIMALS WHOSE EVOLUTIONARY TRAITS HAVE MANY DISADVANTAGES. UTILIZING WHAT ADVANTAGES THEY DID HAVE WHEN FACED WITH EXTINCTION RESULTED IN THEIR SURVIVAL AS THE ONLY MODERN HUMANS.

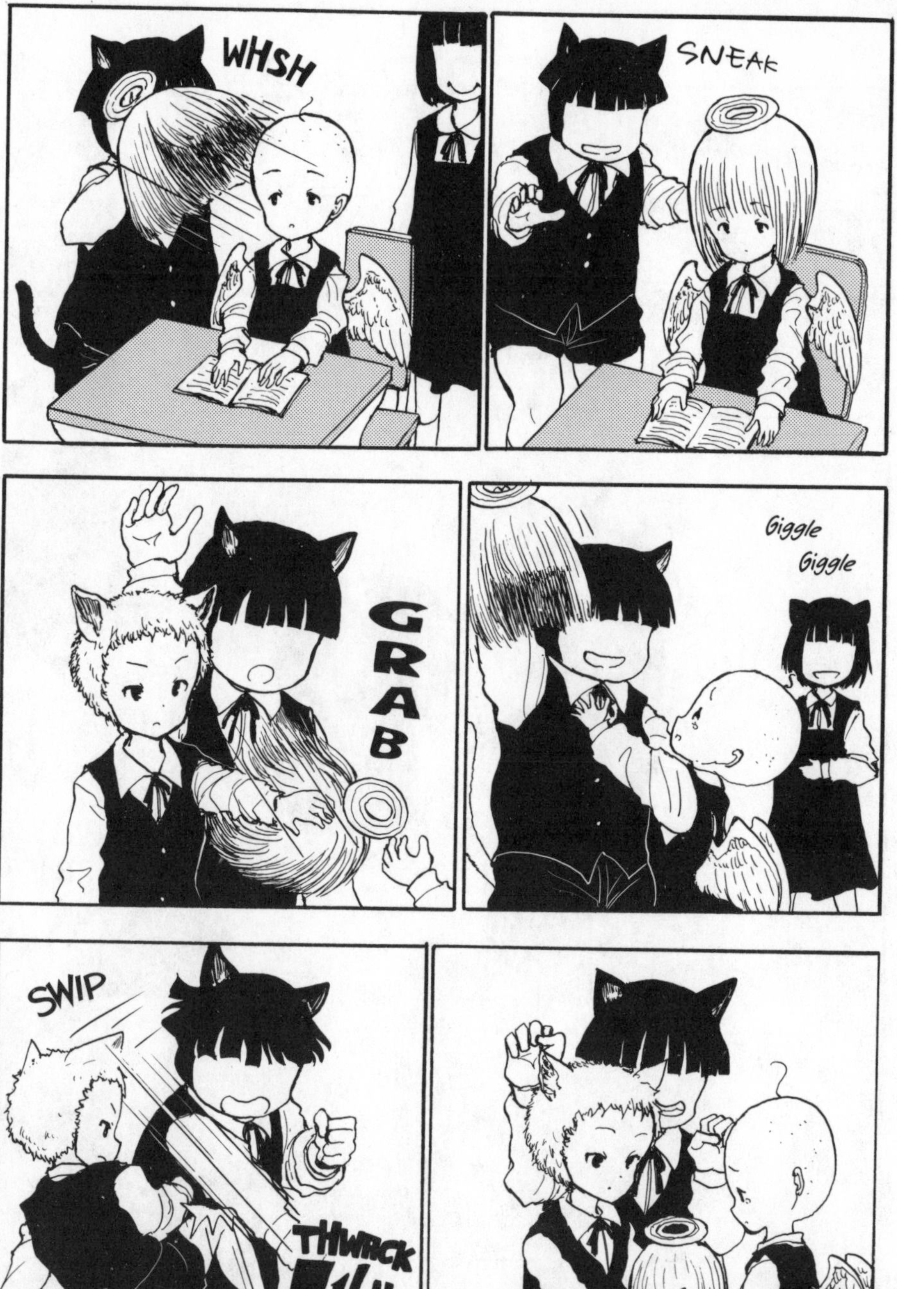
SNEAK
WHSH
Giggle
Giggle
GRAB
SWIP
THWACK

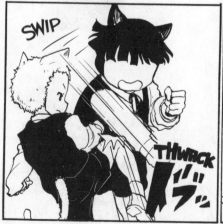

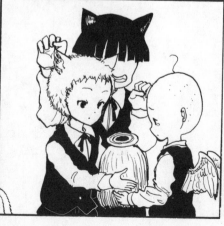

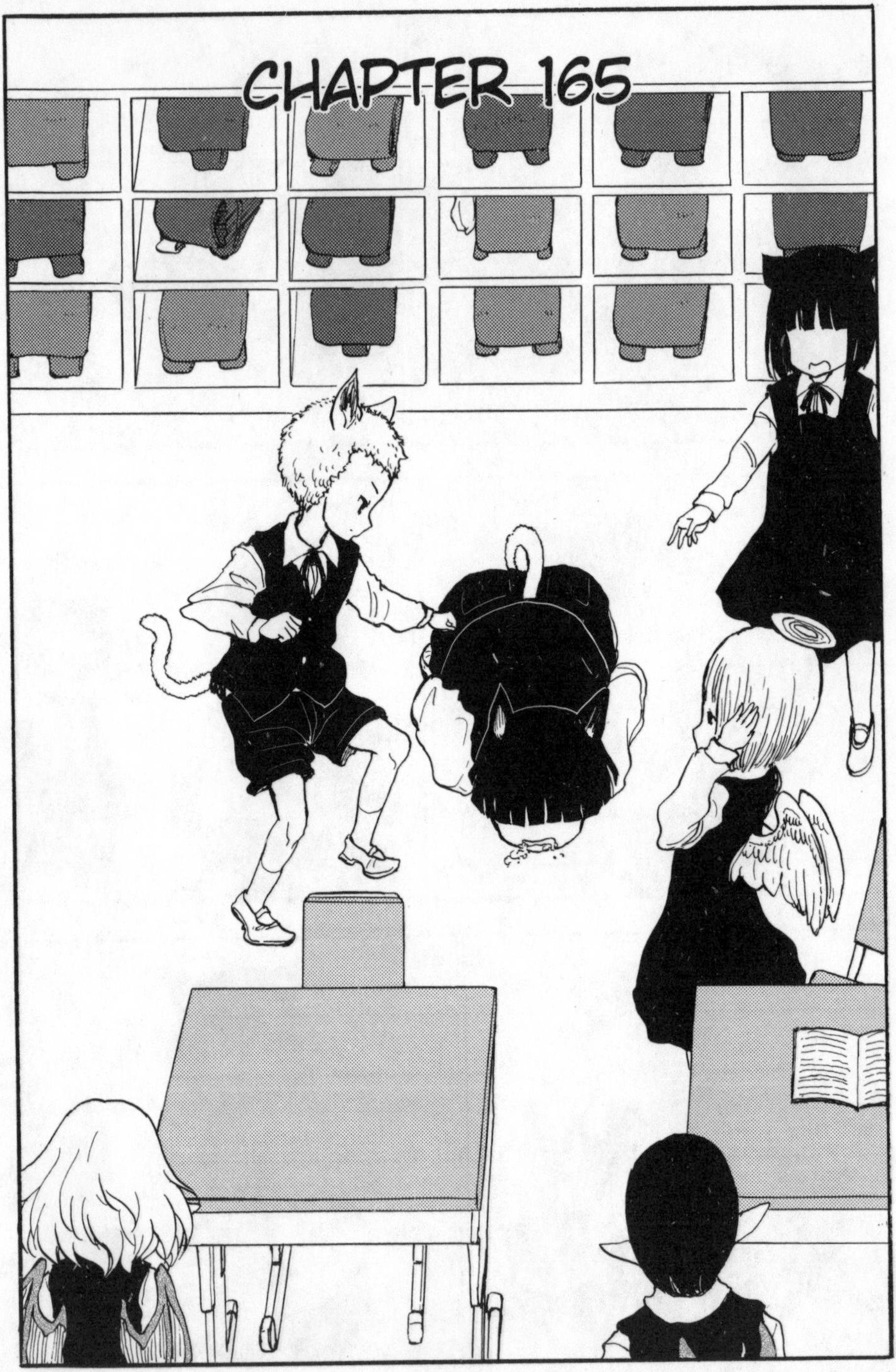
CHAPTER 165

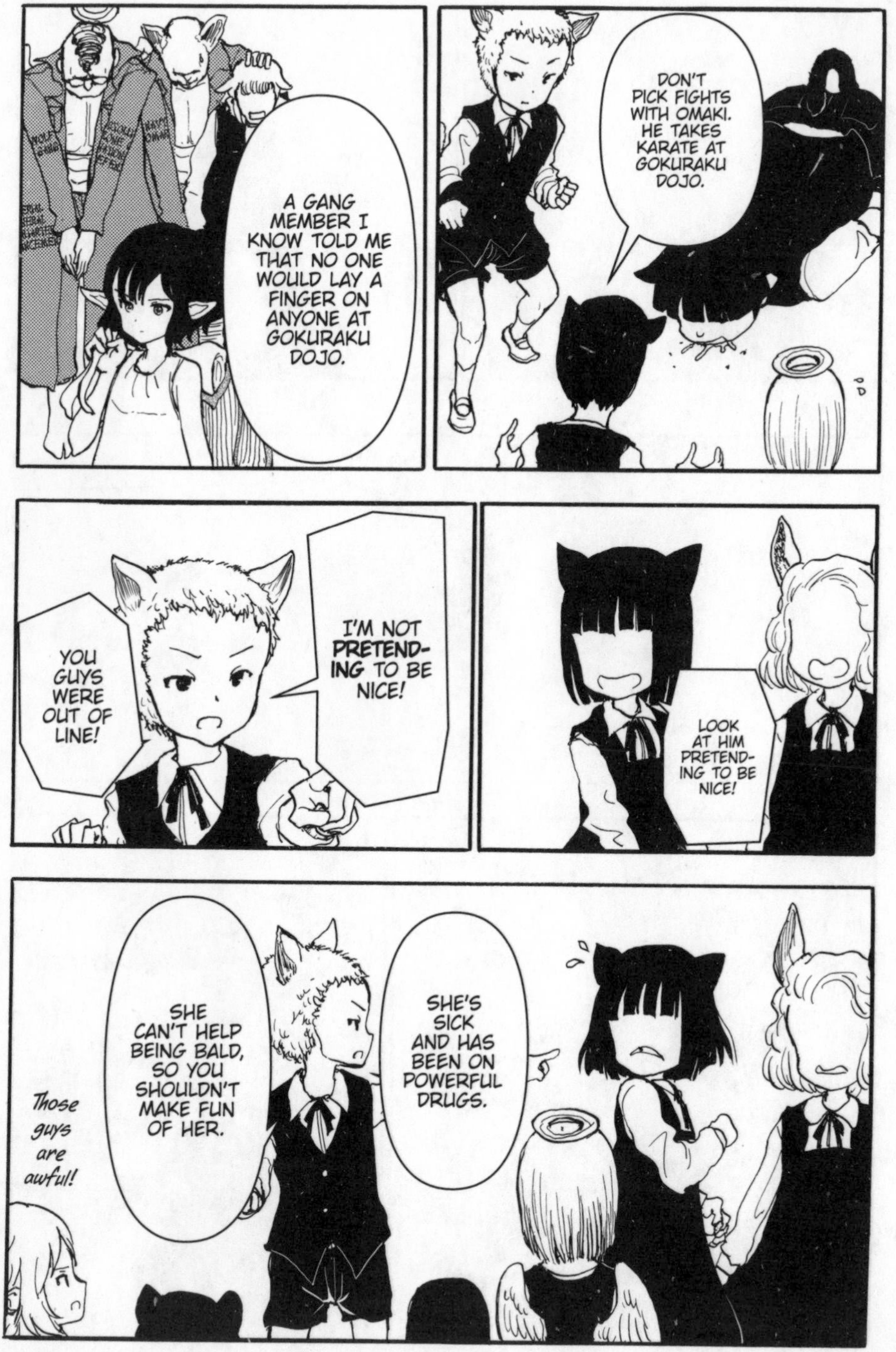
DON'T PICK FIGHTS WITH OMAKI. HE TAKES KARATE AT GOKURAKU DOJO.
A GANG MEMBER I KNOW TOLD ME THAT NO ONE WOULD LAY A FINGER ON ANYONE AT GOKURAKU DOJO.
LOOK AT HIM PRETENDING TO BE NICE!
I'M NOT PRETENDING TO BE NICE!
YOU GUYS WERE OUT OF LINE!
SHE'S SICK AND HAS BEEN ON POWERFUL DRUGS.
SHE CAN'T HELP BEING BALD, SO YOU SHOULDN'T MAKE FUN OF HER.
Those guys are awful!

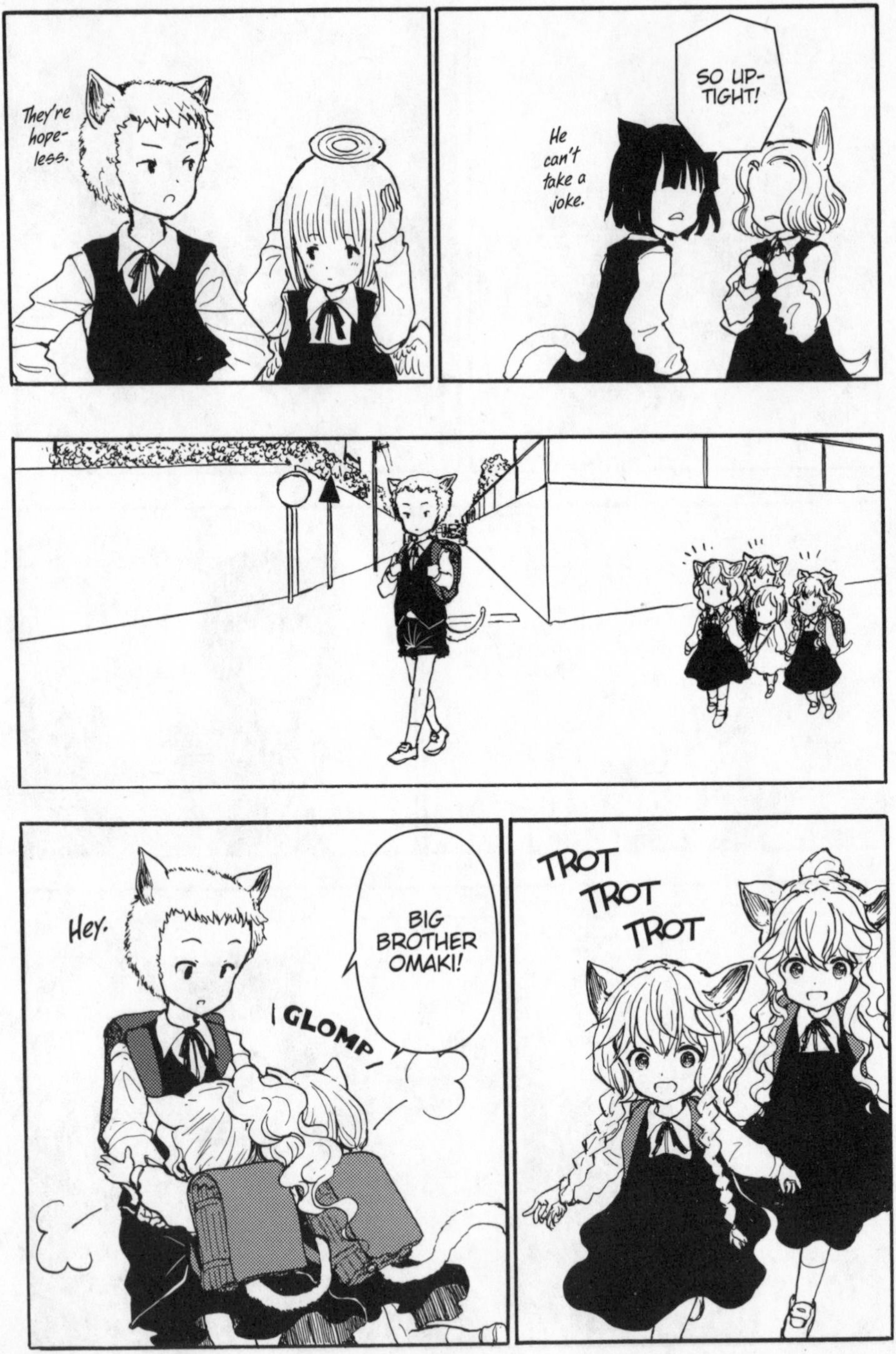
SO UP-TIGHT!
He can't take a joke.
They're hope-less.
TROT TROT TROT
BIG BROTHER OMAKI!
GLOMP!
Hey.

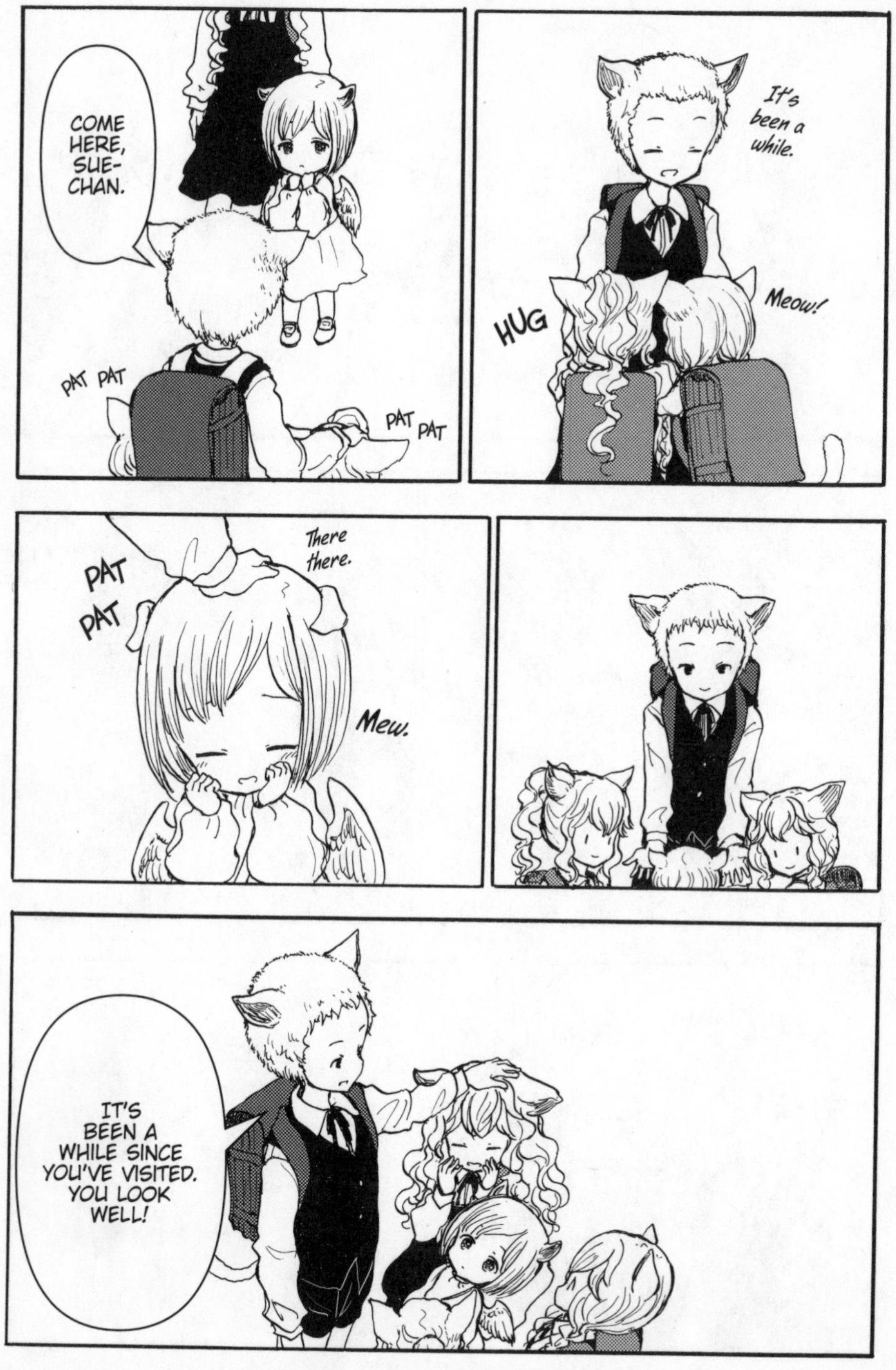
It's been a while.
Meow!
HUG
COME HERE, SUE-CHAN.
PAT PAT
PAT PAT
There there.
PAT PAT
Mew.
IT'S BEEN A WHILE SINCE YOU'VE VISITED. YOU LOOK WELL!

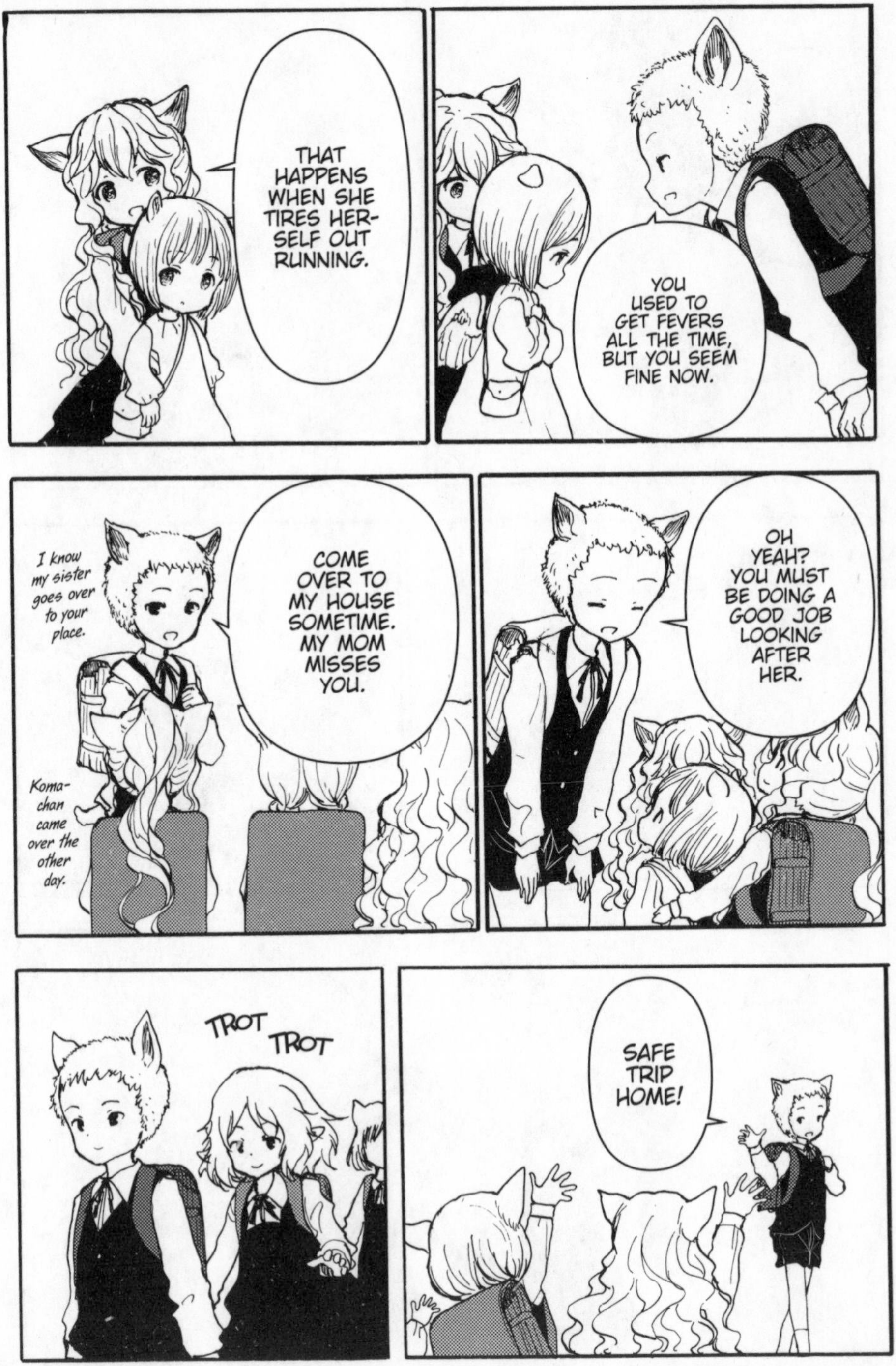
YOU USED TO GET FEVERS ALL THE TIME, BUT YOU SEEM FINE NOW.
THAT HAPPENS WHEN SHE TIRES HER-SELF OUT RUNNING.
OH YEAH? YOU MUST BE DOING A GOOD JOB LOOKING AFTER HER.
COME OVER TO MY HOUSE SOMETIME. MY MOM MISSES YOU.
I know my sister goes over to your place.
Koma-chan came over the other day.
SAFE TRIP HOME!
TROT TROT

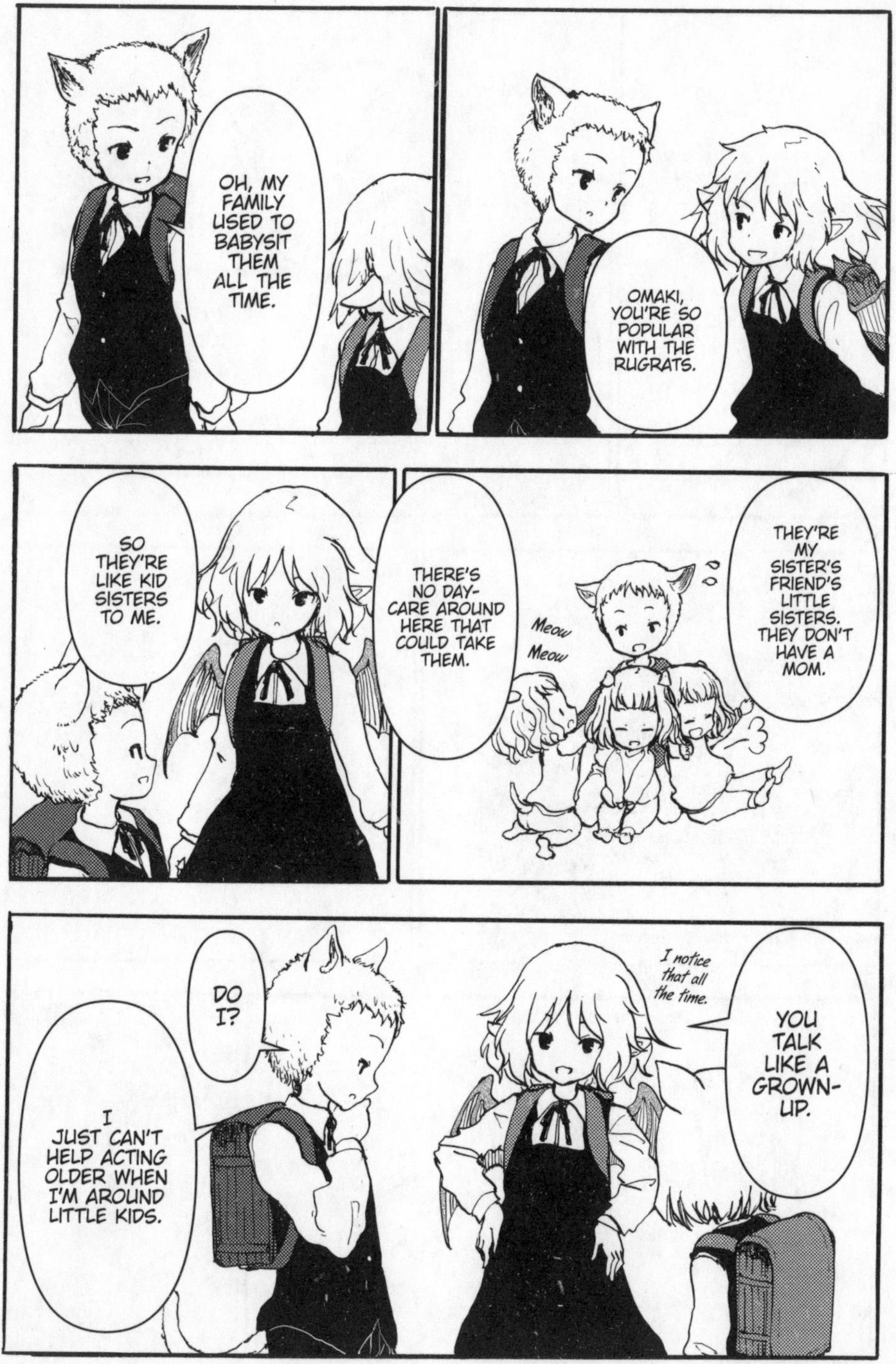
OMAKI, YOU'RE SO POPULAR WITH THE RUGRATS.
OH, MY FAMILY USED TO BABYSIT THEM ALL THE TIME.
THEY'RE MY SISTER'S FRIEND'S LITTLE SISTERS. THEY DON'T HAVE A MOM.
THERE'S NO DAY-CARE AROUND HERE THAT COULD TAKE THEM.
Meow
Meow
SO THEY'RE LIKE KID SISTERS TO ME.
YOU TALK LIKE A GROWN-UP.
I notice that all the time.
DO I?
I JUST CAN'T HELP ACTING OLDER WHEN I'M AROUND LITTLE KIDS.

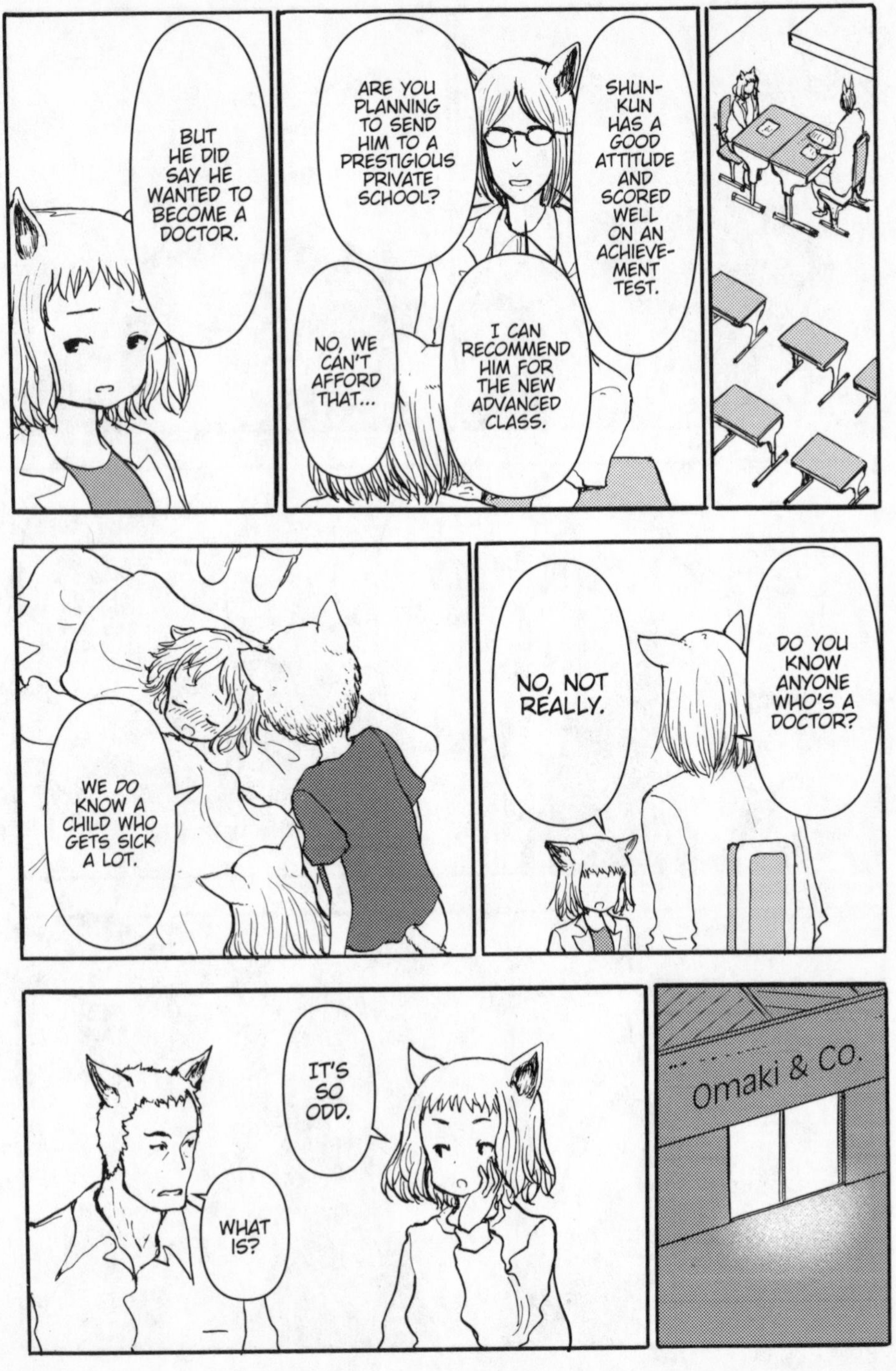
SHUN-KUN HAS A GOOD ATTITUDE AND SCORED WELL ON AN ACHIEVEMENT TEST.
ARE YOU PLANNING TO SEND HIM TO A PRESTIGIOUS PRIVATE SCHOOL?
I CAN RECOMMEND HIM FOR THE NEW ADVANCED CLASS.
NO, WE CAN'T AFFORD THAT...
BUT HE DID SAY HE WANTED TO BECOME A DOCTOR.
DO YOU KNOW ANYONE WHO'S A DOCTOR?
NO, NOT REALLY.
WE DO KNOW A CHILD WHO GETS SICK A LOT.
Omaki & Co.
IT'S SO ODD.
WHAT IS?

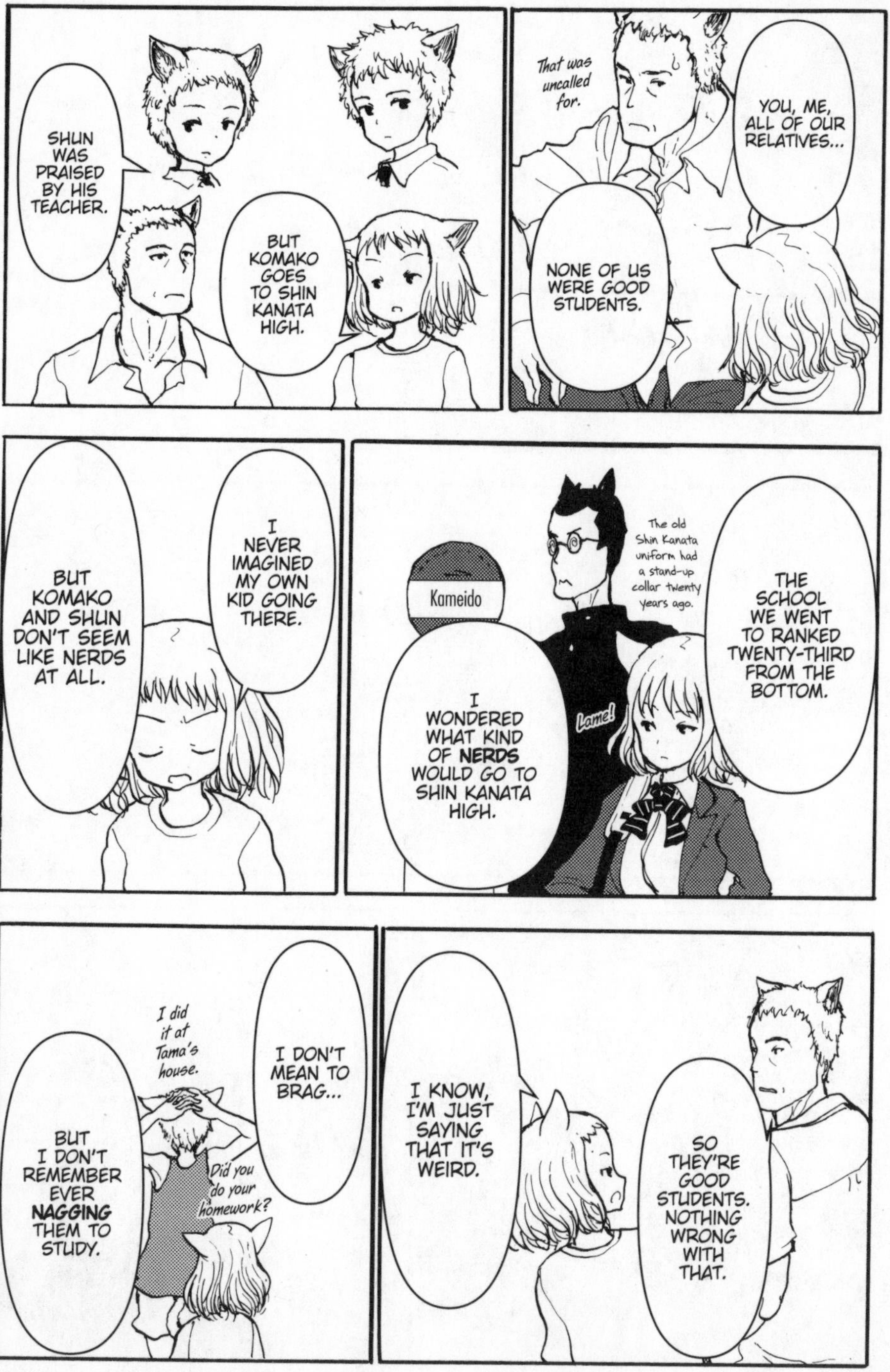
YOU, ME, ALL OF OUR RELATIVES...
That was uncalled for.
NONE OF US WERE GOOD STUDENTS.
SHUN WAS PRAISED BY HIS TEACHER.
BUT KOMAKO GOES TO SHIN KANATA HIGH.
THE SCHOOL WE WENT TO RANKED TWENTY-THIRD FROM THE BOTTOM.
The old Shin Kanata uniform had a stand-up collar twenty years ago.
Kameido
Lame!
I WONDERED WHAT KIND OF NERDS WOULD GO TO SHIN KANATA HIGH.
I NEVER IMAGINED MY OWN KID GOING THERE.
BUT KOMAKO AND SHUN DON'T SEEM LIKE NERDS AT ALL.
SO THEY'RE GOOD STUDENTS. NOTHING WRONG WITH THAT.
I KNOW, I'M JUST SAYING THAT IT'S WEIRD.
I DON'T MEAN TO BRAG...
I did it at Tama's house.
Did you do your homework?
BUT I DON'T REMEMBER EVER NAGGING THEM TO STUDY.

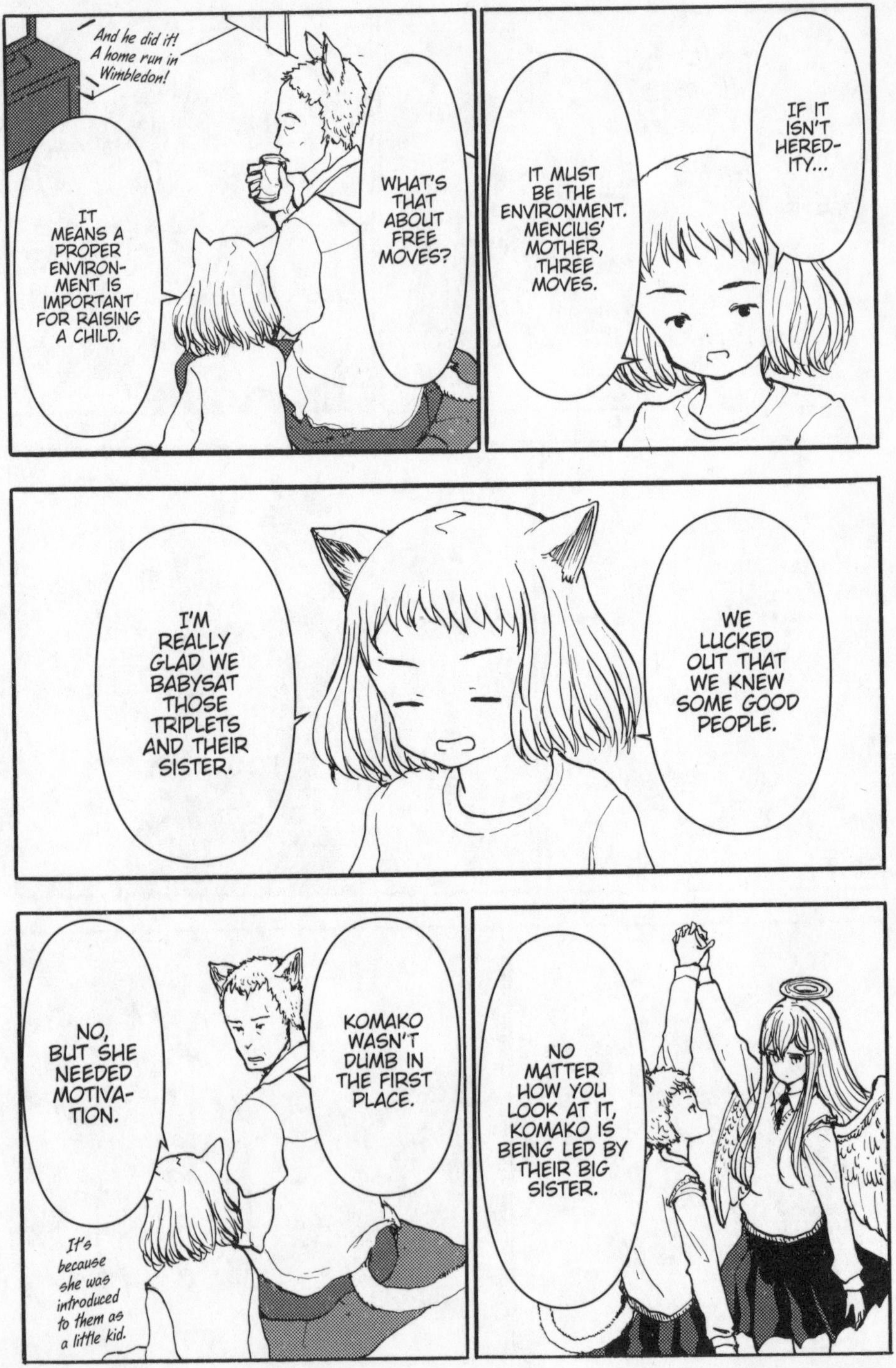
IF IT ISN'T HEREDITY...
IT MUST BE THE ENVIRONMENT. MENCIUS' MOTHER, THREE MOVES.
WHAT'S THAT ABOUT FREE MOVES?
And he did it! A home run in Wimbledon!
IT MEANS A PROPER ENVIRONMENT IS IMPORTANT FOR RAISING A CHILD.
WE LUCKED OUT THAT WE KNEW SOME GOOD PEOPLE.
I'M REALLY GLAD WE BABYSAT THOSE TRIPLETS AND THEIR SISTER.
NO MATTER HOW YOU LOOK AT IT, KOMAKO IS BEING LED BY THEIR BIG SISTER.
KOMAKO WASN'T DUMB IN THE FIRST PLACE.
NO, BUT SHE NEEDED MOTIVATION.
It's because she was introduced to them as a little kid.

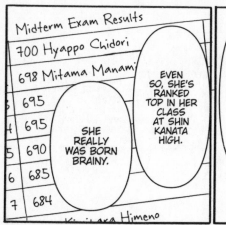

Midterm Exam Results	
700	Hyappo Chidori
698	Mitama Manami
3	695
4	695
5	690
6	685
7	684
	Kirikara Himeno

SHE REALLY WAS BORN BRAINY.

EVEN SO, SHE'S RANKED TOP IN HER CLASS AT SHIN KANATA HIGH.

God, I'm so busy.

OF COURSE NOT. SHE DOESN'T HAVE *TIME* TO STUDY LIKE CRAZY.

THAT GIRL DOESN'T LOOK LIKE A NERD TO ME.

AND THEY GET SMARTER IN A SMART ENVIRONMENT.

ORDINARY PEOPLE GET DUMBER AROUND DUMB PEOPLE.

Woo!

A KID WITH NATURAL TALENT LIKE THAT PUSHED HERSELF TO THE TOP WHEN NO ONE ELSE CARED.

KOMAKO AND SHUN WOULD'VE PLAYED HOOKY LIKE WE DID, NO MATTER WHAT WE DID.

IF WE HADN'T BABY-SAT THE TRIPLETS AND THEIR SISTER...

YES, BECAUSE THEY'RE *OUR* KIDS.

ARE OUR KIDS ORDINARY?

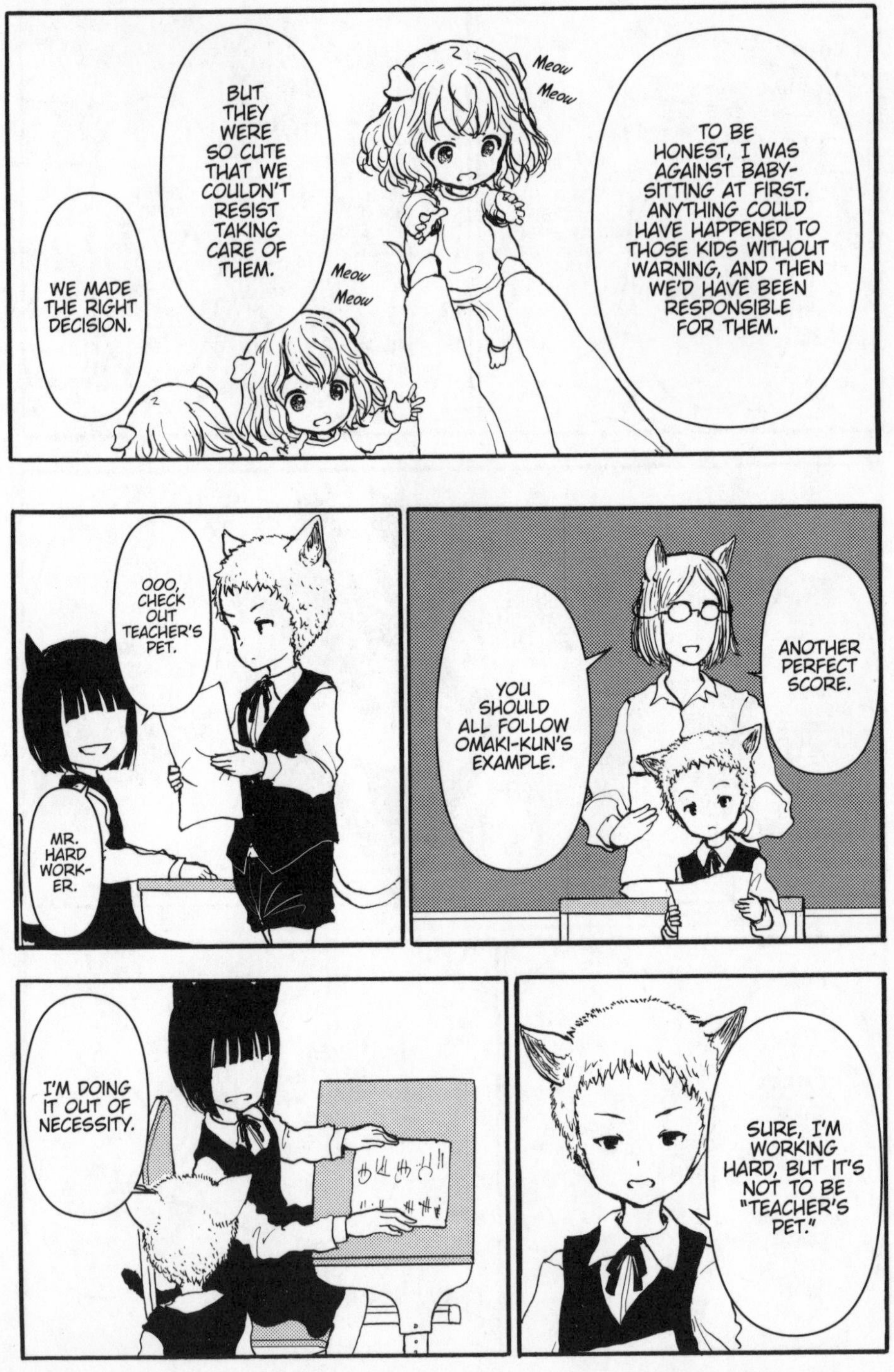
TO BE HONEST, I WAS AGAINST BABY-SITTING AT FIRST. ANYTHING COULD HAVE HAPPENED TO THOSE KIDS WITHOUT WARNING, AND THEN WE'D HAVE BEEN RESPONSIBLE FOR THEM.
Meow Meow
BUT THEY WERE SO CUTE THAT WE COULDN'T RESIST TAKING CARE OF THEM.
Meow Meow
WE MADE THE RIGHT DECISION.
ANOTHER PERFECT SCORE.
YOU SHOULD ALL FOLLOW OMAKI-KUN'S EXAMPLE.
OOO, CHECK OUT TEACHER'S PET.
MR. HARD WORK-ER.
SURE, I'M WORKING HARD, BUT IT'S NOT TO BE "TEACHER'S PET."
I'M DOING IT OUT OF NECESSITY.

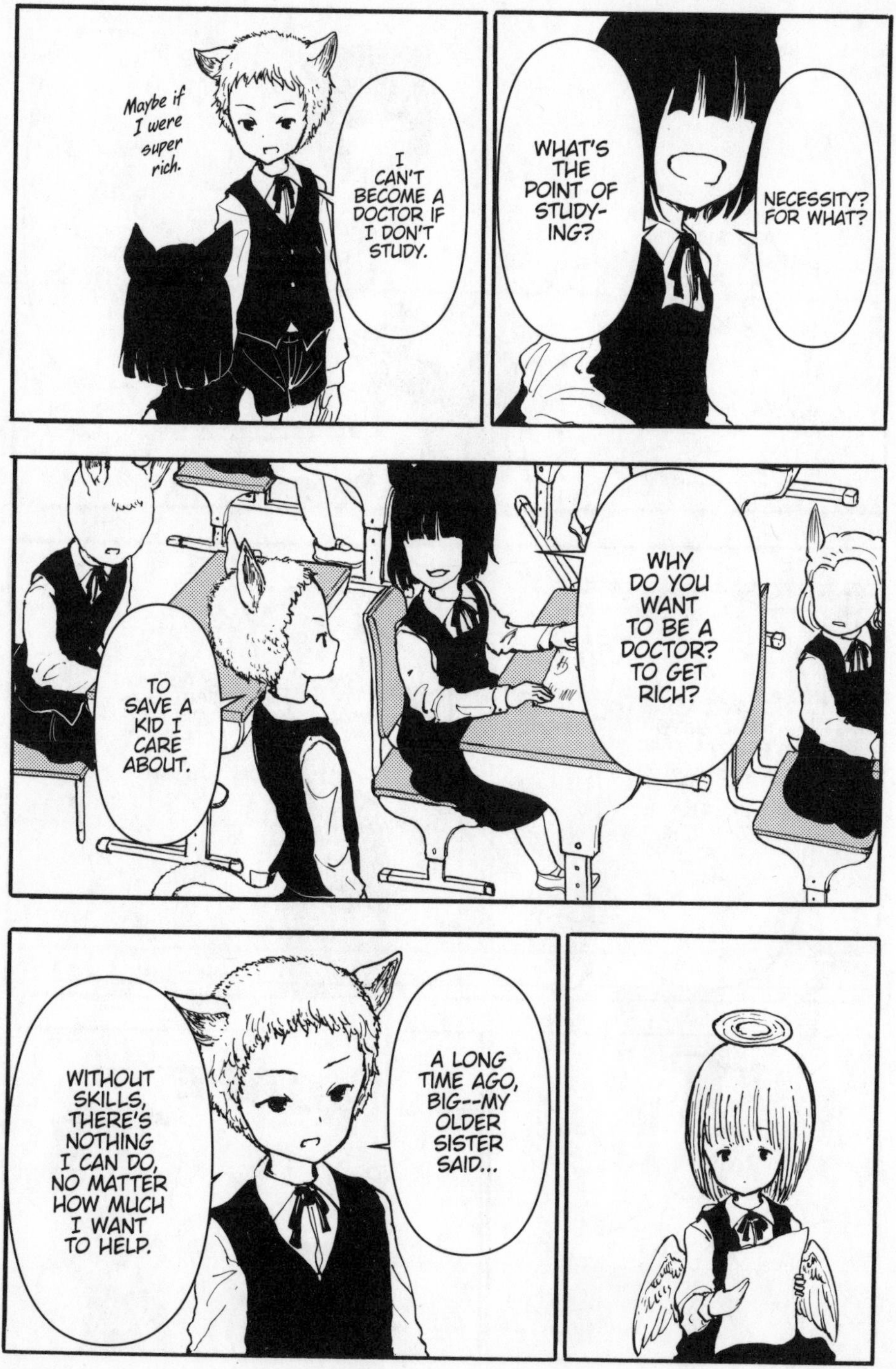
NECESSITY? FOR WHAT?
WHAT'S THE POINT OF STUDY-ING?
I CAN'T BECOME A DOCTOR IF I DON'T STUDY.
Maybe if I were super rich.
WHY DO YOU WANT TO BE A DOCTOR? TO GET RICH?
TO SAVE A KID I CARE ABOUT.
A LONG TIME AGO, BIG--MY OLDER SISTER SAID...
WITHOUT SKILLS, THERE'S NOTHING I CAN DO, NO MATTER HOW MUCH I WANT TO HELP.

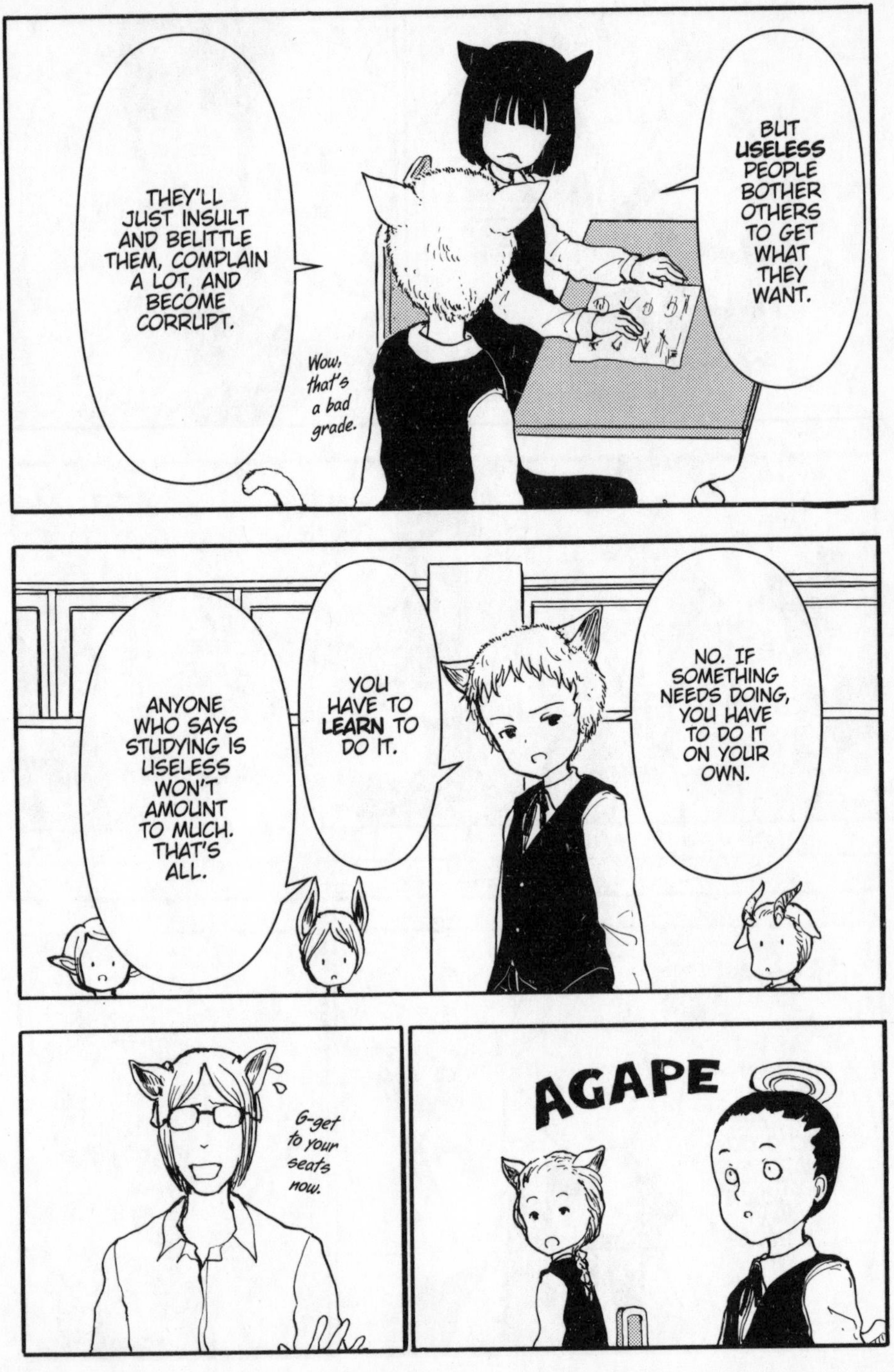
BUT USELESS PEOPLE BOTHER OTHERS TO GET WHAT THEY WANT.
THEY'LL JUST INSULT AND BELITTLE THEM, COMPLAIN A LOT, AND BECOME CORRUPT.
Wow, that's a bad grade.
NO. IF SOMETHING NEEDS DOING, YOU HAVE TO DO IT ON YOUR OWN.
YOU HAVE TO LEARN TO DO IT.
ANYONE WHO SAYS STUDYING IS USELESS WON'T AMOUNT TO MUCH. THAT'S ALL.
AGAPE
G-get to your seats now.

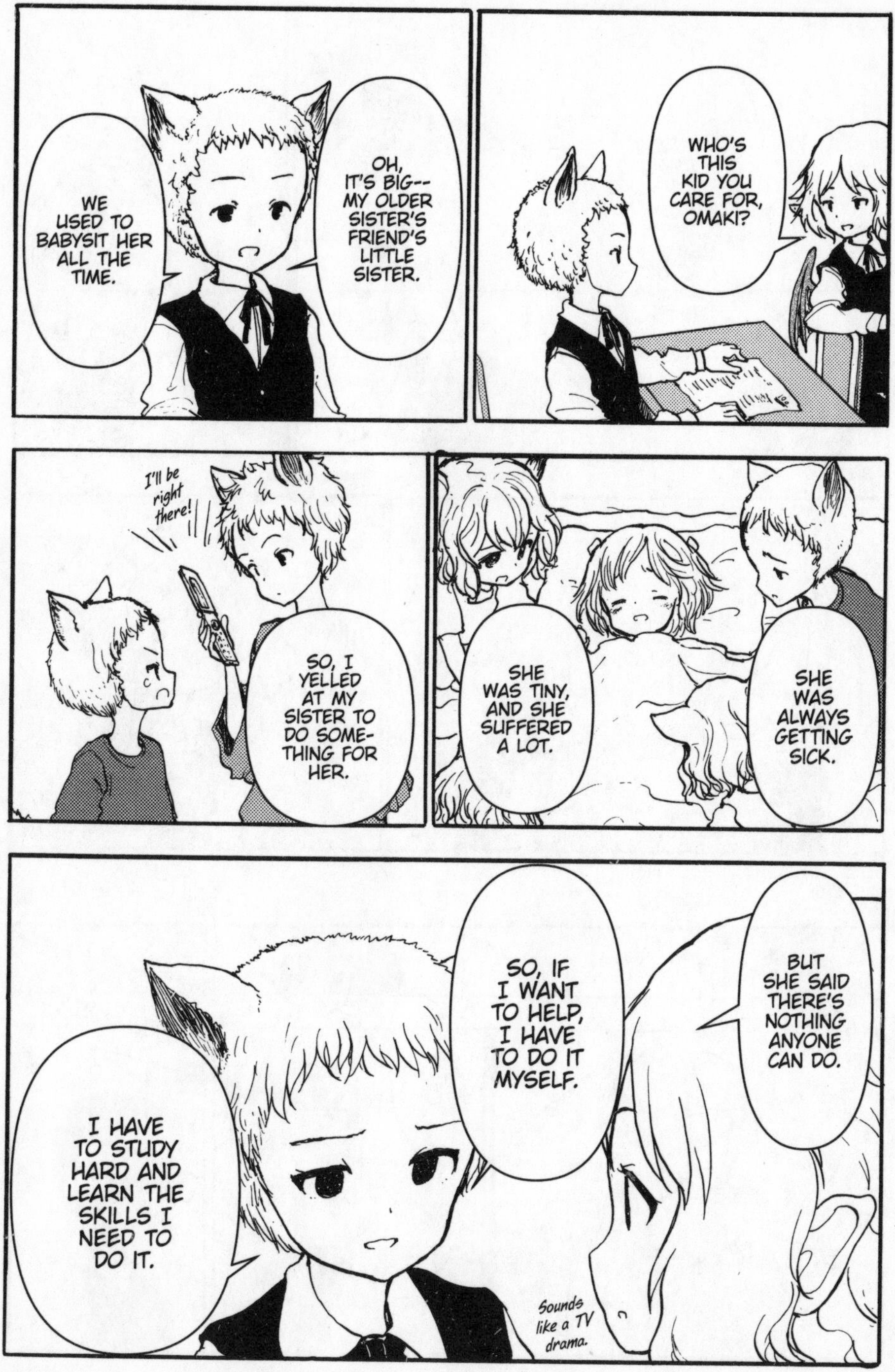
WHO'S THIS KID YOU CARE FOR, OMAKI?
OH, IT'S BIG-- MY OLDER SISTER'S FRIEND'S LITTLE SISTER.
WE USED TO BABYSIT HER ALL THE TIME.
SHE WAS ALWAYS GETTING SICK.
SHE WAS TINY, AND SHE SUFFERED A LOT.
I'll be right there!
SO, I YELLED AT MY SISTER TO DO SOMETHING FOR HER.
BUT SHE SAID THERE'S NOTHING ANYONE CAN DO.
SO, IF I WANT TO HELP, I HAVE TO DO IT MYSELF.
I HAVE TO STUDY HARD AND LEARN THE SKILLS I NEED TO DO IT.
Sounds like a TV drama.

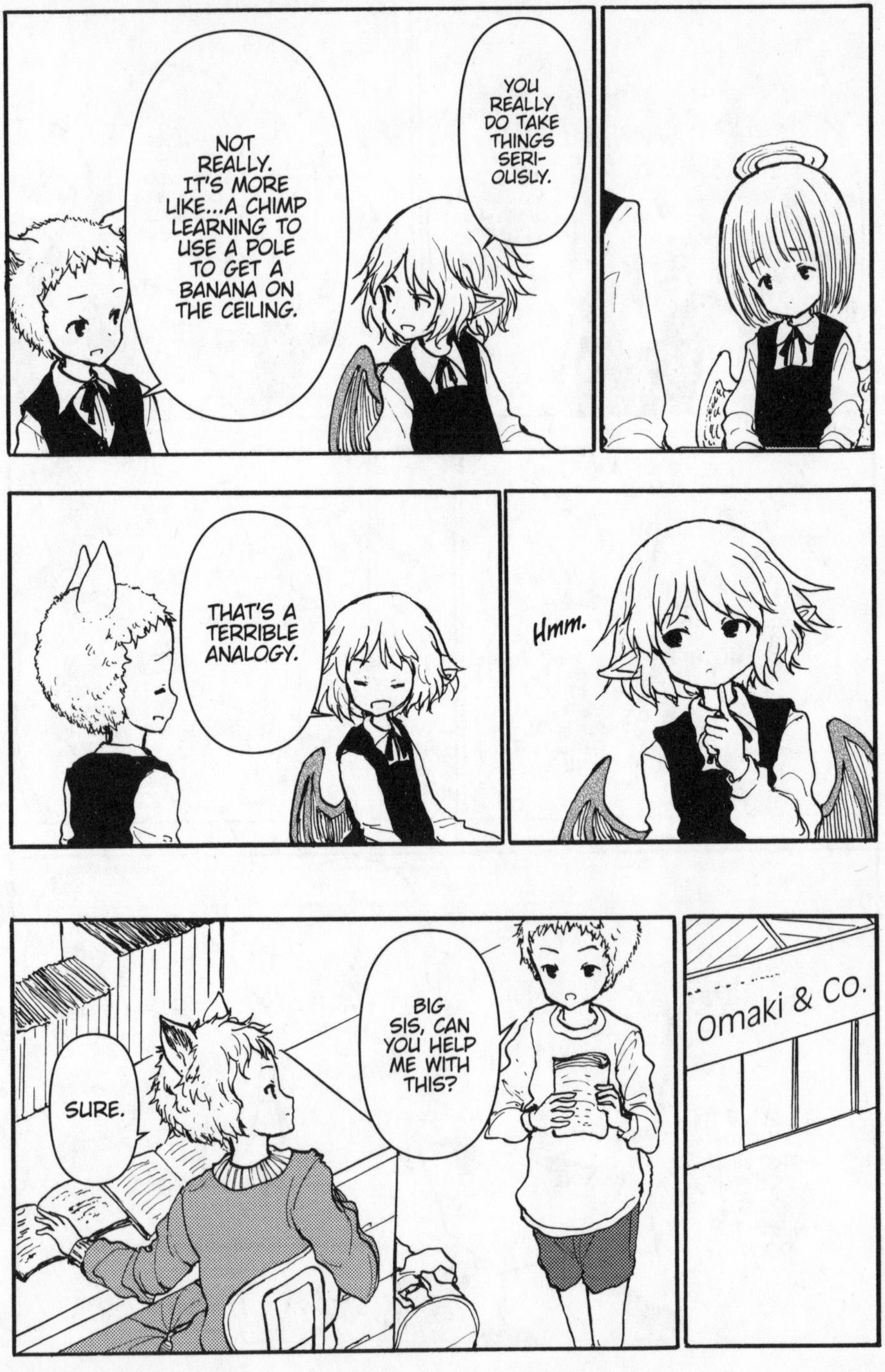
YOU REALLY DO TAKE THINGS SERI-OUSLY.
NOT REALLY. IT'S MORE LIKE...A CHIMP LEARNING TO USE A POLE TO GET A BANANA ON THE CEILING.
Hmm.
THAT'S A TERRIBLE ANALOGY.
Omaki & Co.
BIG SIS, CAN YOU HELP ME WITH THIS?
SURE.

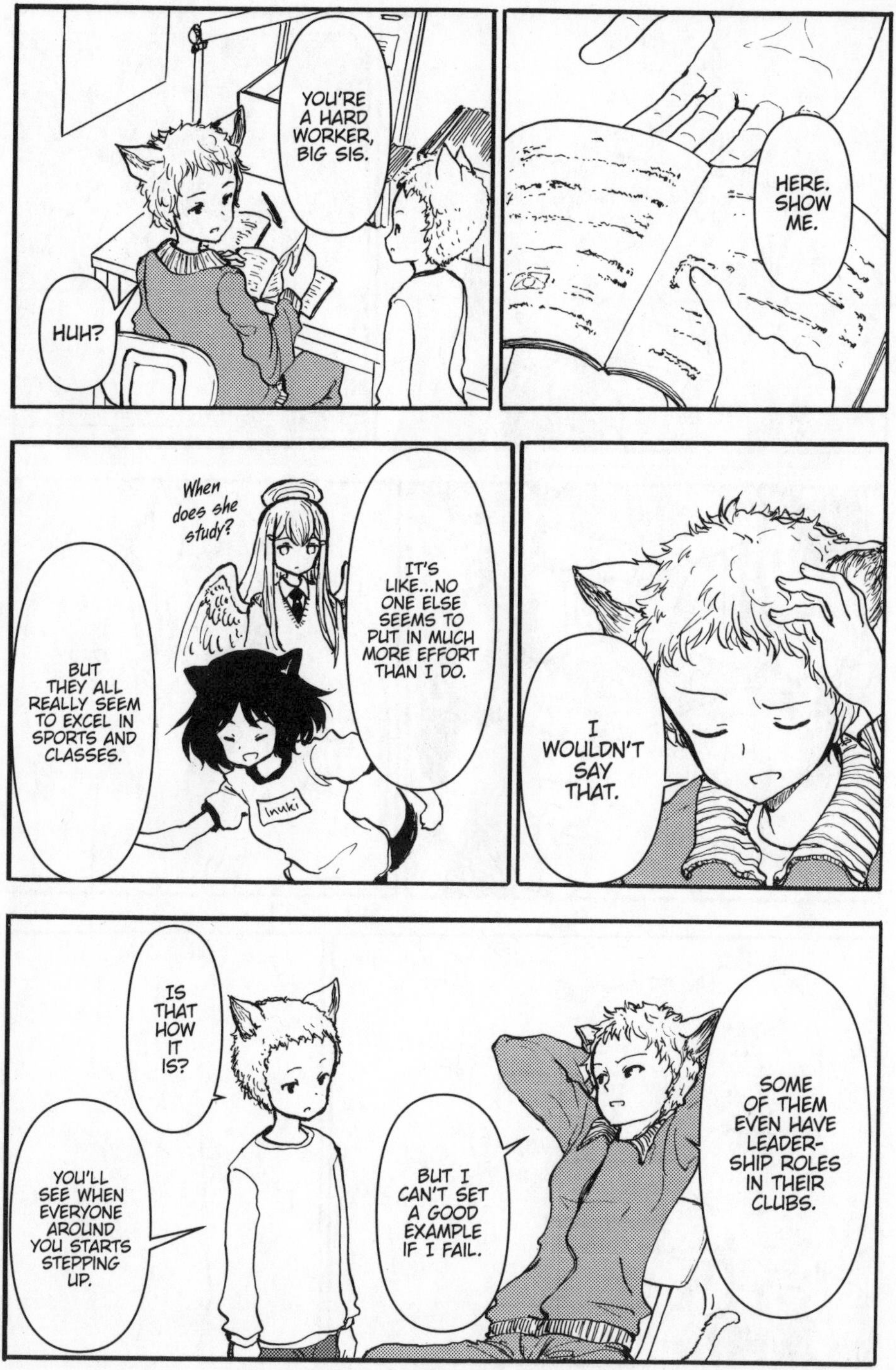
HERE. SHOW ME.
YOU'RE A HARD WORKER, BIG SIS.
HUH?
I WOULDN'T SAY THAT.
IT'S LIKE...NO ONE ELSE SEEMS TO PUT IN MUCH MORE EFFORT THAN I DO.
When does she study?
BUT THEY ALL REALLY SEEM TO EXCEL IN SPORTS AND CLASSES.
Inuki
SOME OF THEM EVEN HAVE LEADER-SHIP ROLES IN THEIR CLUBS.
BUT I CAN'T SET A GOOD EXAMPLE IF I FAIL.
IS THAT HOW IT IS?
YOU'LL SEE WHEN EVERYONE AROUND YOU STARTS STEPPING UP.

KYOUSAWA-SAN WILL BE ABSENT FOR A WHILE.

WHO'S CLOSE TO KYOU-SAWA-SAN?

OKAY, FOLKS.

THEN I'LL LEAVE IT UP TO YOU, OMAKI-KUN.

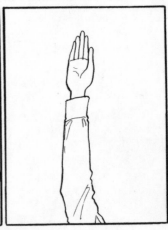

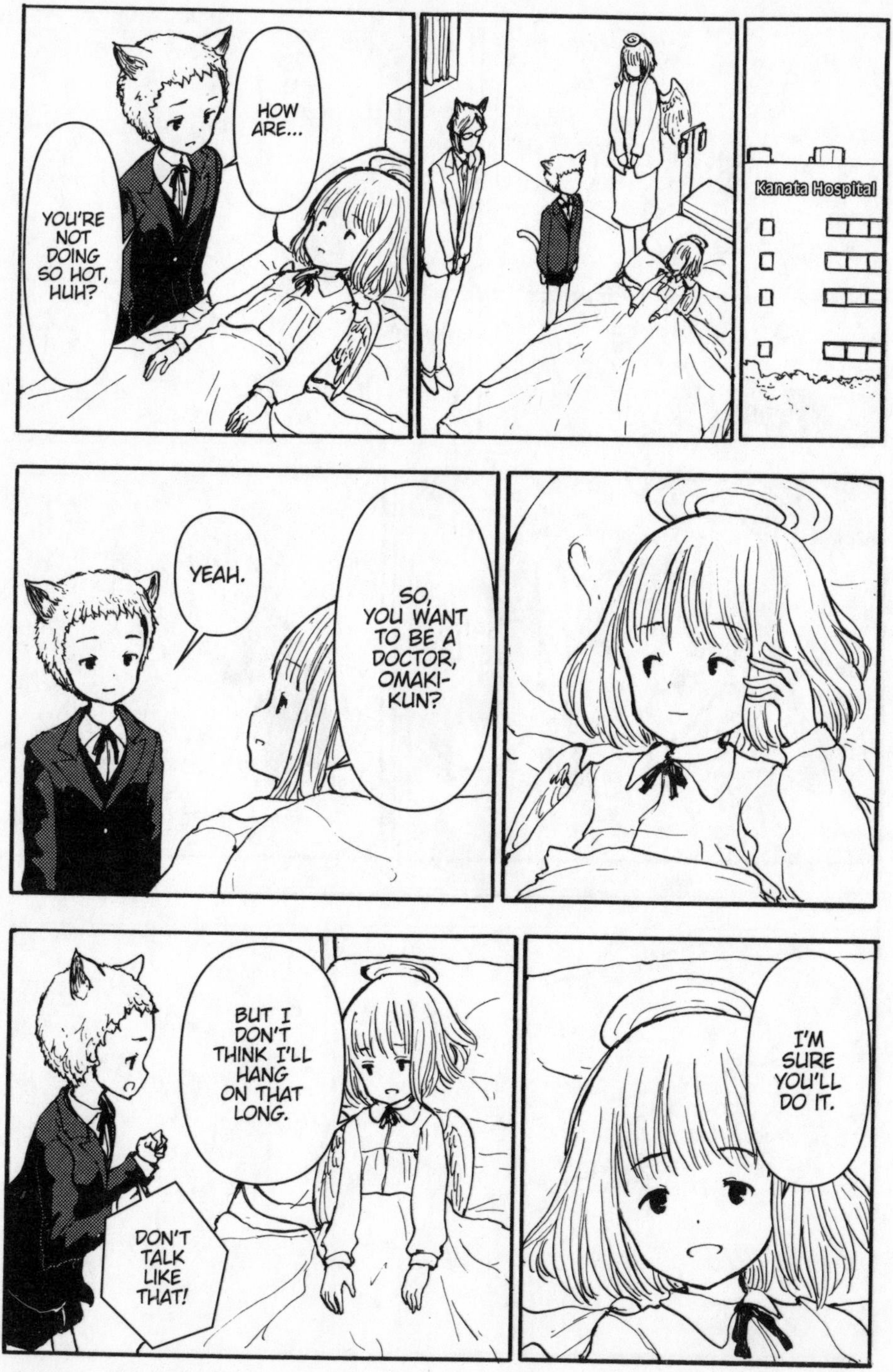
Kanata Hospital
HOW ARE...
YOU'RE NOT DOING SO HOT, HUH?
SO, YOU WANT TO BE A DOCTOR, OMAKI-KUN?
YEAH.
I'M SURE YOU'LL DO IT.
BUT I DON'T THINK I'LL HANG ON THAT LONG.
DON'T TALK LIKE THAT!

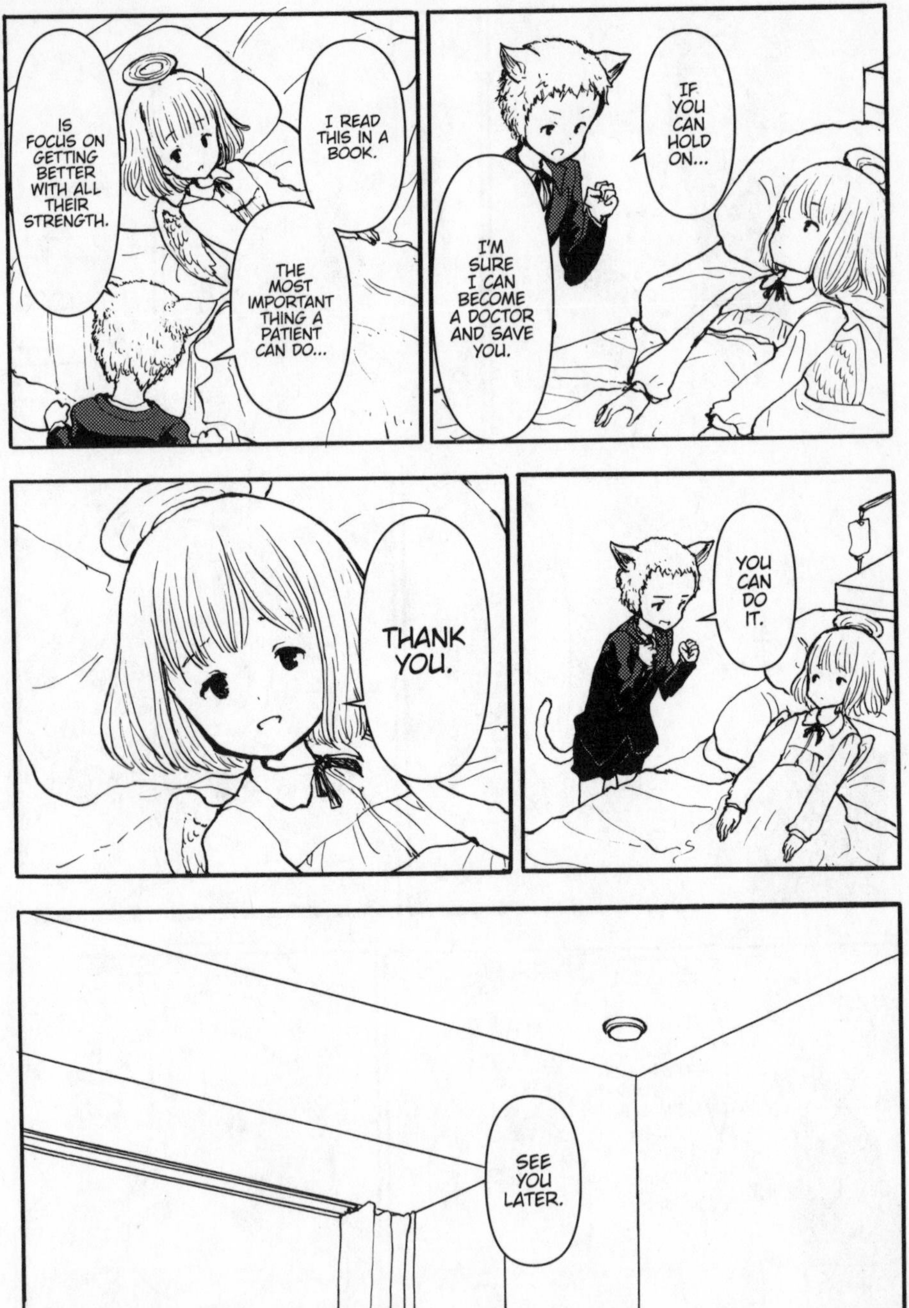
IF YOU CAN HOLD ON...
I'M SURE I CAN BECOME A DOCTOR AND SAVE YOU.
I READ THIS IN A BOOK.
THE MOST IMPORTANT THING A PATIENT CAN DO...
IS FOCUS ON GETTING BETTER WITH ALL THEIR STRENGTH.
YOU CAN DO IT.
THANK YOU.
SEE YOU LATER.

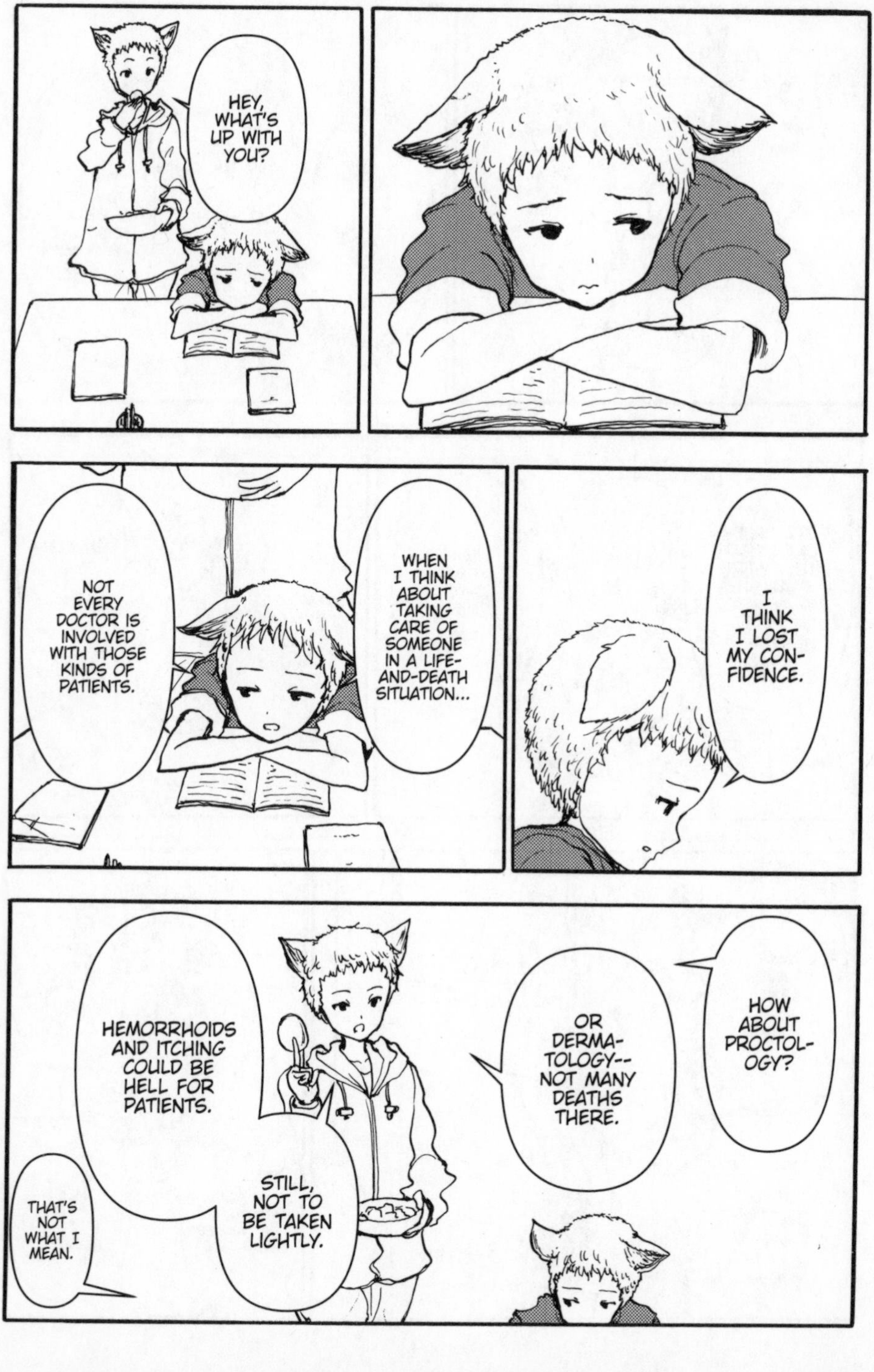
HEY, WHAT'S UP WITH YOU?
I THINK I LOST MY CONFIDENCE.
WHEN I THINK ABOUT TAKING CARE OF SOMEONE IN A LIFE-AND-DEATH SITUATION...
NOT EVERY DOCTOR IS INVOLVED WITH THOSE KINDS OF PATIENTS.
HOW ABOUT PROCTOLOGY?
OR DERMATOLOGY--NOT MANY DEATHS THERE.
HEMORRHOIDS AND ITCHING COULD BE HELL FOR PATIENTS.
STILL, NOT TO BE TAKEN LIGHTLY.
THAT'S NOT WHAT I MEAN.

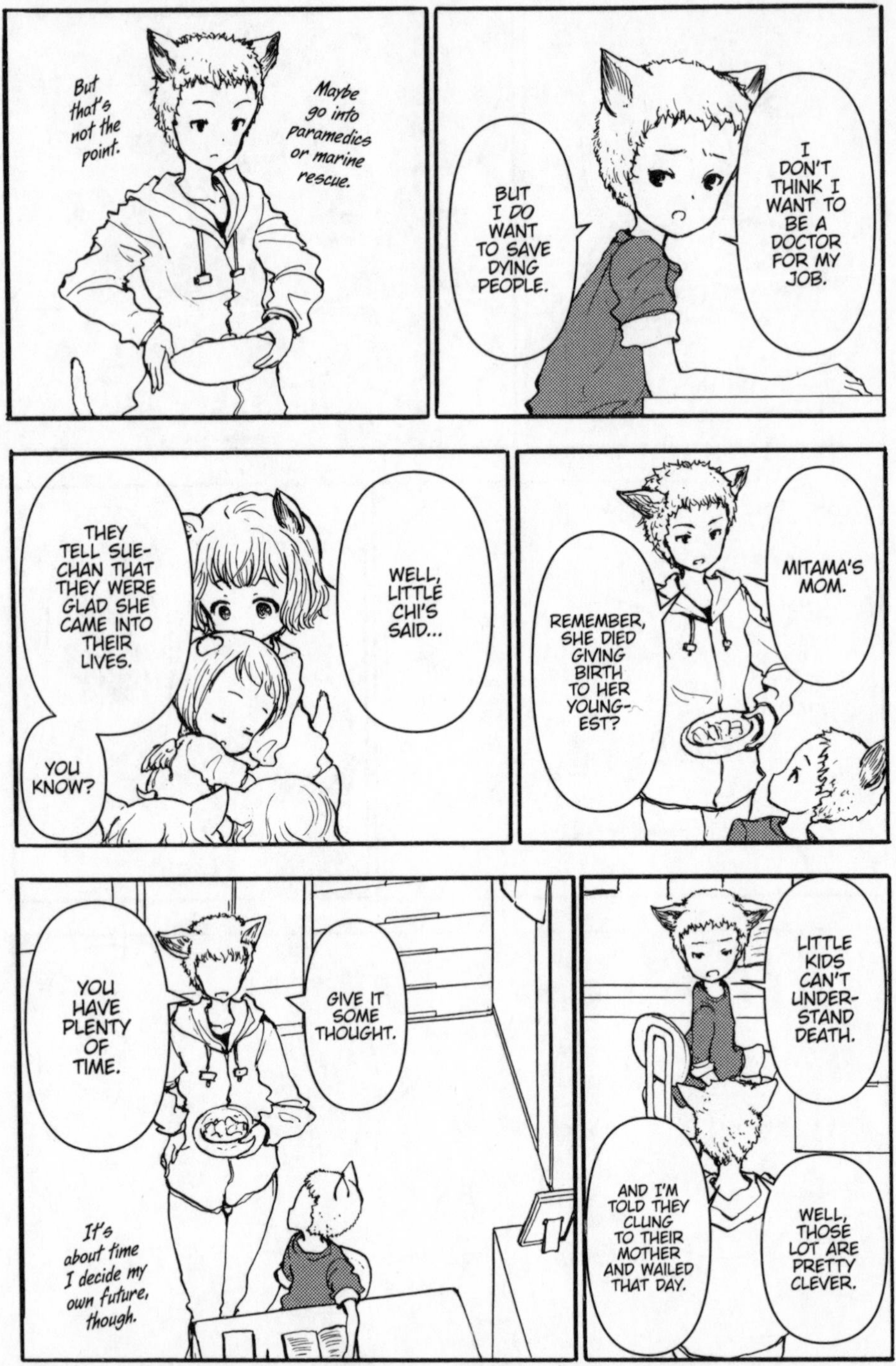
I DON'T THINK I WANT TO BE A DOCTOR FOR MY JOB.
BUT I DO WANT TO SAVE DYING PEOPLE.
Maybe go into paramedics or marine rescue.
But that's not the point.
MITAMA'S MOM.
REMEMBER, SHE DIED GIVING BIRTH TO HER YOUNG-EST?
WELL, LITTLE CHI'S SAID...
THEY TELL SUE-CHAN THAT THEY WERE GLAD SHE CAME INTO THEIR LIVES.
YOU KNOW?
LITTLE KIDS CAN'T UNDER-STAND DEATH.
WELL, THOSE LOT ARE PRETTY CLEVER.
AND I'M TOLD THEY CLUNG TO THEIR MOTHER AND WAILED THAT DAY.
GIVE IT SOME THOUGHT.
YOU HAVE PLENTY OF TIME.
It's about time I decide my own future, though.

A Centaur's Life

RELEARNING THE ORIGIN OF MAMMALIAN HUMANS
7. HOW MODERN HUMANS BECAME THE ONLY MAMMALIAN HUMAN SPECIES

MAMMALIAN HUMANS FACED A NUMBER OF ORDEALS, ONE OF THEM BEING THE ICE AGE. HAVING INFORMATION, SUCH AS BEHAVIOR AND MIGRATION ROUTES OF PREY ANIMALS, OR UNDERSTANDING THE USEFULNESS OF PLANTS AND WHERE TO FIND THEM, WOULD WORK IN THE FAVOR OF ANY CREATURE TRYING TO SURVIVE IN SUCH A HARSH ENVIRONMENT. AS CREATURES WITH LARGE BRAINS, MODERN HUMANS WERE CAPABLE OF CONDENSING INFORMATION BY ABSTRACTION OR SHARING IT THROUGH VERBAL COMMUNICATION, WHICH GAVE THEM A SIGNIFICANT ADVANTAGE OVER OTHER HUMAN SPECIES. THEY STOCKPILED FOOD IN ANTICIPATION OF FUTURE SHORTAGES, AND THEY MADE CHANGES IN THEIR ENVIRONMENT WITH CLOTHES AND HOUSING. MODERN HUMANS ALSO MAINTAINED MULTIPLE FORMS WITHOUT UNDERGOING SPECIATION. UTILIZING THESE DIFFERENCES IN THE DIVISION OF LABOR HELPED THEM SURVIVE. TIGERFOLK, WHO REMAINED ISOLATED FROM OTHER SPECIES, BECAME EXTINCT 100,000 YEARS AGO DESPITE BEING A SPECIES OF THE GENUS *HOMO*.

THE TRAITS AND ABILITIES MODERN HUMANS GAINED IN EXCHANGE FOR EVOLUTIONARY DISADVANTAGES WERE EXPLOITED DURING THE ICE AGE. IF THE WORLD HAD REMAINED AN ENVIRONMENT BEST DOMINATED BY PHYSICAL STRENGTH AND INSTINCTUAL BEHAVIOR--WITHOUT A SHORTAGE OF FOOD DUE TO GLOBAL COOLING--MODERN HUMANS MIGHT HAVE BECOME MINOR ANIMALS IN SPECIFIC REGIONS AT BEST OR DIMINISHED ALONG WITH THE OTHER MAMMALIAN HUMANS. NEANDERTHALS HAD A MORE ROBUST BODY THAN MODERN HUMANS AND MIGHT HAVE SURVIVED AND EVEN DOMINATED.

HOWEVER, NEANDERTHALS DID *NOT* SURVIVE. MODERN HUMANS PROSPERED AFTER THEIR RIVALS PERISHED.

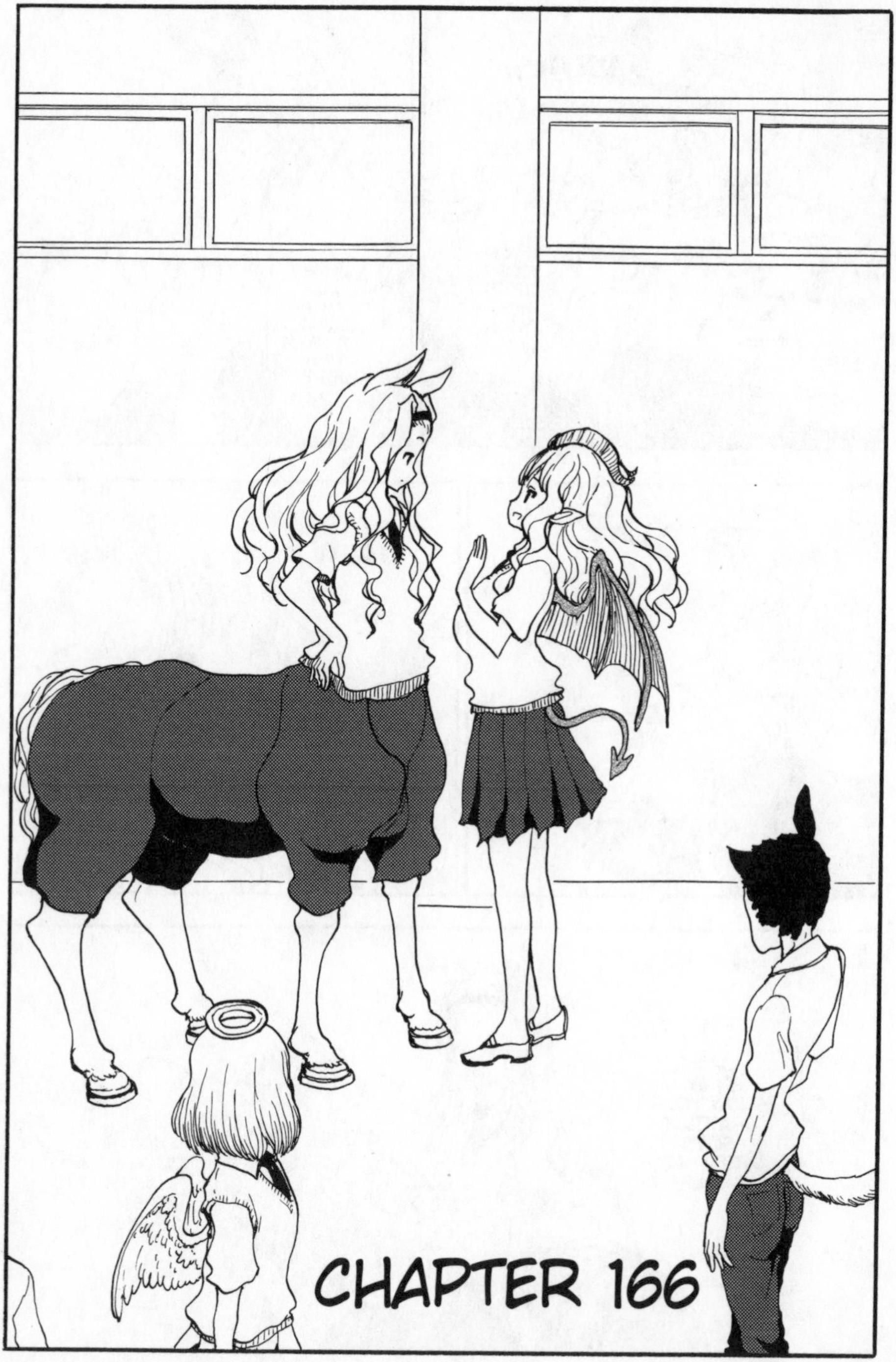
CHAPTER 166

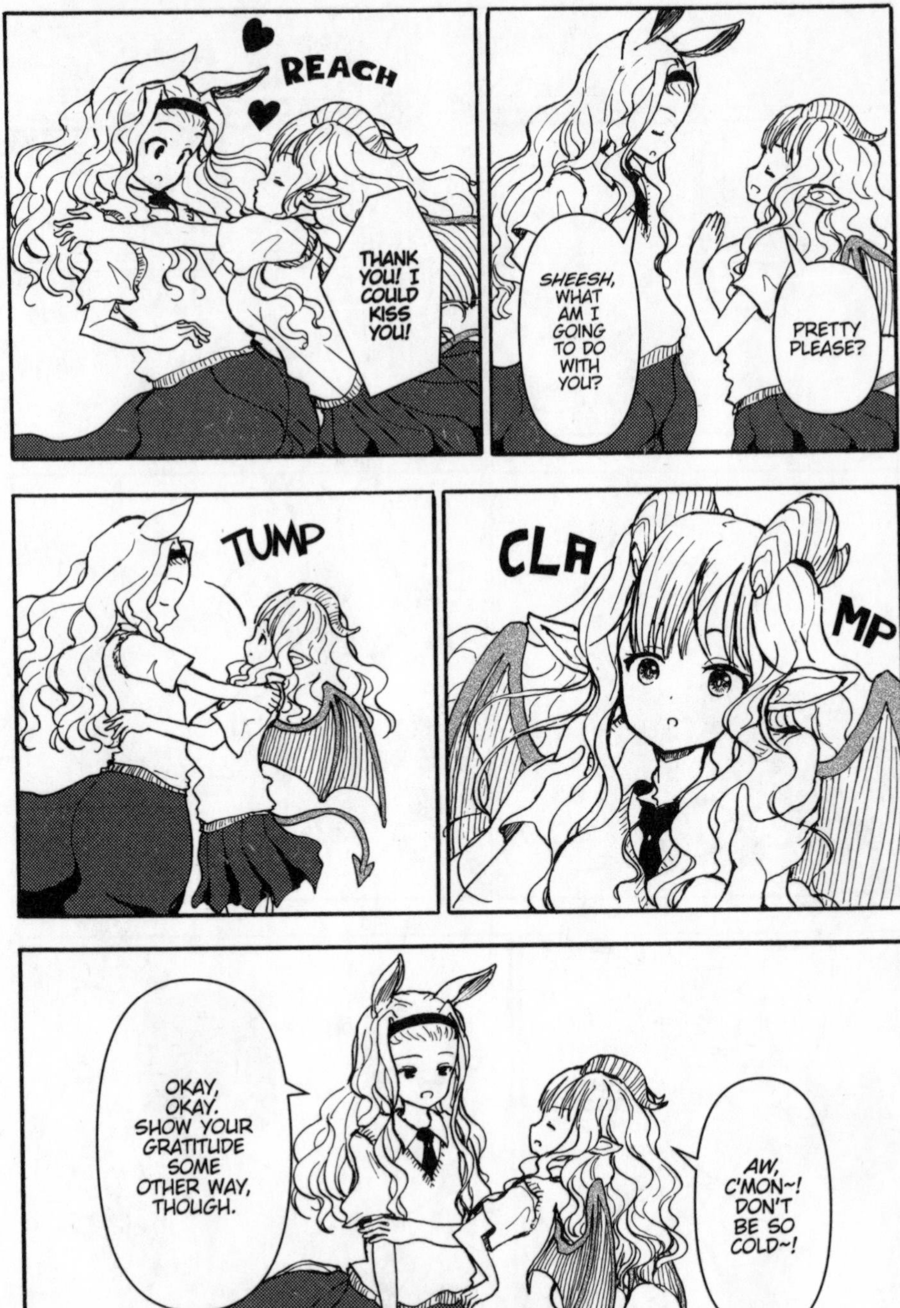
PRETTY PLEASE?
SHEESH, WHAT AM I GOING TO DO WITH YOU?
REACH
THANK YOU! I COULD KISS YOU!
CLA
MP
TUMP
AW, C'MON~! DON'T BE SO COLD~!
OKAY, OKAY. SHOW YOUR GRATITUDE SOME OTHER WAY, THOUGH.

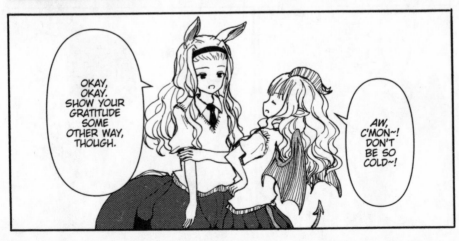

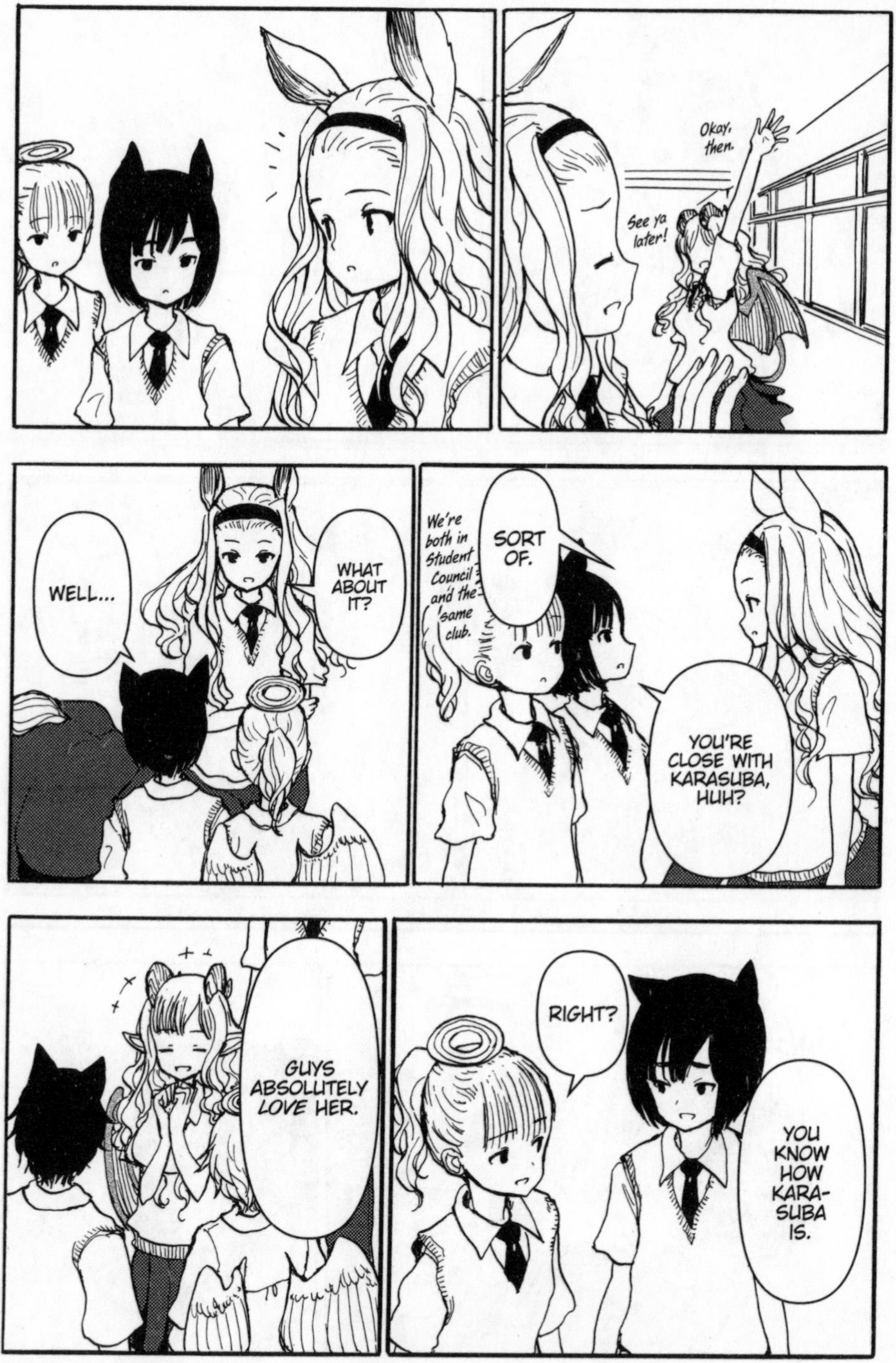
Okay, then.
See ya later!
YOU'RE CLOSE WITH KARASUBA, HUH?
SORT OF.
We're both in Student Council and the same club.
WHAT ABOUT IT?
WELL...
YOU KNOW HOW KARA-SUBA IS.
RIGHT?
GUYS ABSOLUTELY LOVE HER.

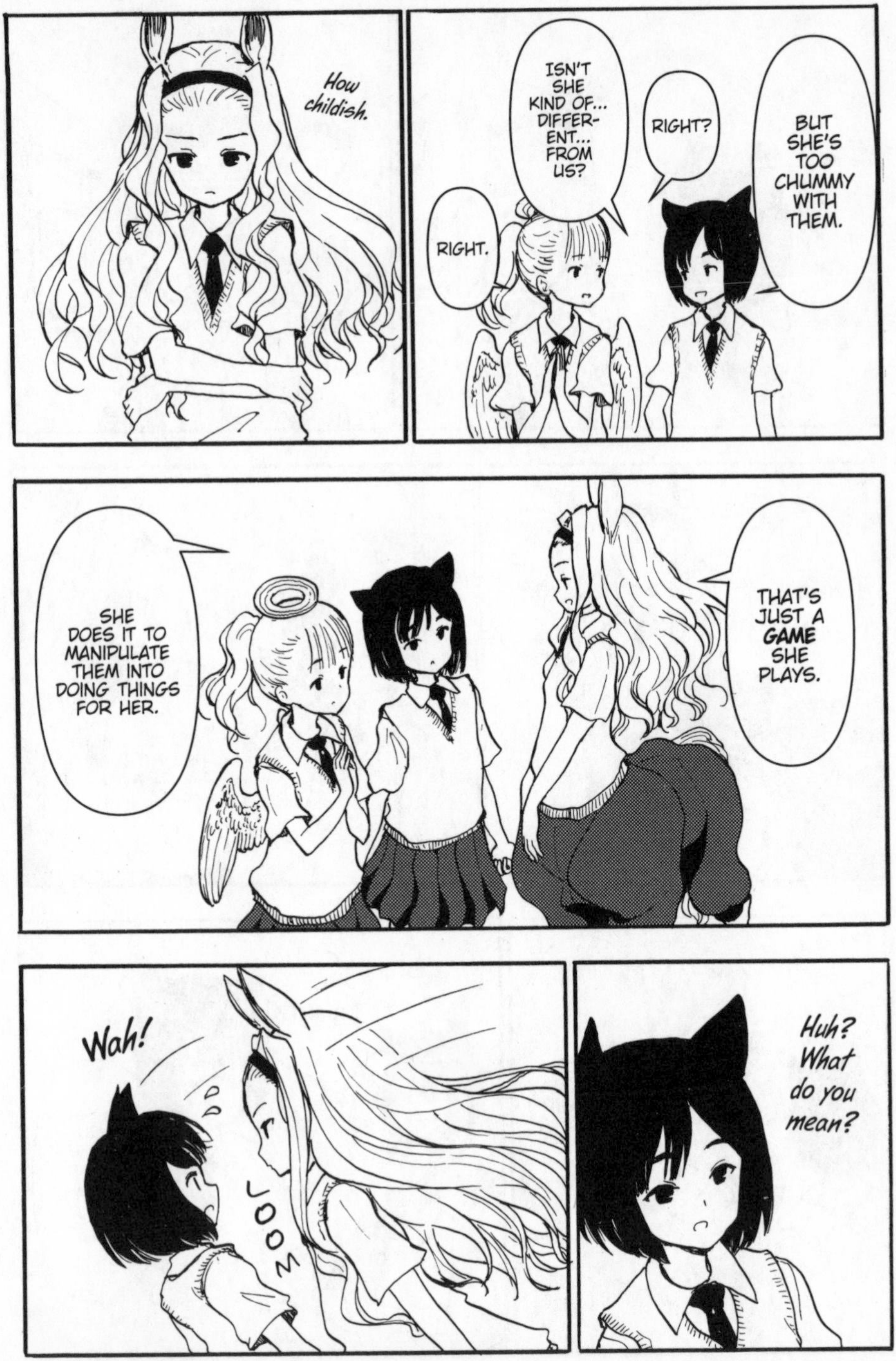
BUT SHE'S TOO CHUMMY WITH THEM.
RIGHT?
ISN'T SHE KIND OF... DIFFER-ENT... FROM US?
RIGHT.
How childish.
THAT'S JUST A GAME SHE PLAYS.
SHE DOES IT TO MANIPULATE THEM INTO DOING THINGS FOR HER.
Huh? What do you mean?
Wah!
VOOM

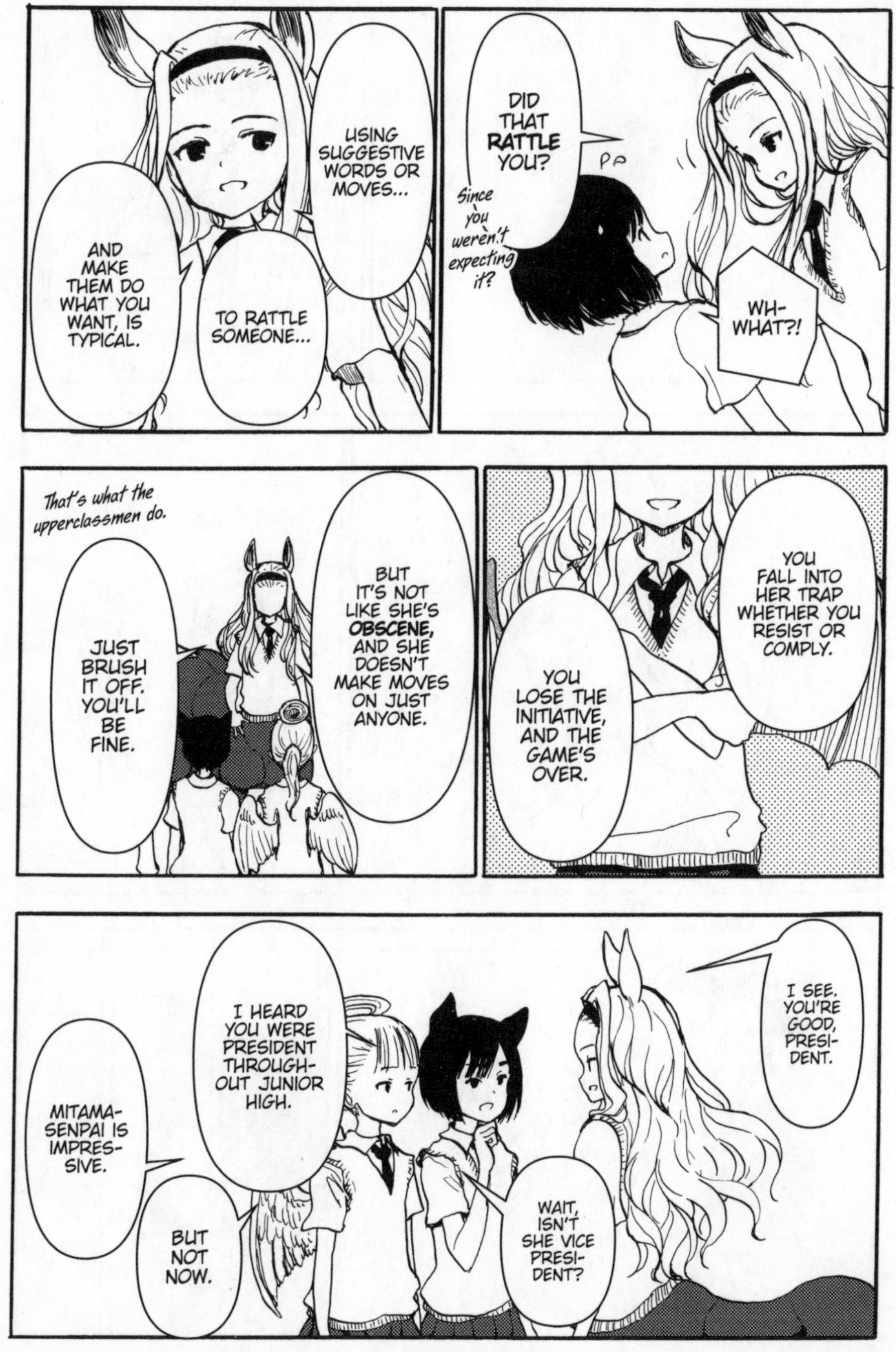
DID THAT RATTLE YOU?
Since you weren't expecting it?
WH- WHAT?!
USING SUGGESTIVE WORDS OR MOVES...
TO RATTLE SOMEONE...
AND MAKE THEM DO WHAT YOU WANT, IS TYPICAL.
YOU FALL INTO HER TRAP WHETHER YOU RESIST OR COMPLY.
YOU LOSE THE INITIATIVE, AND THE GAME'S OVER.
BUT IT'S NOT LIKE SHE'S OBSCENE, AND SHE DOESN'T MAKE MOVES ON JUST ANYONE.
JUST BRUSH IT OFF. YOU'LL BE FINE.
That's what the upperclassmen do.
I SEE. YOU'RE GOOD, PRESIDENT.
I HEARD YOU WERE PRESIDENT THROUGHOUT JUNIOR HIGH.
WAIT, ISN'T SHE VICE PRESIDENT?
MITAMA-SENPAI IS IMPRESSIVE.
BUT NOT NOW.

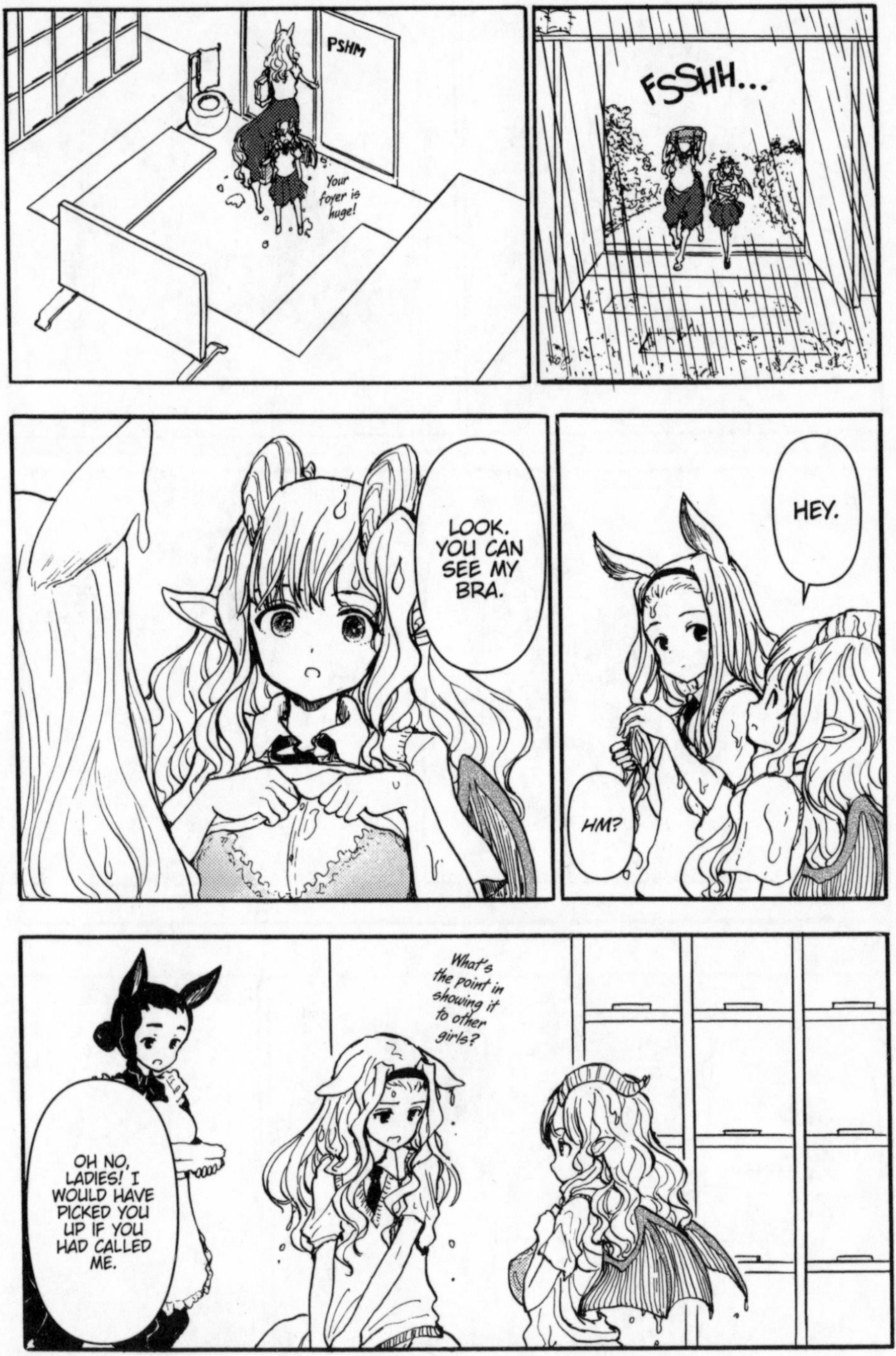
FSSHH...
PSHM
Your foyer is huge!
HEY.
HM?
LOOK. YOU CAN SEE MY BRA.
What's the point in showing it to other girls?
OH NO, LADIES! I WOULD HAVE PICKED YOU UP IF YOU HAD CALLED ME.

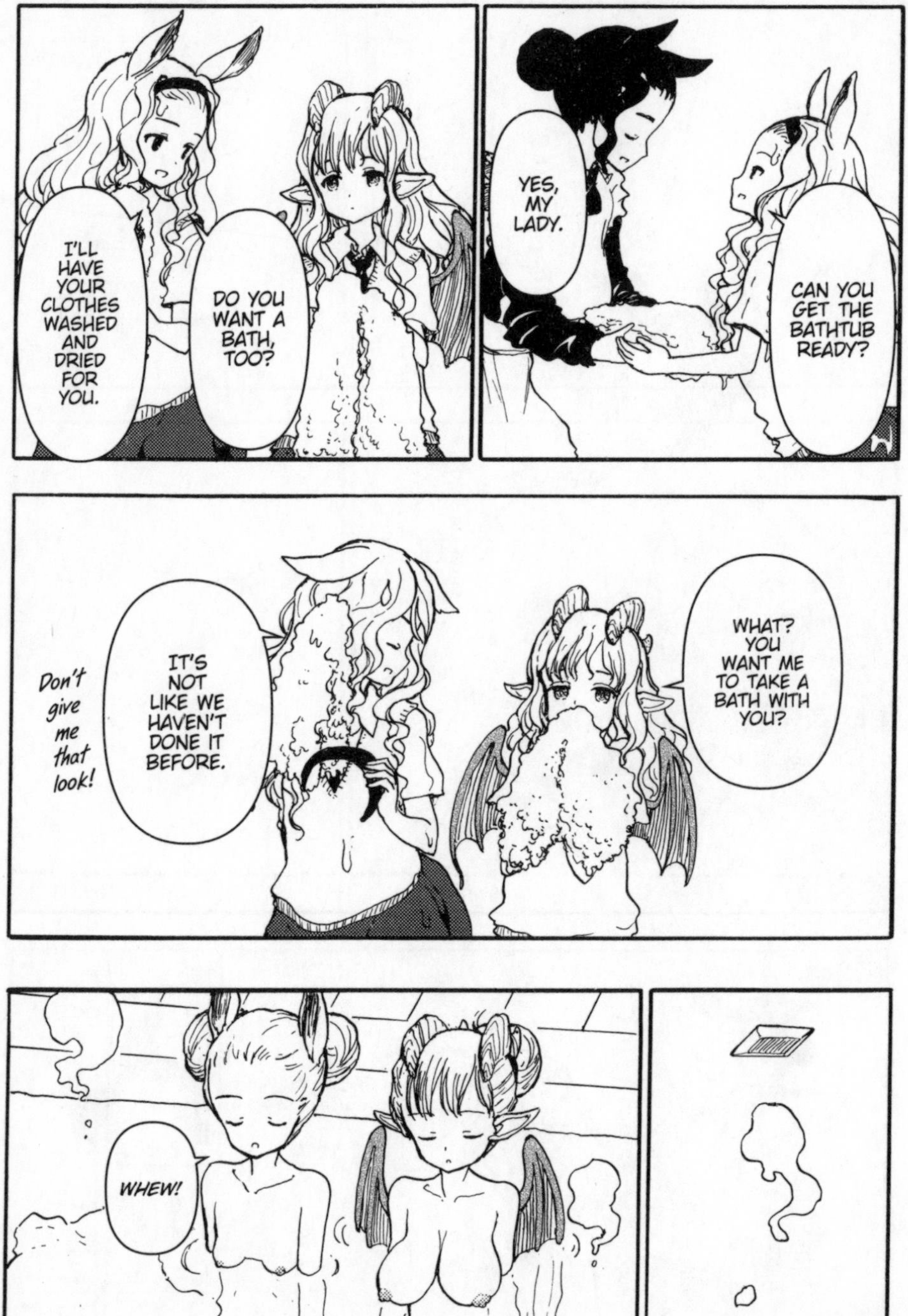
CAN YOU GET THE BATHTUB READY?
YES, MY LADY.
DO YOU WANT A BATH, TOO?
I'LL HAVE YOUR CLOTHES WASHED AND DRIED FOR YOU.
WHAT? YOU WANT ME TO TAKE A BATH WITH YOU?
IT'S NOT LIKE WE HAVEN'T DONE IT BEFORE.
Don't give me that look!
WHEW!

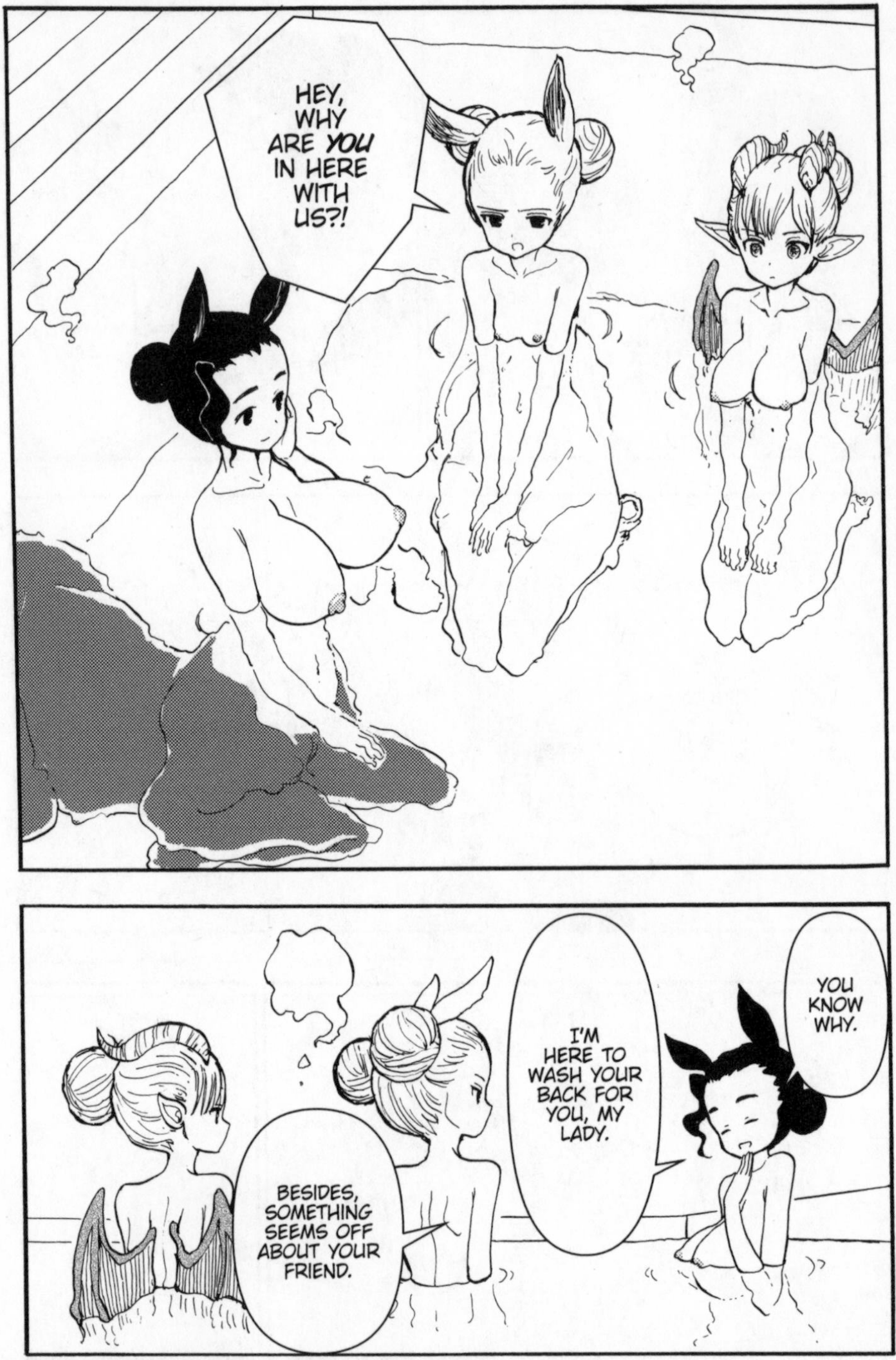
HEY, WHY ARE *YOU* IN HERE WITH US?!
YOU KNOW WHY.
I'M HERE TO WASH YOUR BACK FOR YOU, MY LADY.
BESIDES, SOMETHING SEEMS OFF ABOUT YOUR FRIEND.

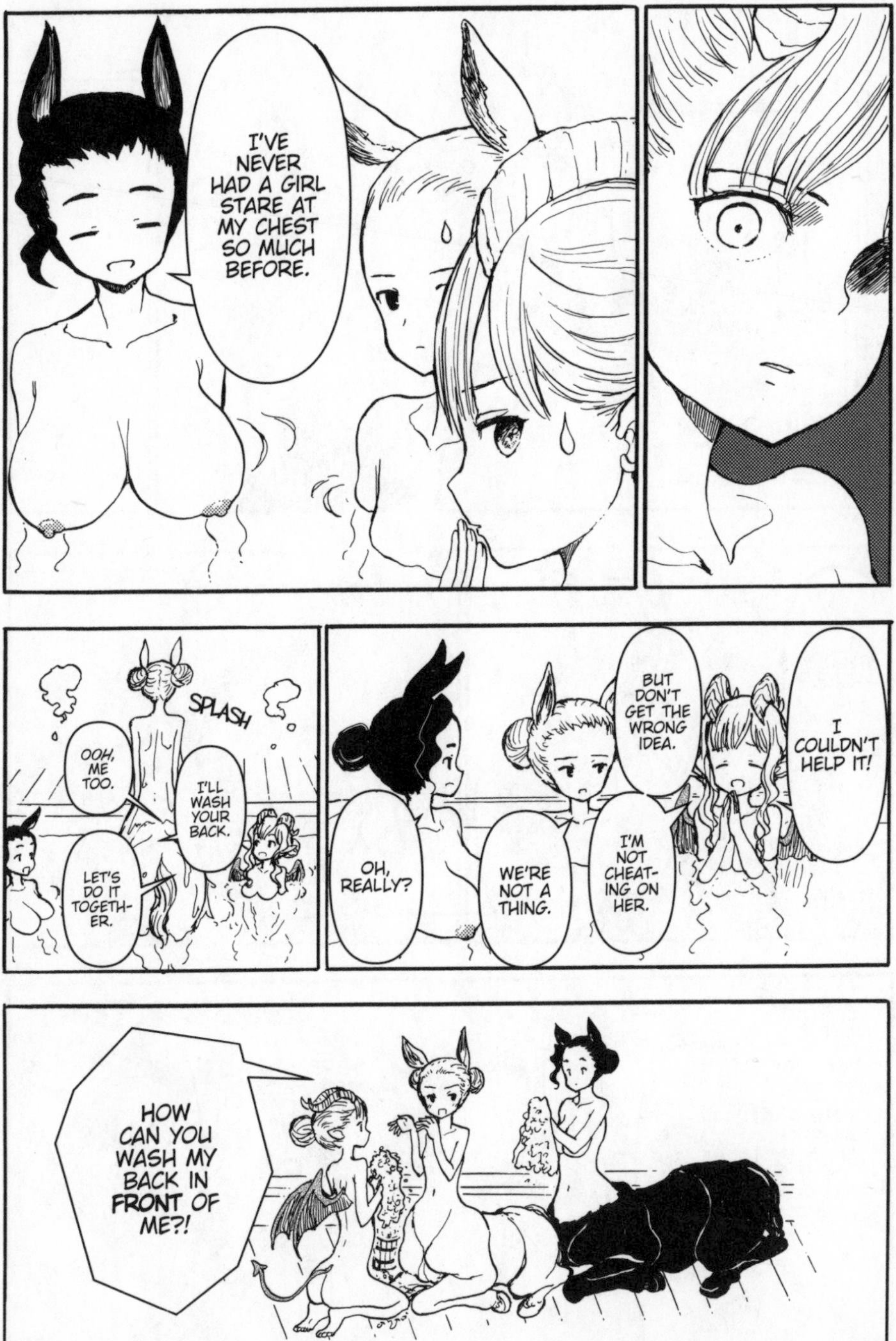
I'VE NEVER HAD A GIRL STARE AT MY CHEST SO MUCH BEFORE.
I COULDN'T HELP IT!
BUT DON'T GET THE WRONG IDEA.
I'M NOT CHEATING ON HER.
WE'RE NOT A THING.
OH, REALLY?
SPLASH
I'LL WASH YOUR BACK.
OOH, ME TOO.
LET'S DO IT TOGETHER.
HOW CAN YOU WASH MY BACK IN FRONT OF ME?!

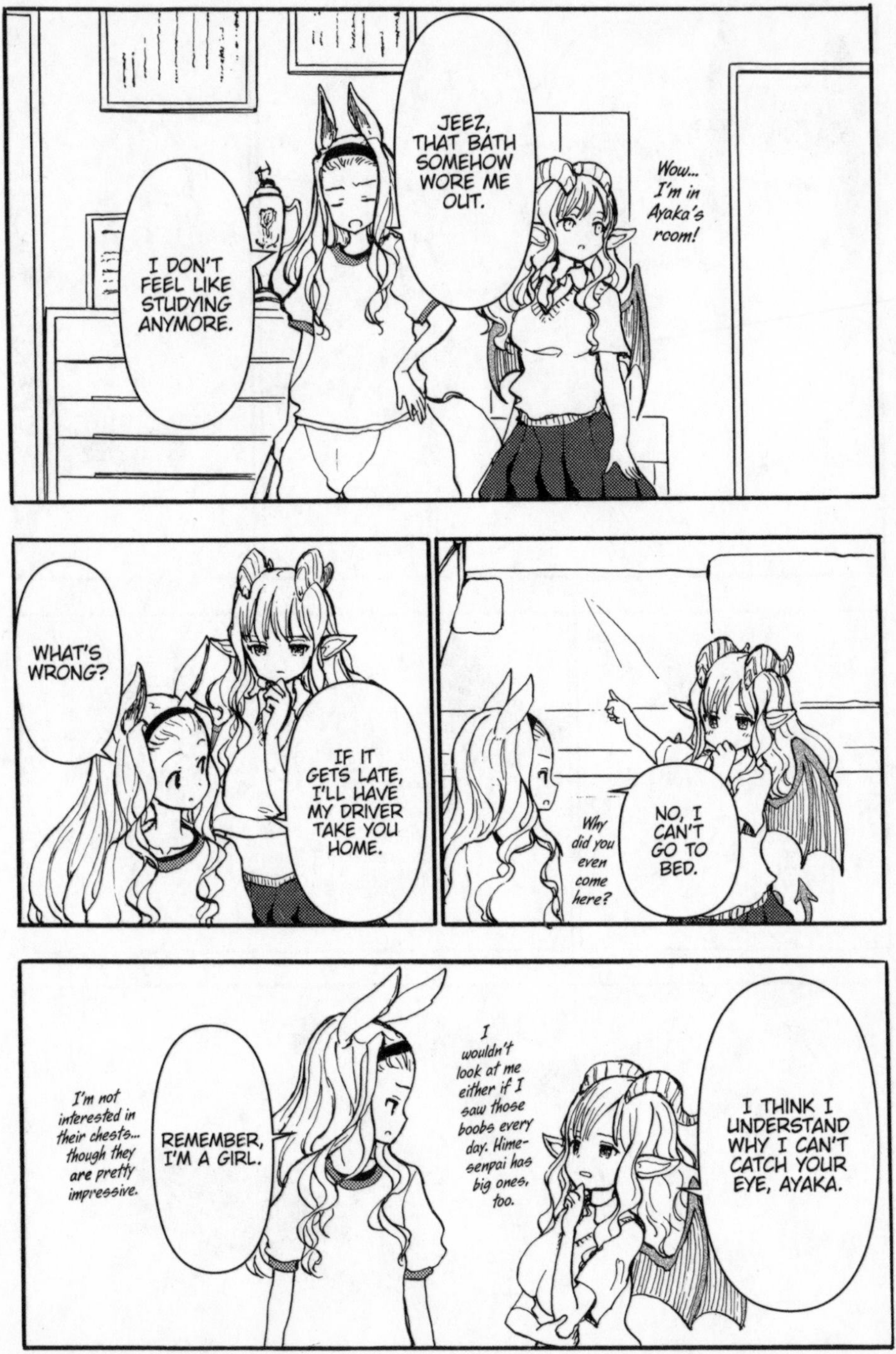
Wow... I'm in Ayaka's room!
JEEZ, THAT BATH SOMEHOW WORE ME OUT.
I DON'T FEEL LIKE STUDYING ANYMORE.
NO, I CAN'T GO TO BED.
Why did you even come here?
IF IT GETS LATE, I'LL HAVE MY DRIVER TAKE YOU HOME.
WHAT'S WRONG?
I THINK I UNDERSTAND WHY I CAN'T CATCH YOUR EYE, AYAKA.
I wouldn't look at me either if I saw those boobs every day. Hime-senpai has big ones, too.
REMEMBER, I'M A GIRL.
I'm not interested in their chests... though they are pretty impressive.

A Centaur's Life

RELEARNING THE ORIGIN OF MAMMALIAN HUMANS
8. WHAT MAKES HUMAN BEINGS HUMAN?

ANYONE WHO HAS READ UP TO THIS POINT HAS
PROBABLY BEEN FREED FROM MYTHS OR OUTDATED
INFORMATION ABOUT HUMAN EVOLUTION AND GAINED A
NEW PERSPECTIVE. THEY MUST HAVE LEARNED WHAT MADE
MAMMALIAN HUMANS UNIQUE AND WHAT MADE MODERN HUMANS
WHAT THEY ARE. THE UPRIGHT POSTURE MADE THE FIRST MAMMALIAN
HUMAN AND ITS DESCENDANTS UNIQUE. LARGE BRAINS, WHICH PRODUCED
THE ABSTRACT THINKING AND VERBAL COMMUNICATION SKILLS THAT MADE
THE COEXISTENCE OF MULTIPLE RACES POSSIBLE, MADE MODERN HUMANS
WHAT THEY ARE. IF ANY OF THESE FACTORS HAD BEEN LOST, WE COULD
HAVE BECOME EXTINCT OURSELVES. THE TREND OF IGNORING THIS FACT WILL
REQUIRE A THOROUGH REEDUCATION CAMPAIGN. HOWEVER INTENSE THIS
REEDUCATION MAY BE, IT SHOULDN'T BE CONSIDERED CRUEL. AN IDEOLOGY
CAN'T BE BLAMED FOR IT, EITHER. IT'S NOTHING BUT A NECESSITY AND
A DESIRE TO LEAVE SOMETHING MEANINGFUL FOR THE FUTURE.

PRIMATES WERE PUT THROUGH A
REEDUCATION PROGRAM AT THE SOCIAL
CONSERVANCY BUREAU, AND THEY LEARNED
TO HAVE A SUCCESSFUL CONVERSATION UTILIZING
MANY FACIAL EXPRESSIONS. CONTRARY TO SOME
UNFAVORABLE REPORTS, IT CAN BE SAID THAT
THE PROGRAM PROVED QUITE EFFECTIVE.

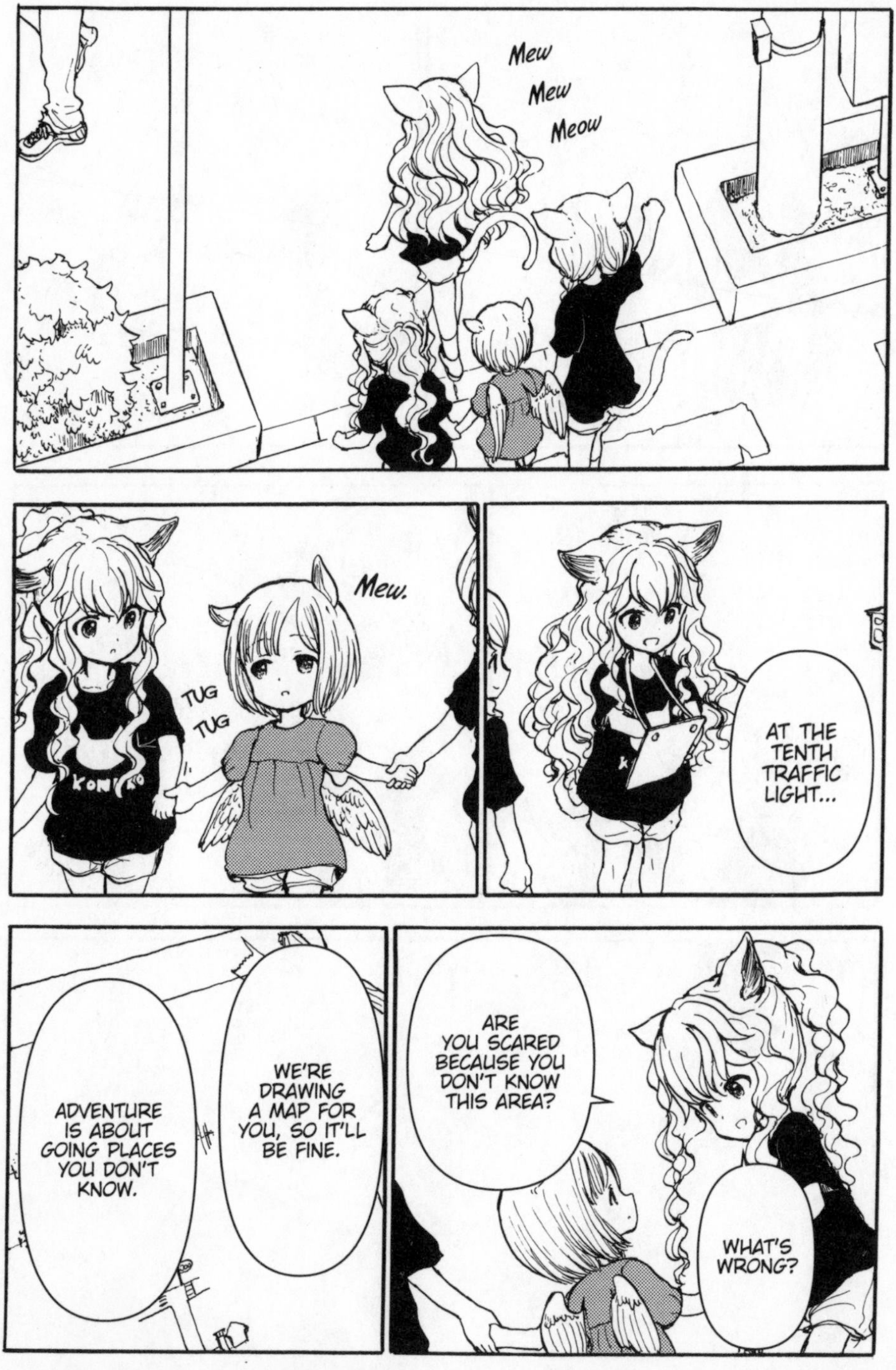
Mew
Mew
Meow
AT THE TENTH TRAFFIC LIGHT...
Mew.
TUG
TUG
WHAT'S WRONG?
ARE YOU SCARED BECAUSE YOU DON'T KNOW THIS AREA?
WE'RE DRAWING A MAP FOR YOU, SO IT'LL BE FINE.
ADVENTURE IS ABOUT GOING PLACES YOU DON'T KNOW.

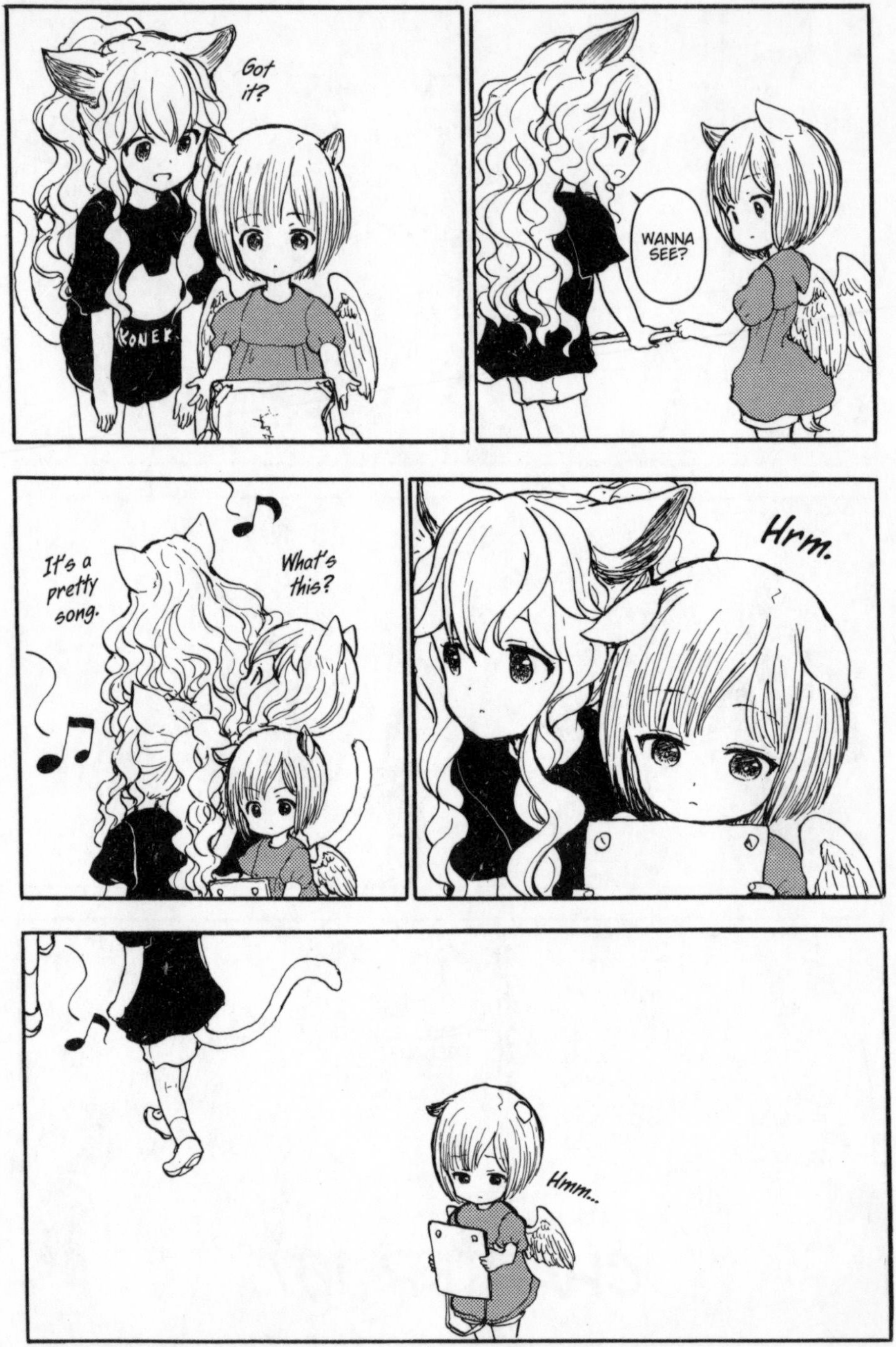
WANNA SEE?
Got it?
Hrm.
What's this?
It's a pretty song.
Hmm...

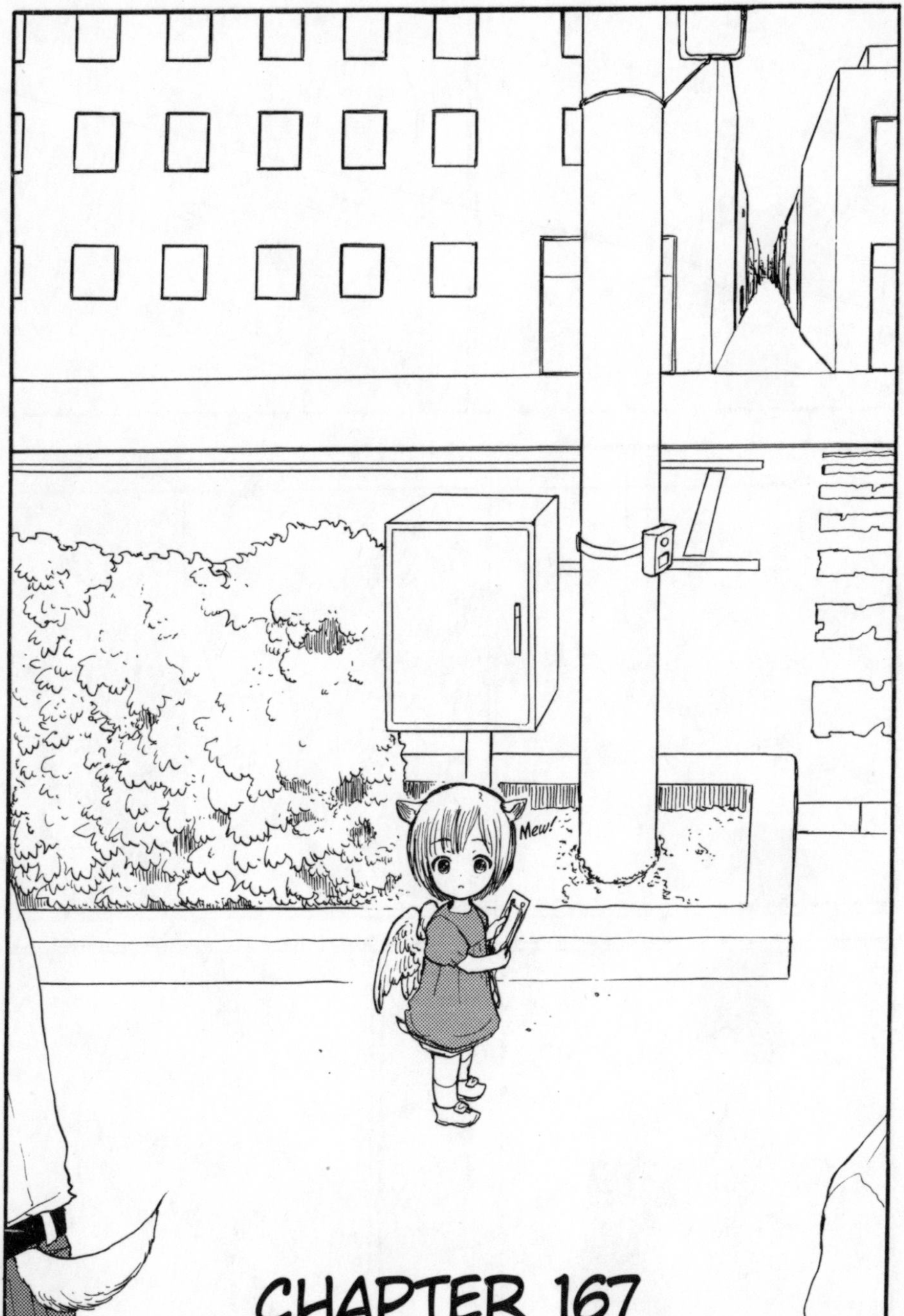
Mew!
CHAPTER 167

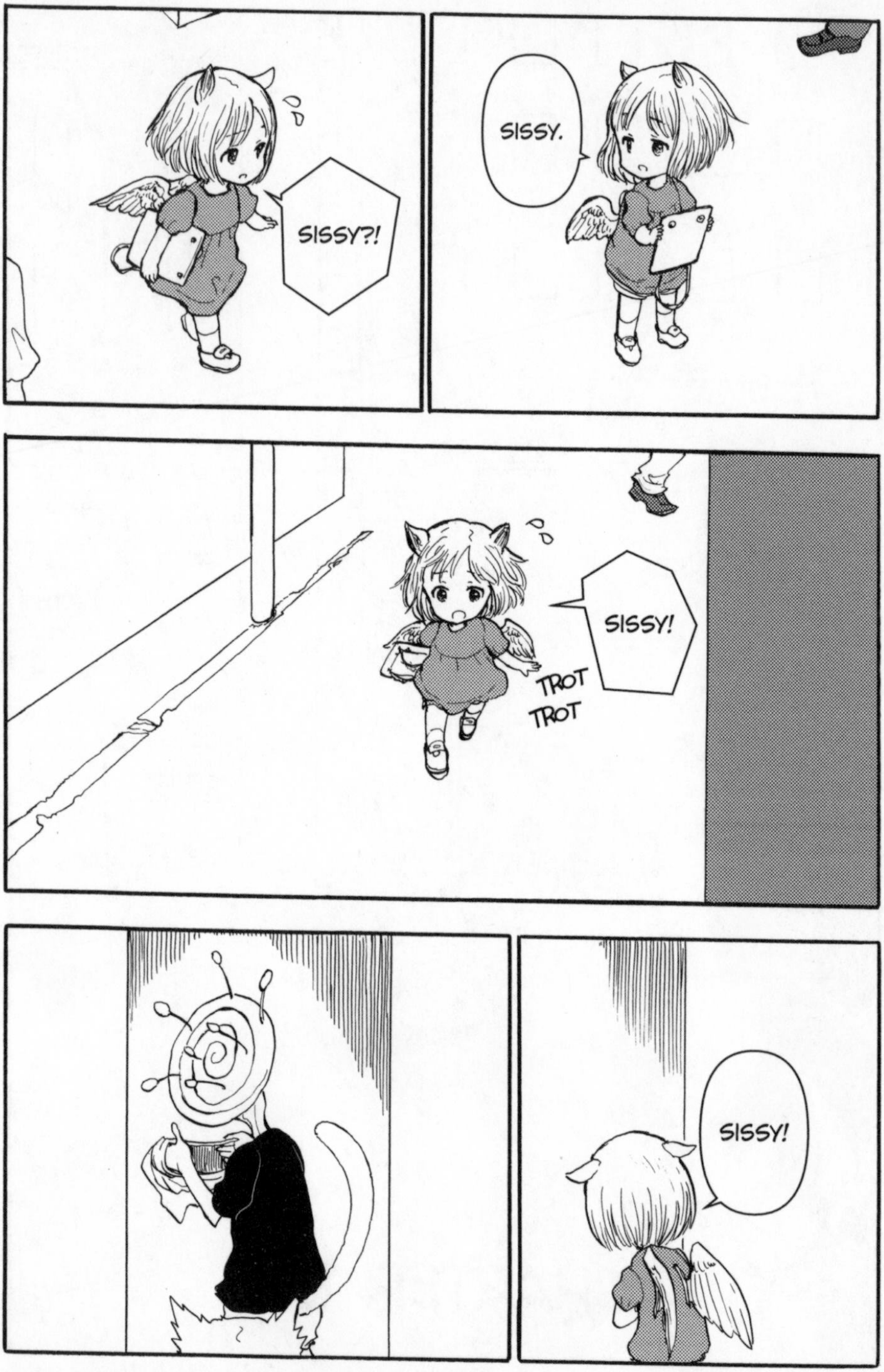
SISSY.
SISSY?!
SISSY!
TROT TROT
SISSY!

Sniffle

PLOP

CREEP

Too weak to cry out loud.

Hic hic...

LOOM

Meee

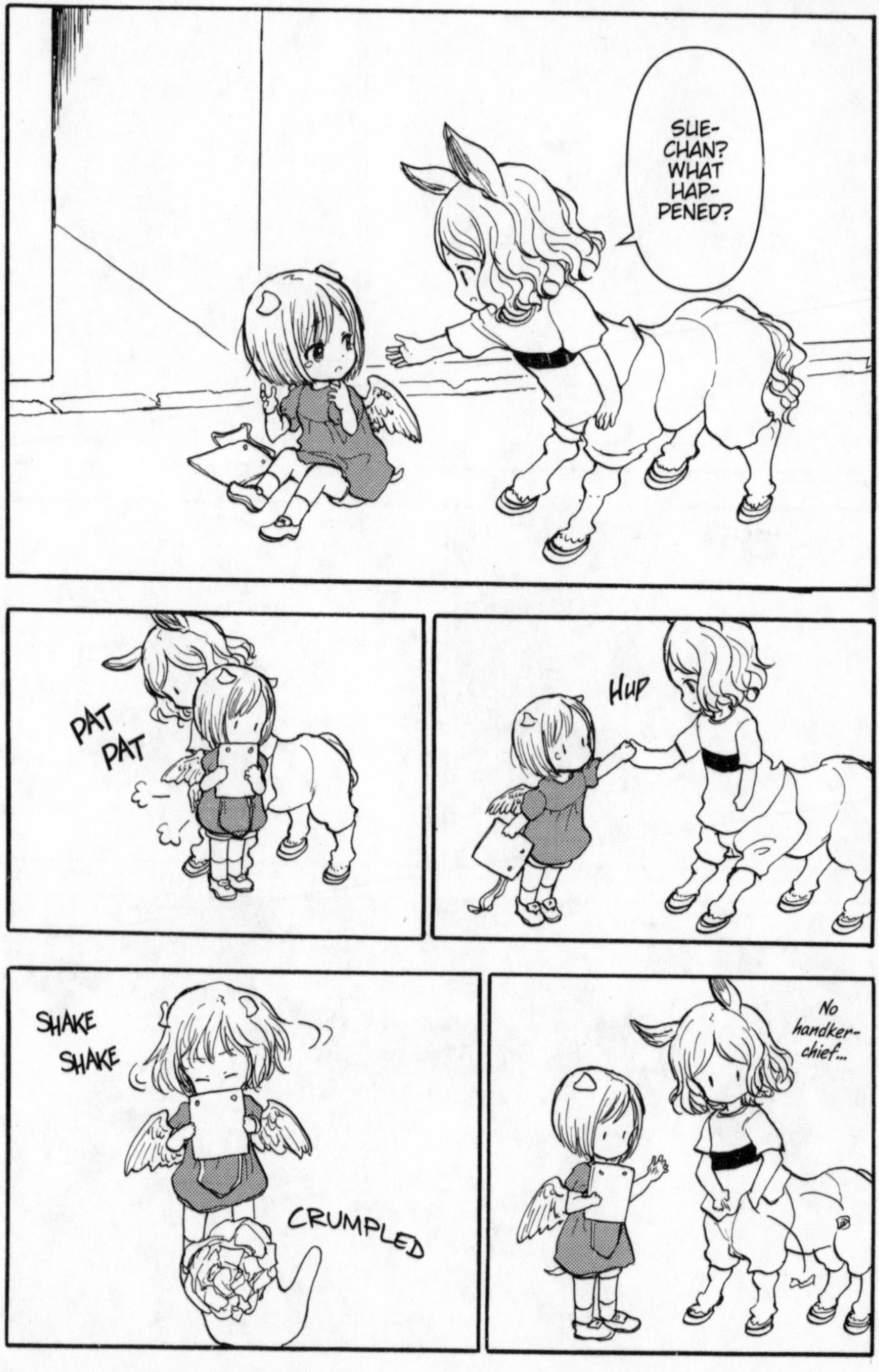
SUE-CHAN? WHAT HAP-PENED?
HUP
PAT PAT
No handker-chief...
SHAKE SHAKE
CRUMPLED

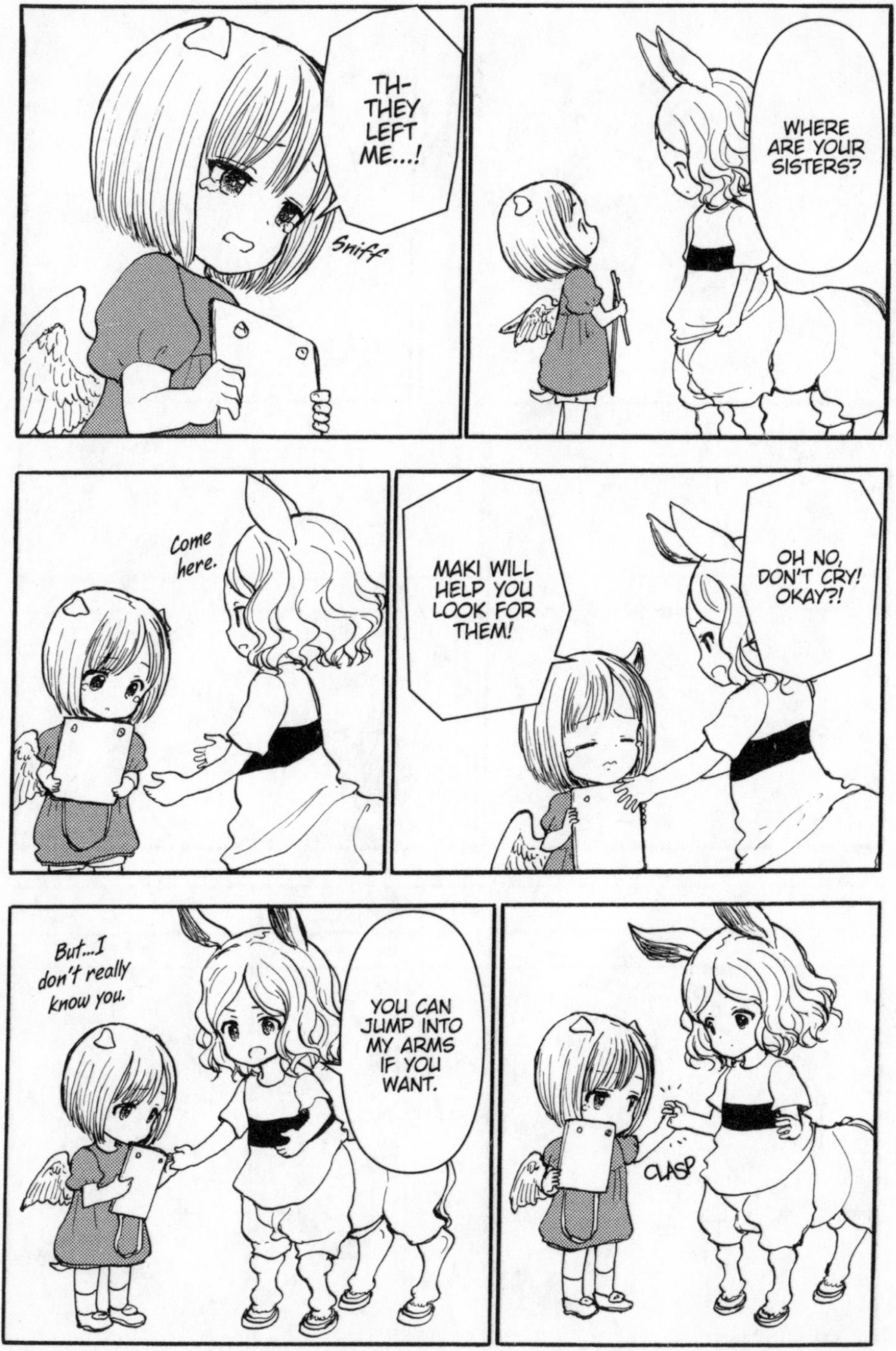
WHERE ARE YOUR SISTERS?
TH-THEY LEFT ME...!
Sniff
OH NO, DON'T CRY! OKAY?!
MAKI WILL HELP YOU LOOK FOR THEM!
Come here.
CLASP
YOU CAN JUMP INTO MY ARMS IF YOU WANT.
But...I don't really know you.

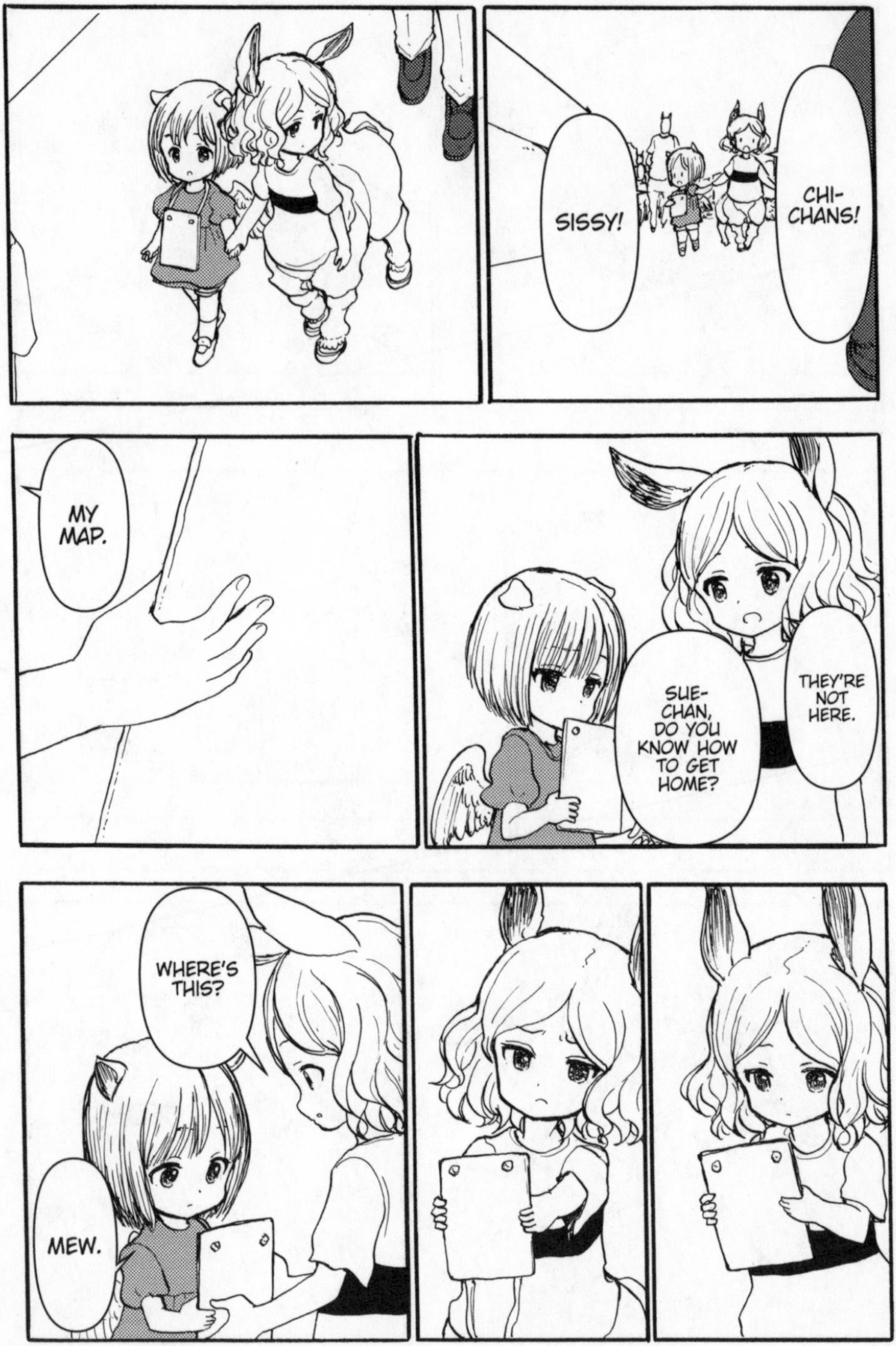
CHI-CHANS!
SISSY!
THEY'RE NOT HERE.
SUE-CHAN, DO YOU KNOW HOW TO GET HOME?
MY MAP.
WHERE'S THIS?
MEW.

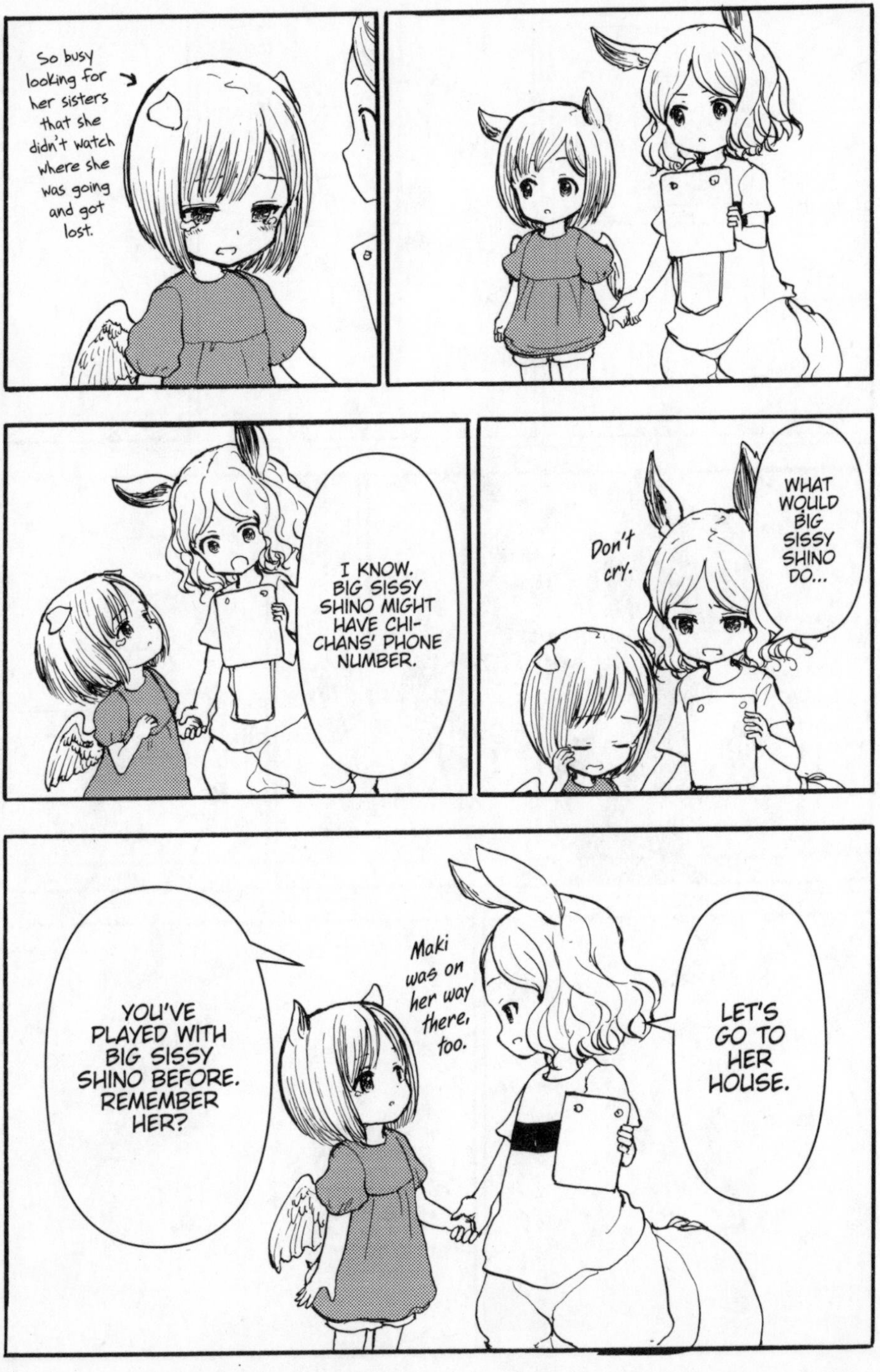
So busy looking for her sisters that she didn't watch where she was going and got lost.
WHAT WOULD BIG SISSY SHINO DO...
Don't cry.
I KNOW. BIG SISSY SHINO MIGHT HAVE CHI-CHANS' PHONE NUMBER.
LET'S GO TO HER HOUSE.
Maki was on her way there, too.
YOU'VE PLAYED WITH BIG SISSY SHINO BEFORE. REMEMBER HER?

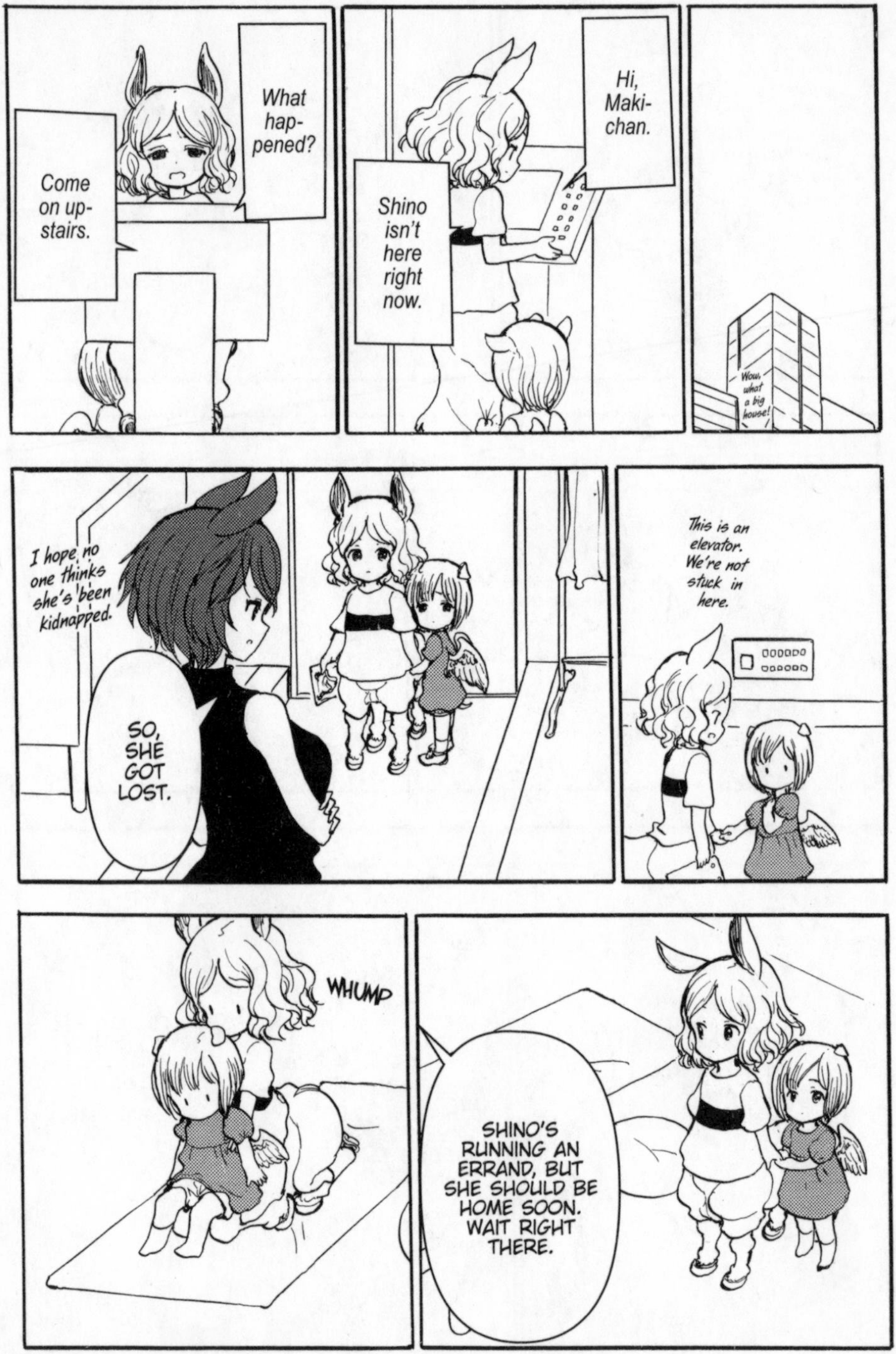
Wow, what a big house!
Hi, Maki-chan.
Shino isn't here right now.
What hap-pened?
Come on up-stairs.
This is an elevator. We're not stuck in here.
I hope no one thinks she's been kidnapped.
SO, SHE GOT LOST.
SHINO'S RUNNING AN ERRAND, BUT SHE SHOULD BE HOME SOON. WAIT RIGHT THERE.
WHUMP

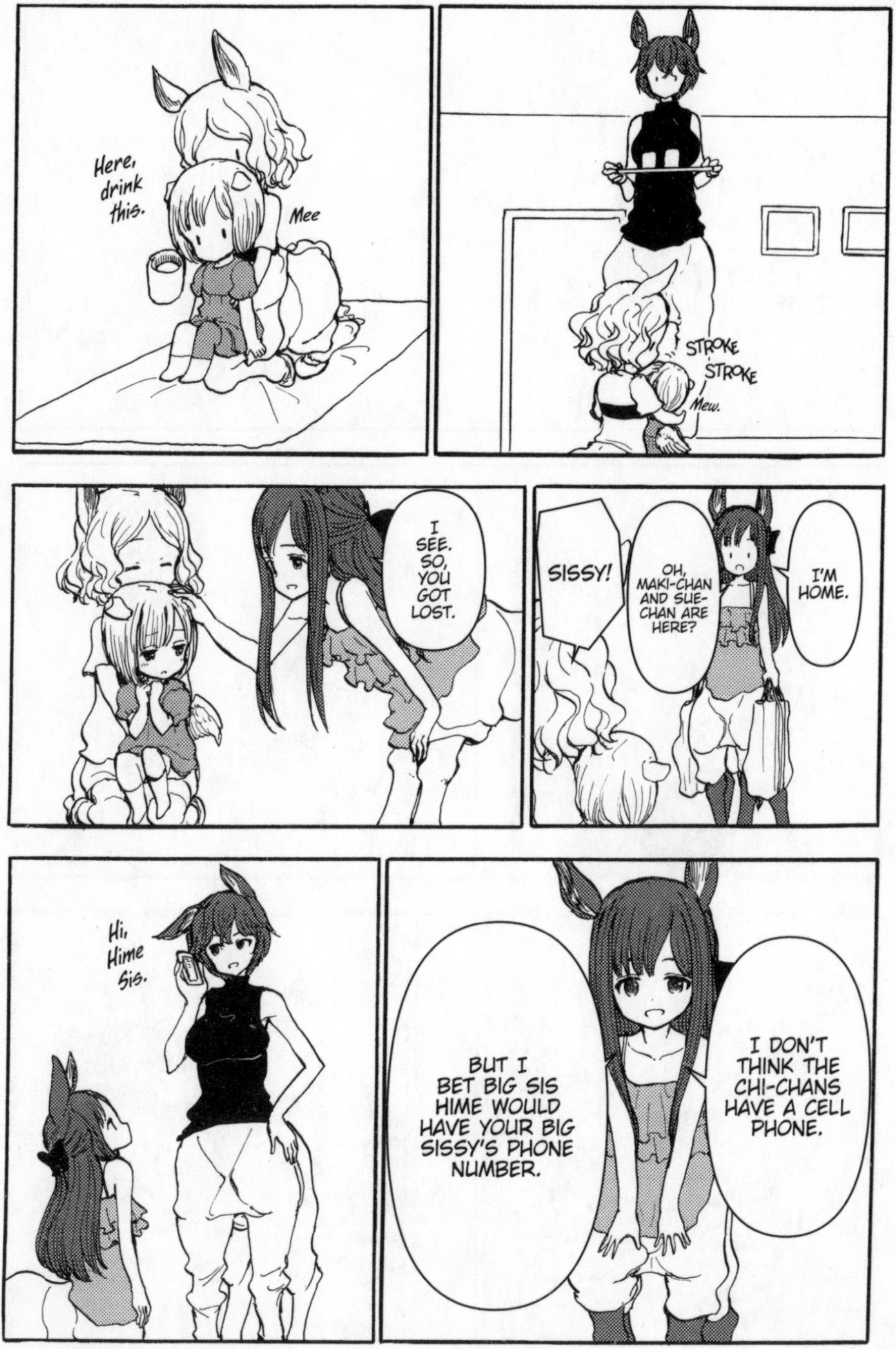
STROKE
STROKE
Mew.
Here, drink this.
Mee
I'M HOME.
OH, MAKI-CHAN AND SUE-CHAN ARE HERE?
SISSY!
I SEE. SO, YOU GOT LOST.
I DON'T THINK THE CHI-CHANS HAVE A CELL PHONE.
BUT I BET BIG SIS HIME WOULD HAVE YOUR BIG SISSY'S PHONE NUMBER.
Hi, Hime Sis.

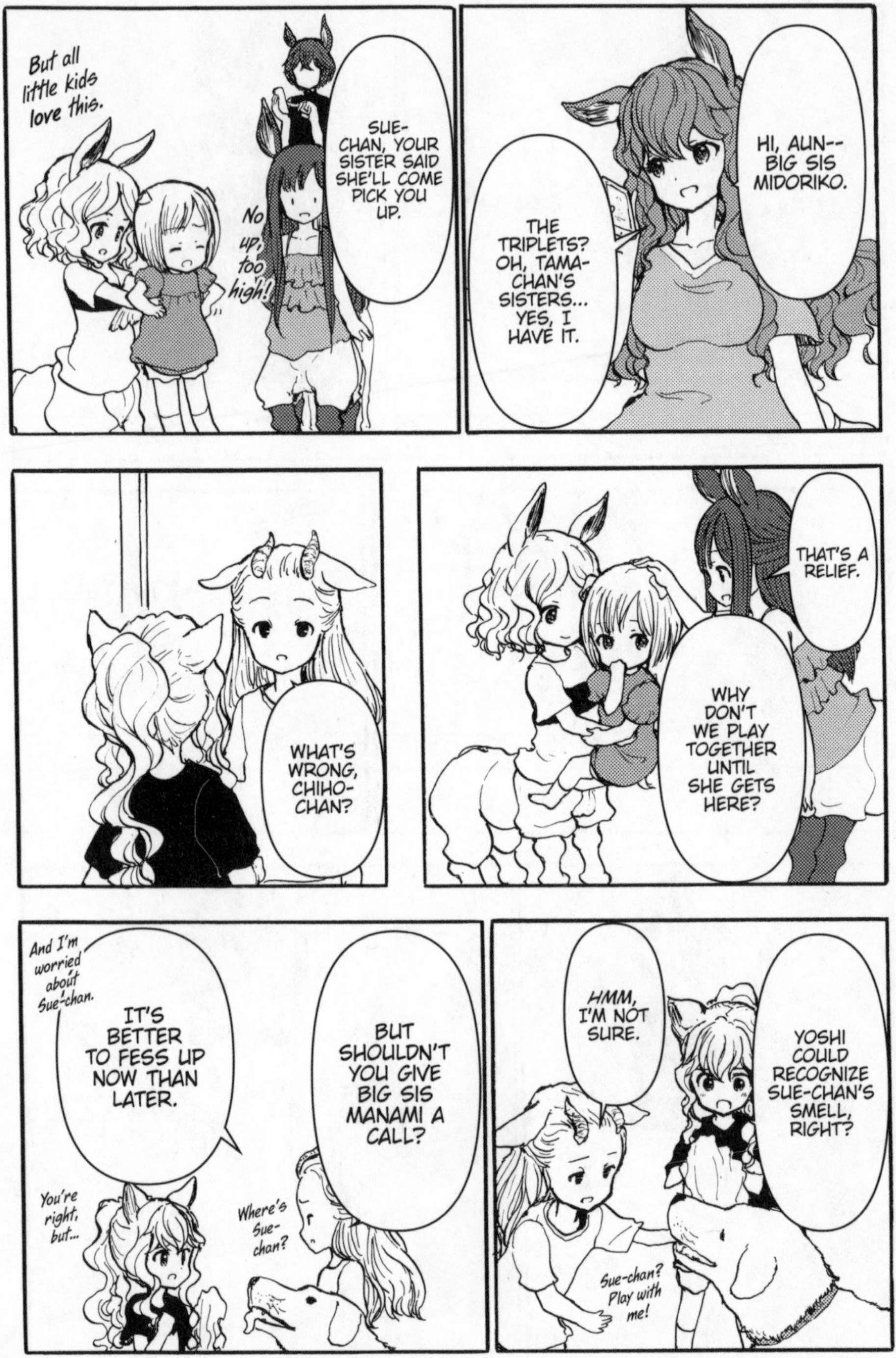
HI, AUN-- BIG SIS MIDORIKO.
THE TRIPLETS? OH, TAMA-CHAN'S SISTERS... YES, I HAVE IT.
SUE-CHAN, YOUR SISTER SAID SHE'LL COME PICK YOU UP.
But all little kids love this.
No up, too high!
THAT'S A RELIEF.
WHY DON'T WE PLAY TOGETHER UNTIL SHE GETS HERE?
WHAT'S WRONG, CHIHO-CHAN?
YOSHI COULD RECOGNIZE SUE-CHAN'S SMELL, RIGHT?
HMM, I'M NOT SURE.
Sue-chan? Play with me!
BUT SHOULDN'T YOU GIVE BIG SIS MANAMI A CALL?
And I'm worried about Sue-chan.
IT'S BETTER TO FESS UP NOW THAN LATER.
Where's Sue-chan?
You're right, but...

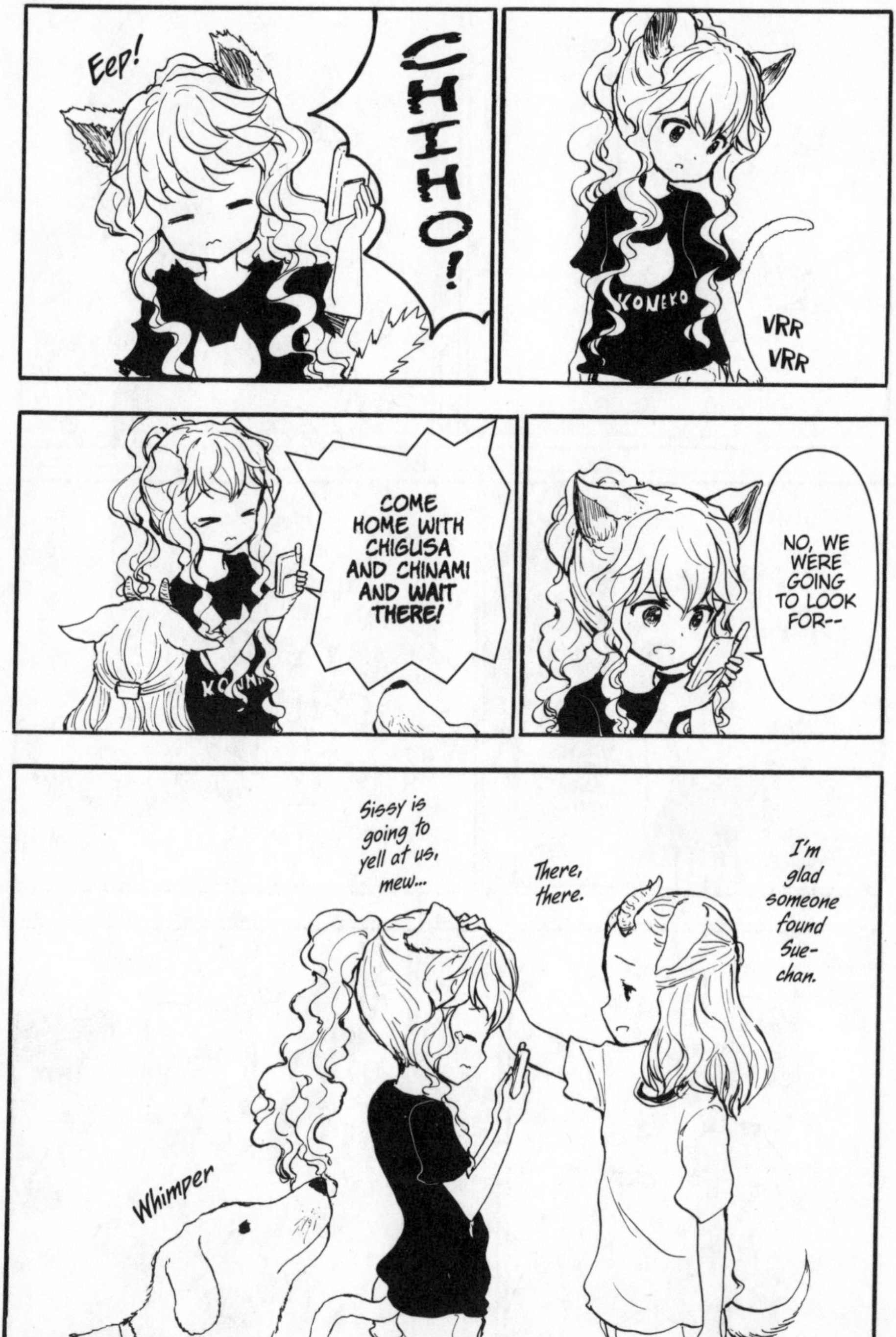
KONEKO
VRR VRR
CHIHO!
Eep!
NO, WE WERE GOING TO LOOK FOR--
COME HOME WITH CHIGUSA AND CHINAMI AND WAIT THERE!
I'm glad someone found Sue-chan.
There, there.
Sissy is going to yell at us, mew...
Whimper

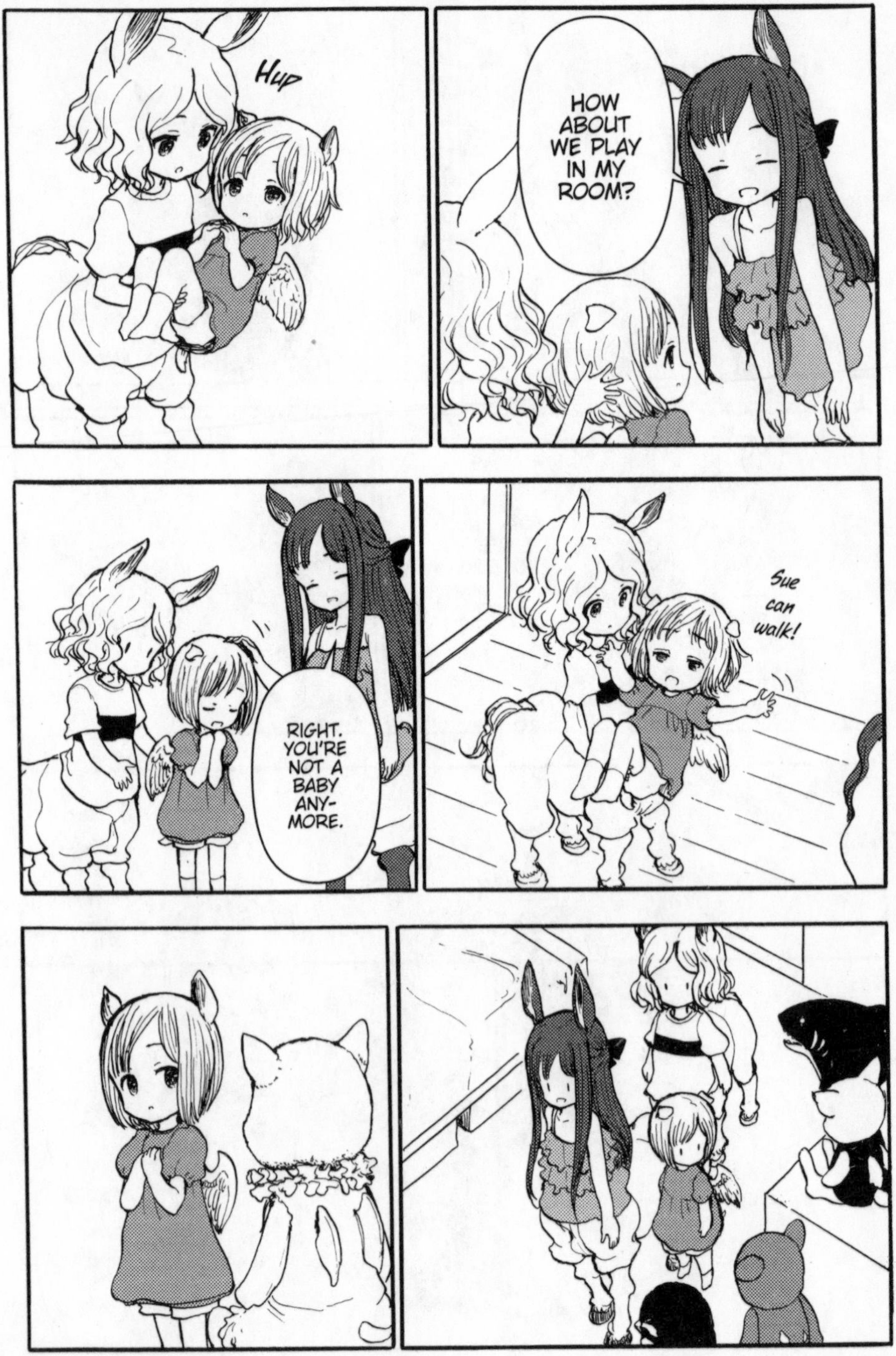
HOW ABOUT WE PLAY IN MY ROOM?
Hup
Sue can walk!
RIGHT. YOU'RE NOT A BABY ANY-MORE.

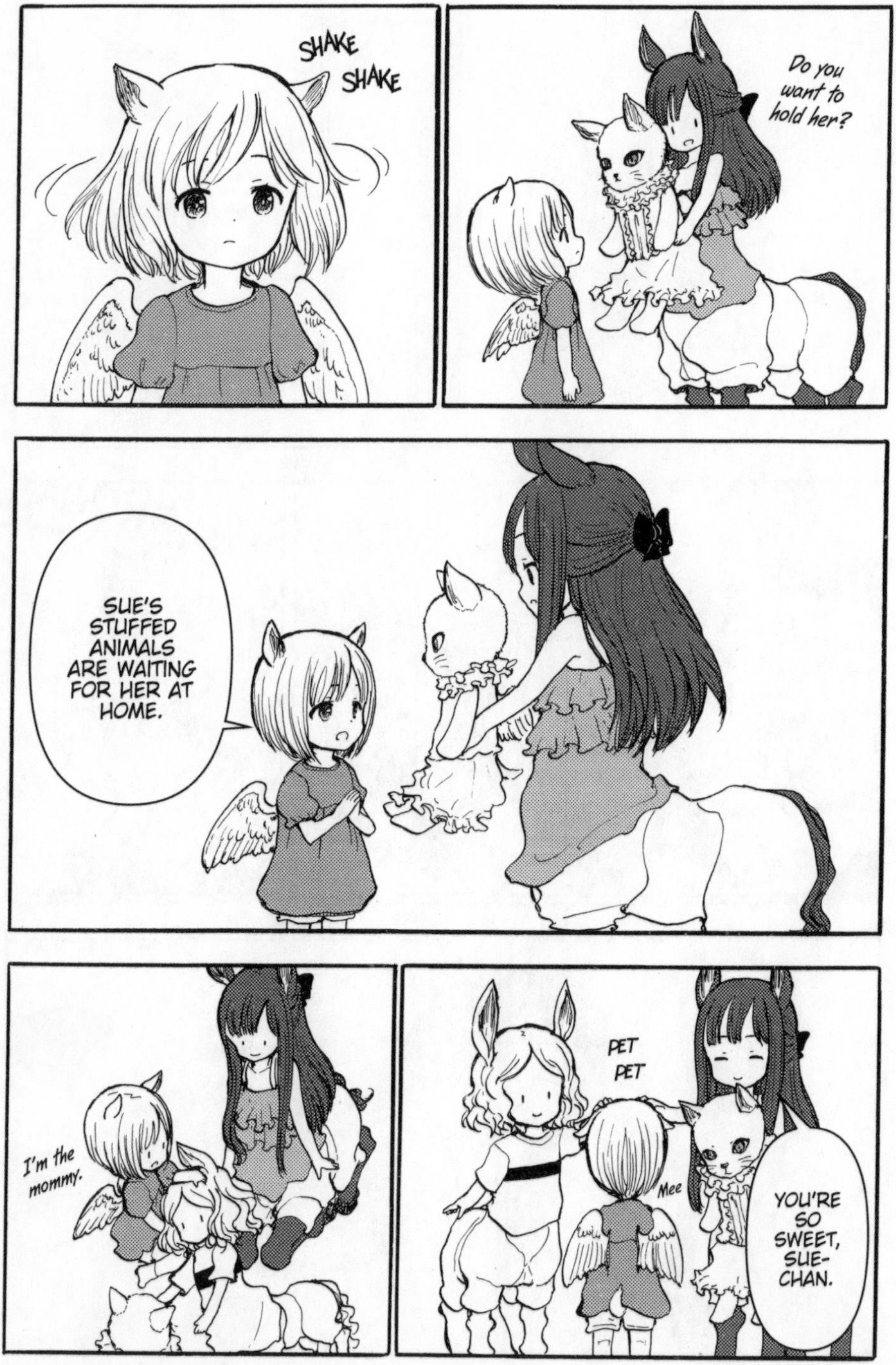
Do you want to hold her?
SHAKE SHAKE
SUE'S STUFFED ANIMALS ARE WAITING FOR HER AT HOME.
PET PET
YOU'RE SO SWEET, SUE-CHAN.
Mee
I'm the mommy.

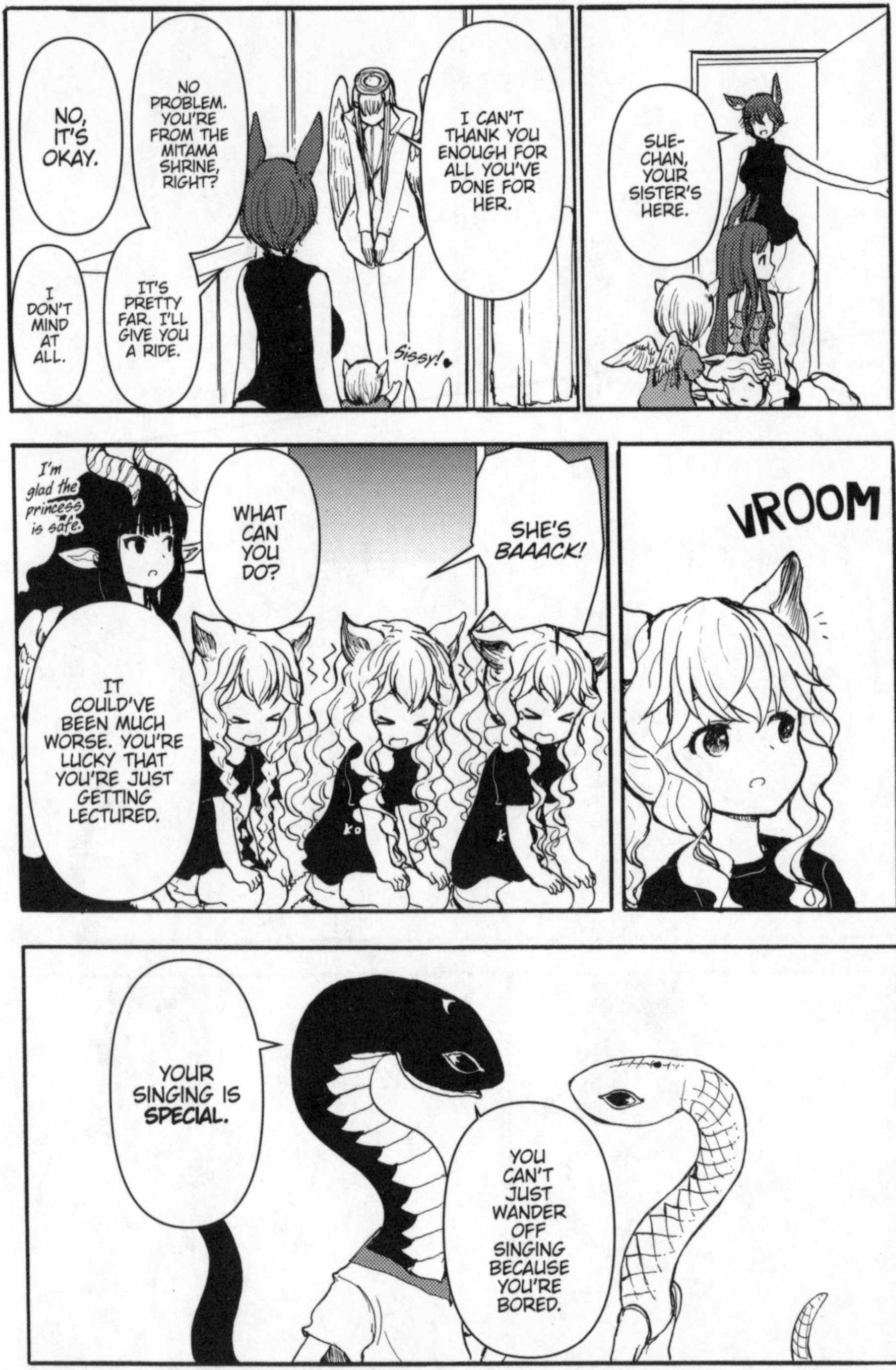
SUE-CHAN, YOUR SISTER'S HERE.
I CAN'T THANK YOU ENOUGH FOR ALL YOU'VE DONE FOR HER.
Sissy! ♥
NO PROBLEM. YOU'RE FROM THE MITAMA SHRINE, RIGHT?
IT'S PRETTY FAR. I'LL GIVE YOU A RIDE.
NO, IT'S OKAY.
I DON'T MIND AT ALL.
VROOM
SHE'S BAAACK!
WHAT CAN YOU DO?
I'm glad the princess is safe.
IT COULD'VE BEEN MUCH WORSE. YOU'RE LUCKY THAT YOU'RE JUST GETTING LECTURED.
YOUR SINGING IS SPECIAL.
YOU CAN'T JUST WANDER OFF SINGING BECAUSE YOU'RE BORED.

A Centaur's Life

AFTERWORD...

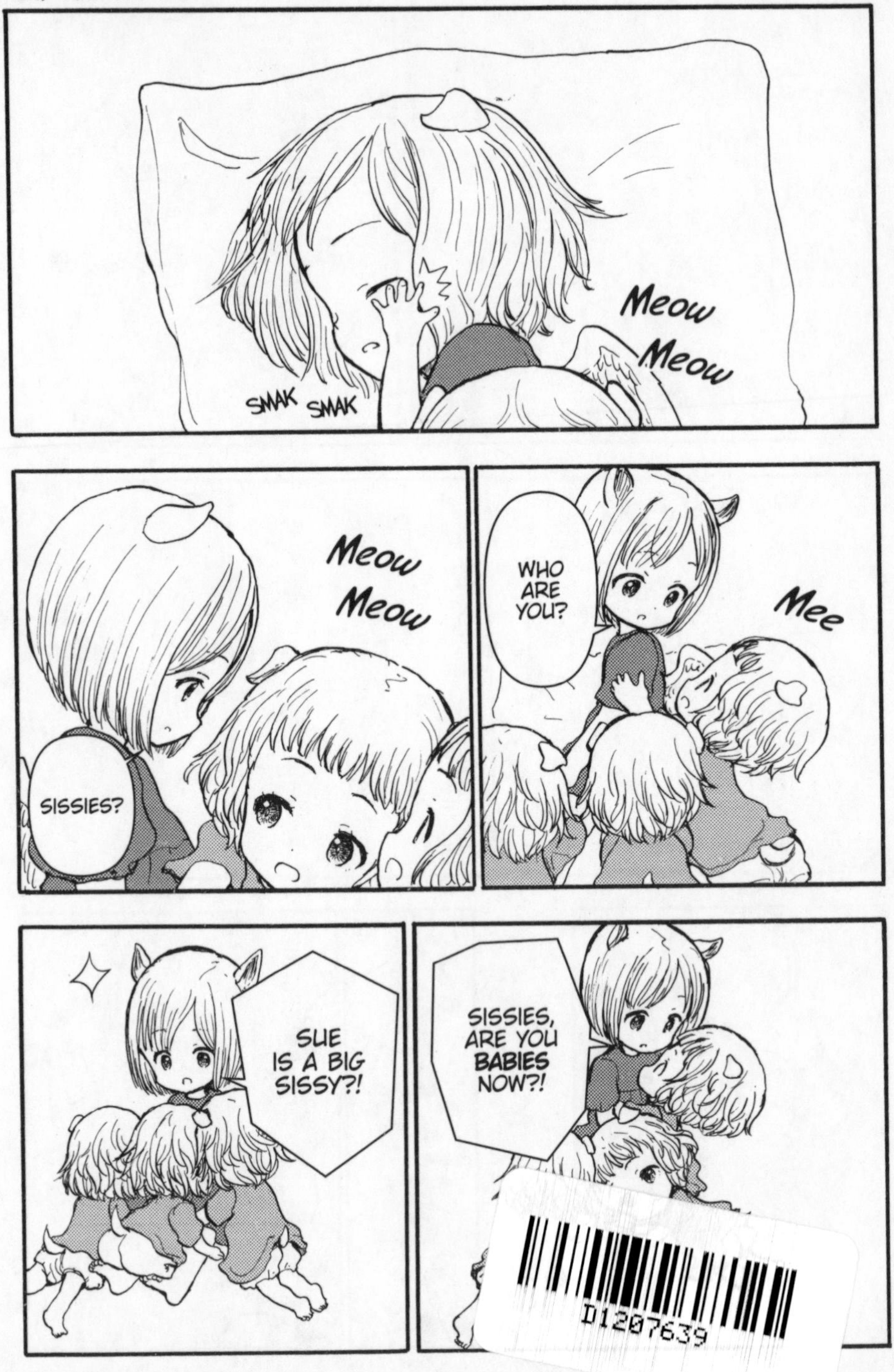
Meow
Meow
SMAK
SMAK
Mee
WHO ARE YOU?
Meow
Meow
SISSIES?
SISSIES, ARE YOU BABIES NOW?!
SUE IS A BIG SISSY?!

Contents

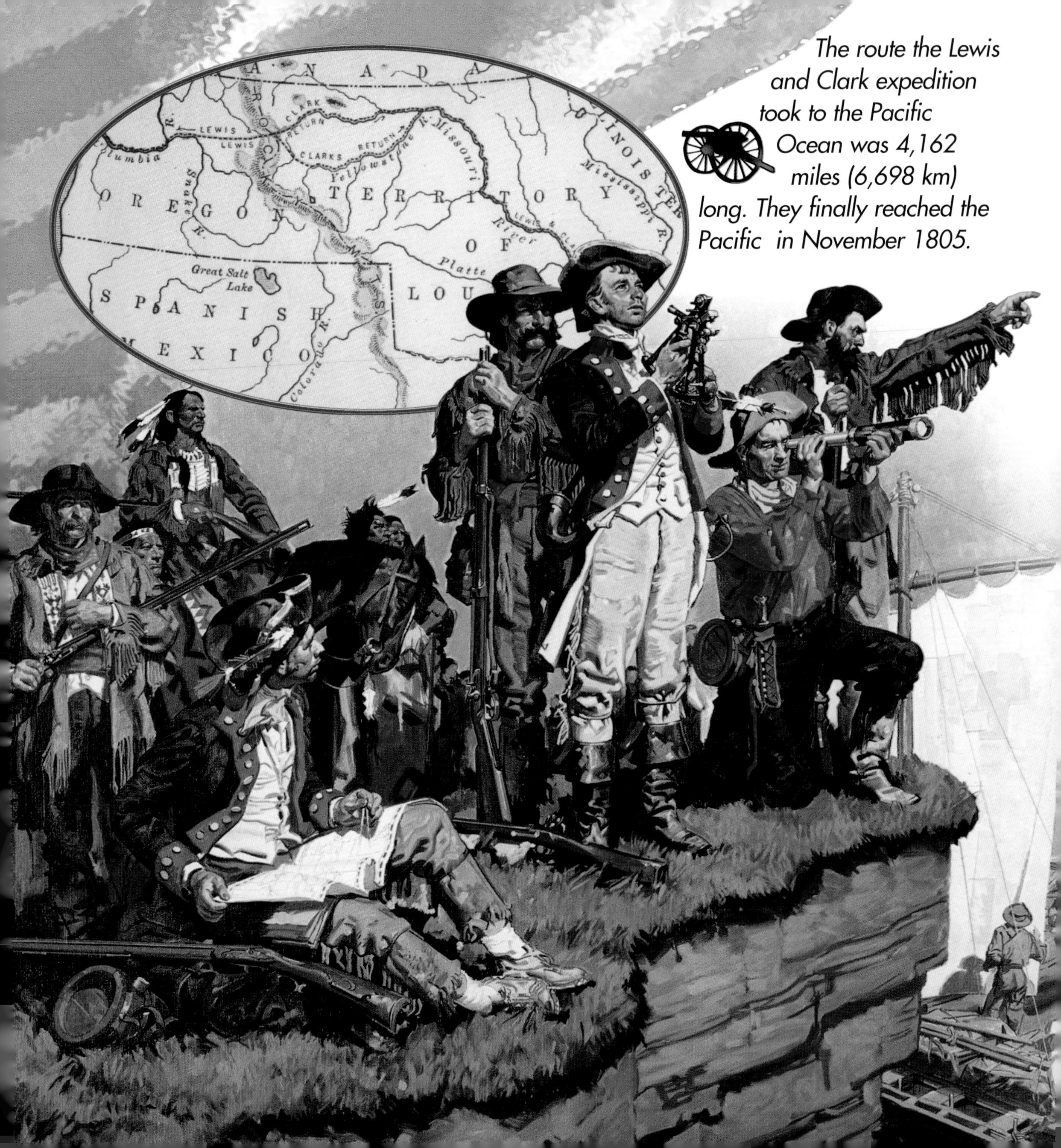

C A N A D A
LEWIS
CLARK
RETURN
CLARKS
Columbia
Snake R.
Yellowstone R.
Missouri
O R E G O N
T E R R I T O R Y
O F
L O U
Mississippi R.
River
Platte
Great Salt Lake
S P A N I S H
M E X I C O
Colorado R.

The route the Lewis and Clark expedition took to the Pacific Ocean was 4,162 miles (6,698 km) long. They finally reached the Pacific in November 1805.

A Route to the Pacific Ocean

In 1804, the United States was a young nation of only 17 states. President Thomas Jefferson sent an **expedition** to explore the land from the Mississippi River west to the Pacific Ocean. Captains Meriwether Lewis and William Clark with a group of about 50 men left the St. Louis area on May 14, 1804. They traveled up the Missouri River in one **keelboat** and two **pirogues**. By November they had journeyed nearly 1,592 miles (2,562 km) into what today is North Dakota. They decided to stay through the cold, harsh winter near the Mandan and Hidatsa peoples. They built a small fort, called Fort Mandan. In the spring some men traveled back to St. Louis with **specimens** and maps for President Jefferson. The rest of the expedition continued west. The explorers kept careful records of all their **adventures**. The group crossed the high Rocky Mountains and then went down the Columbia River to the Pacific Ocean.

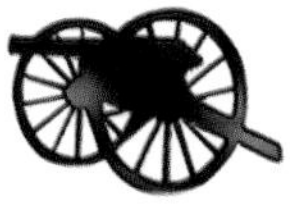

The 33 people who reached the Pacific Coast included many American soldiers, several French Canadian hunters, Clark's African American servant, York, and a Shoshone woman, Sacagawea, her husband, and their baby son.

Building Fort Clatsop

Lewis and Clark reached the Pacific in November 1805, and camped near the ocean. The windy and rainy weather at the coast was hard on the members of the expedition. The captains looked for a good place to spend the winter and asked each person to vote on where to locate their camp. All but one agreed to build a fort on the south side of the Columbia River near the ocean. The men cut the nearby evergreen trees to construct a 50-foot (15-m), square fort. The captains designed the fort with two log buildings facing each other. In one building were three rooms for the men. The opposite building had four rooms: the first for Sacagawea, the Shoshone **interpreter**, and her family, the second for Lewis and Clark, the third for a guardhouse, and the fourth for storage. The captains named the log structure Fort Clatsop for the nearby Native American Clatsop people.

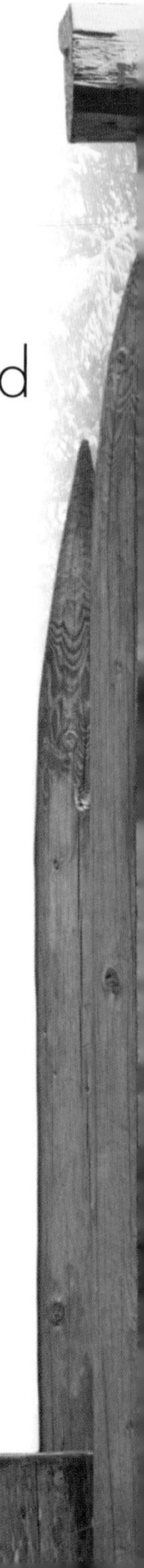

Log walls connected the buildings of Fort Clatsop to form a small parade ground. Gates in both walls provided entrances to the small fort. A spring just outside the fort supplied fresh water.

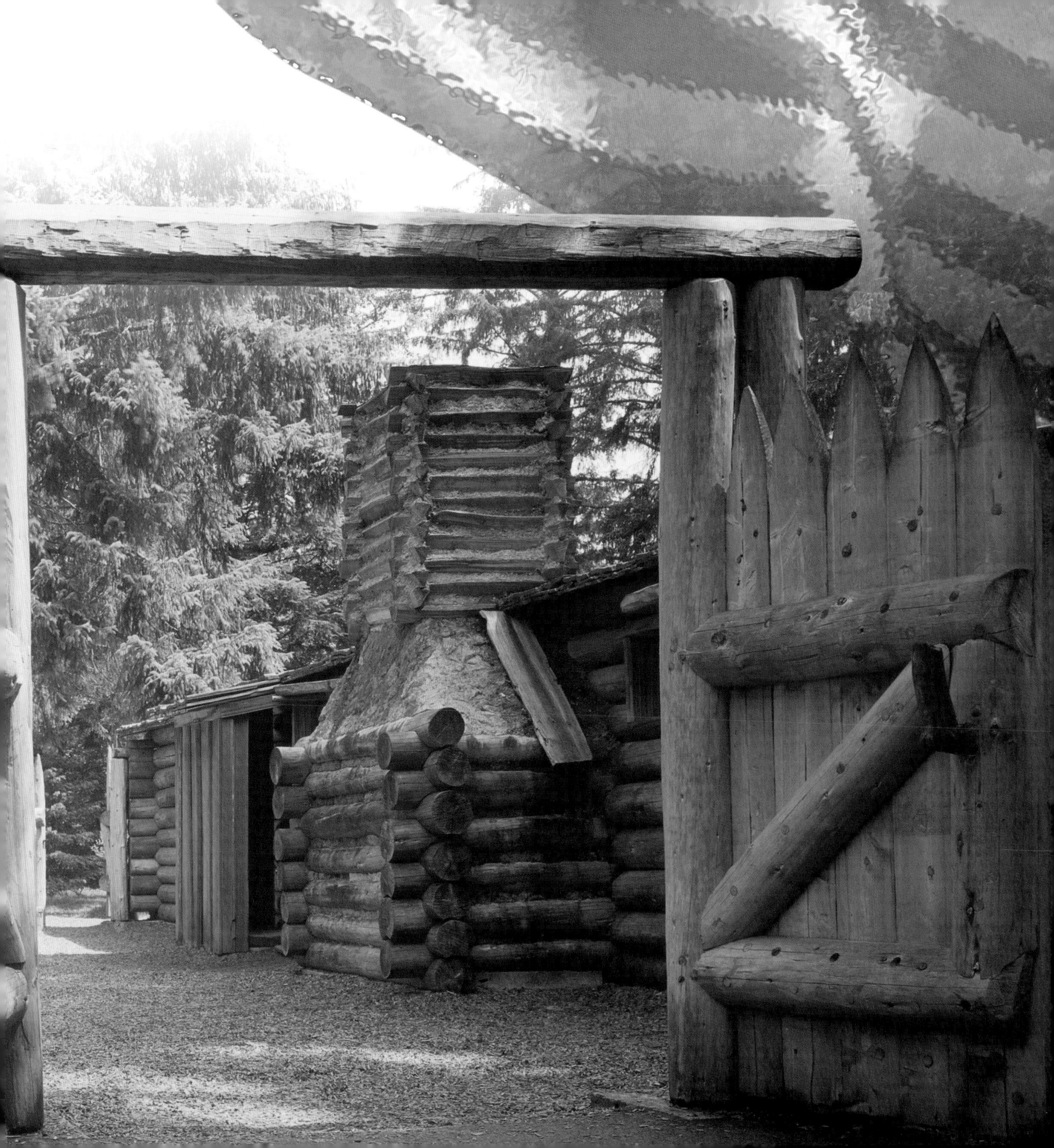

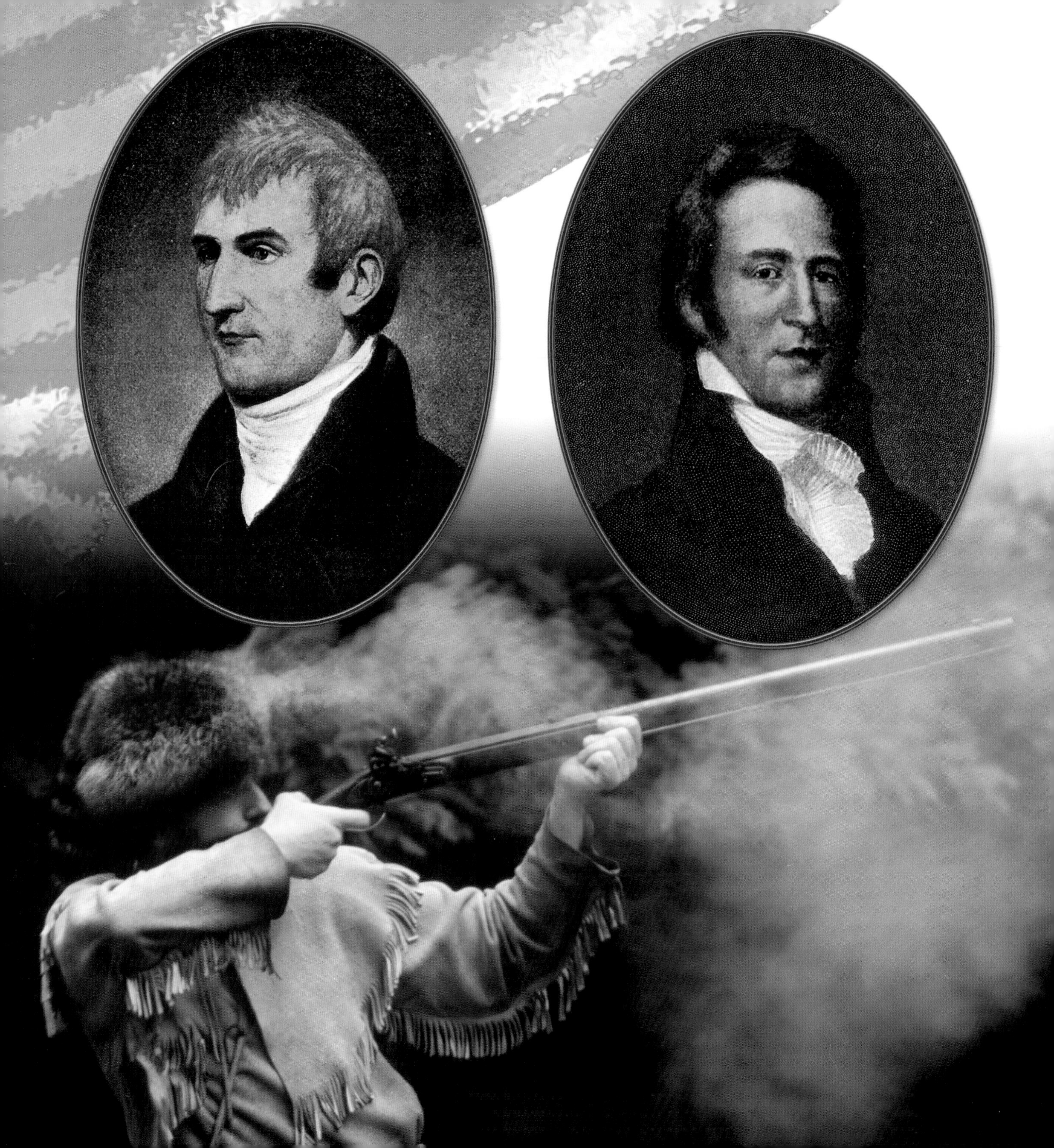

Holidays Away from Home

On Christmas morning, December 25, 1805, Lewis and Clark awoke to laughter, shouting, and the sound of the men shooting their guns in the air. The soldiers celebrated the holiday by singing and dancing to the music of fiddles played by two of the men. The captains gave tobacco and silk handkerchiefs to all the men. Lewis gave Clark woolen underwear, a shirt, and socks. Sacagawea presented Clark with 24 white weasel tails. Others gave him a pair of **moccasins** and a woven basket. They ate elk meat that had started to spoil, dried fish, and roots, perhaps **wapato** roots, which are like potatoes. On January 1, 1806, the day began with shouts and another gun salute. Lewis wrote that all were looking forward to the new year of 1807 when they would eat good food with family and friends back in the East. The homesick men had been away from their homes and families for nearly two years.

Top Left: *In 1801, Meriwether Lewis worked as President Jefferson's assistant. Jefferson chose Lewis to lead the expedition to the Pacific.* Top Right: *Lewis asked William Clark to share the command.* Bottom: *A park ranger fires a rifle into the air at Fort Clatsop during a special program for visitors.*

Making Salt

Salt was important to the Lewis and Clark expedition because it **preserved** meat and made the food taste better. On December 28, five men were sent to find a place to make salt. They located a spot 15 miles (24 km) southwest of Fort Clatsop on the ocean shore where today's Seaside, Oregon, is located. There they built a stone oven for five brass kettles where they boiled ocean water. When all the water had boiled away, only salt remained in the bottom of the kettles.

The men took turns at the saltworks, making about 3 quarts (2.8 liters) of salt each day. After 2 months of boiling a total of about 1,400 gallons (5,300 l) of seawater, almost 3½ bushels (123.3 l) of salt had been made for the trip home. Lewis called the salt "excellent, fine, strong, and white" and "a great treat."

Top: *This is Clark's elkskin-bound journal, or notebook, in which he wrote his daily notes.* Bottom: *Fort Clatsop's saltworks was located along the Oregon coast near today's town of Seaside. The men who worked at the salt camp obtained salt by boiling seawater in large kettles. Today visitors to the camp can watch park rangers make salt like Lewis and Clark's men did.*

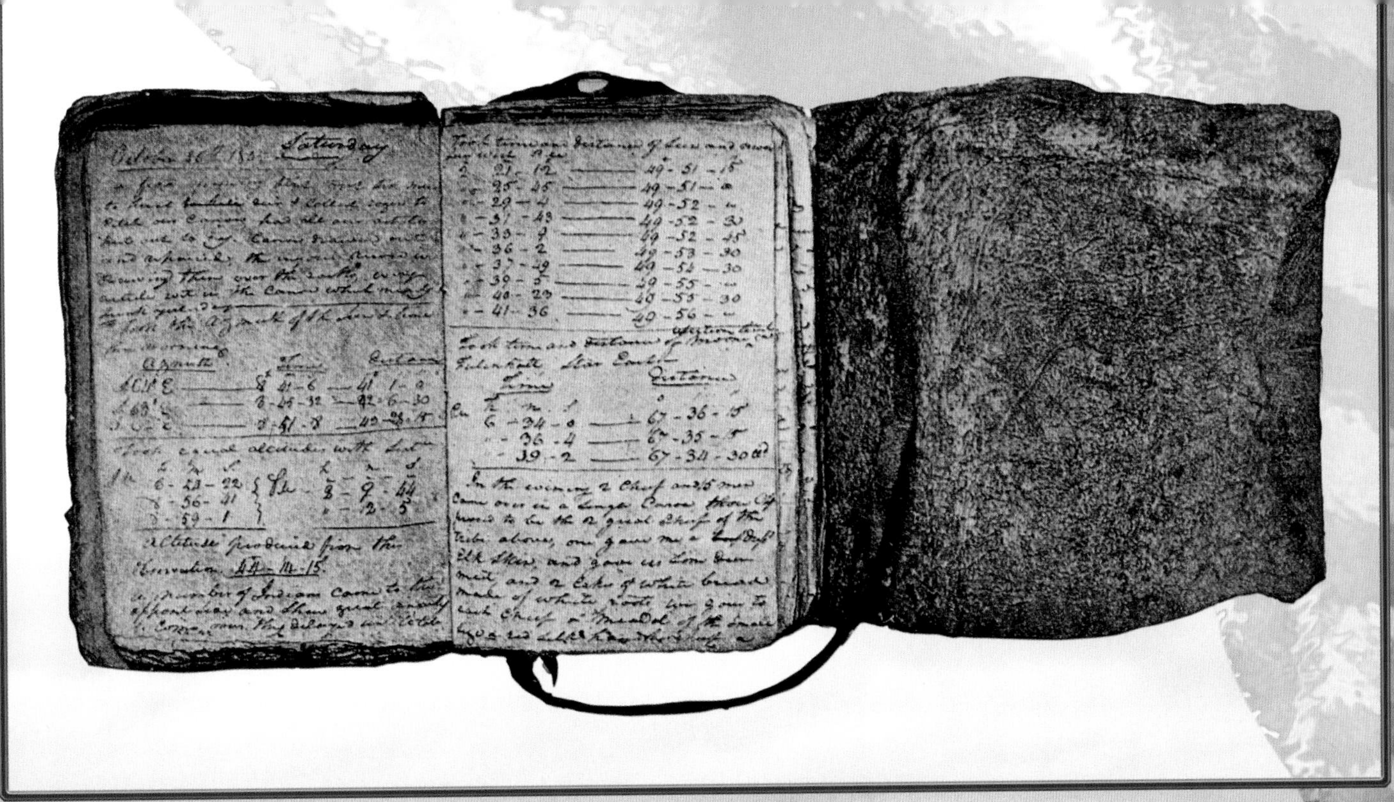

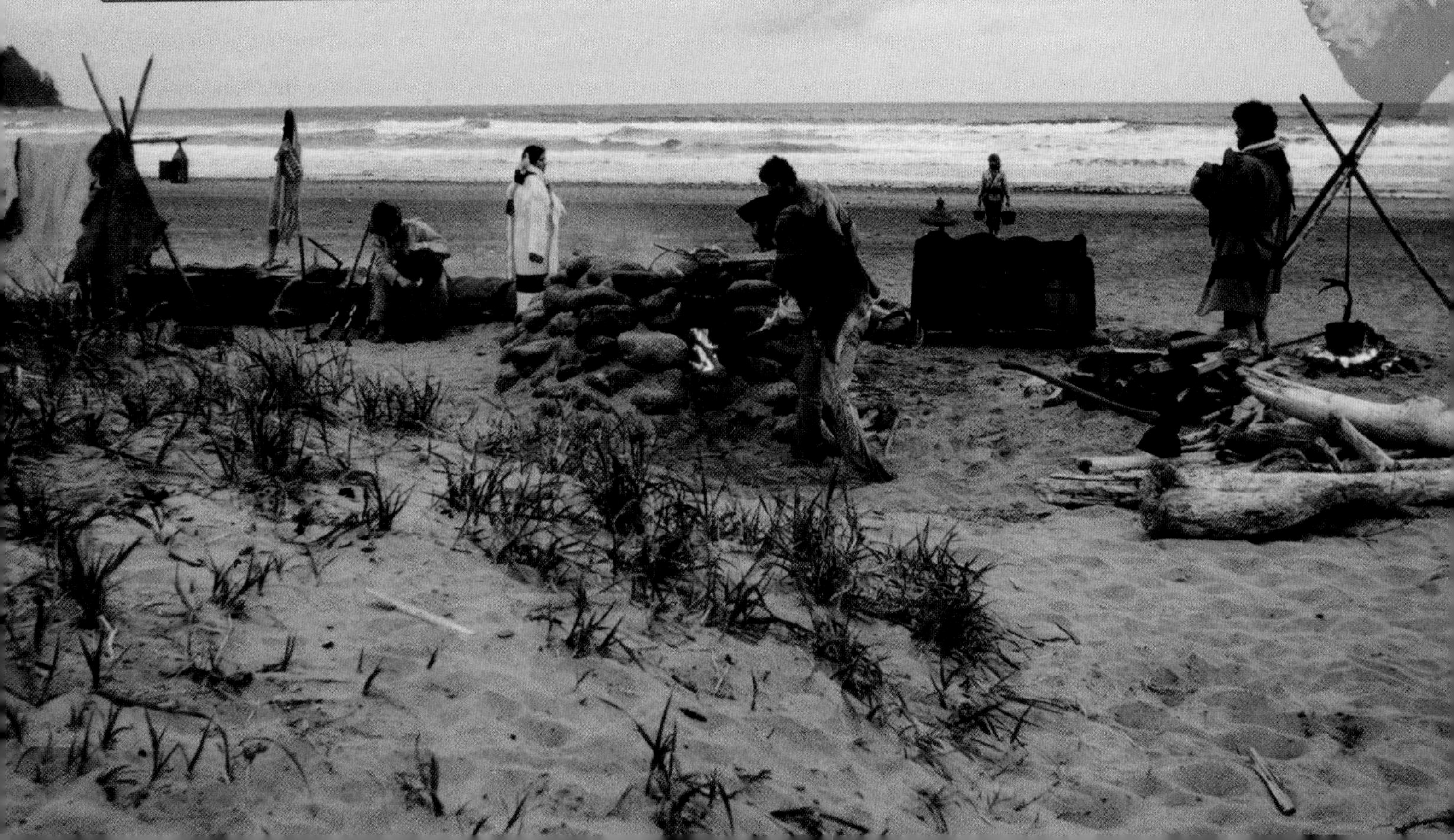

"I . . . thank providence for directing the whale to us; and think him much more kind to us than he was to jonah, having Sent this monster to be Swallowed by us instead of swallowing of us as jonah's did."

William Clark
January 8, 1806

Whale of a Tale

   Some Clatsops brought **blubber** to the salt makers' camp with news of a beached whale. Two men returned to Fort Clatsop with some blubber. The captains decided to send a group with Captain Clark to see the whale and get more blubber to eat. Sacagawea asked to go with the men. On January 6, 1806, Clark, Sacagawea, her husband and her baby, and several of the men traveled to the saltworks, then on south over a high crest to the beach where the whale lay. Tillamook people had already stripped the meat and blubber from the whale. Only its large skeleton, 105 feet (32 m) long, remained. Clark traded with the Tillamook for 300 pounds (136 kg) of blubber and several gallons of whale oil. They returned the 35 miles (56 km) to Fort Clatsop where everyone enjoyed eating the blubber.

Far Left: *Sacagawea said that she had traveled a long way to see "the great waters" of the Pacific Ocean* (background). *Now a large "fish" was to be seen, too, and she wanted the chance to see both.*

Everyday Life at Fort Clatsop

At their winter camp at Fort Clatsop, the men finally were able to rest. Dull tasks filled everyday life during the winter of 1805–06 at Fort Clatsop. The weather was cold and rainy. Of the 106 days at the fort, it rained all but 12. The sun shone on only six days. It was so damp that clothes rotted and nearly everyone got sick. They ate mostly spoiled elk and deer meat with wapato roots and fish. Besides the bad food, sickness, and boredom, fleas were everywhere. Sometimes the men stood in the rain to wash off the fleas.

Work at the fort included making salt, hunting food, and preparing for the trip home. While at the fort, the men stitched 338 pairs of moccasins, sewed elk leather for clothes, and built **dugout canoes**. Some evenings everyone enjoyed fiddle music played by two of the men before sleeping under elk hides and wool blankets on bunks in their cramped quarters.

Far Left: *This rifle was used by one of the explorers during the journey.*
Top: *This picture shows how cramped the living quarters were at Fort Clatsop.*
Far Right: *Today at Fort Clatsop, park rangers make dugout canoes like the ones Lewis and Clark made.*

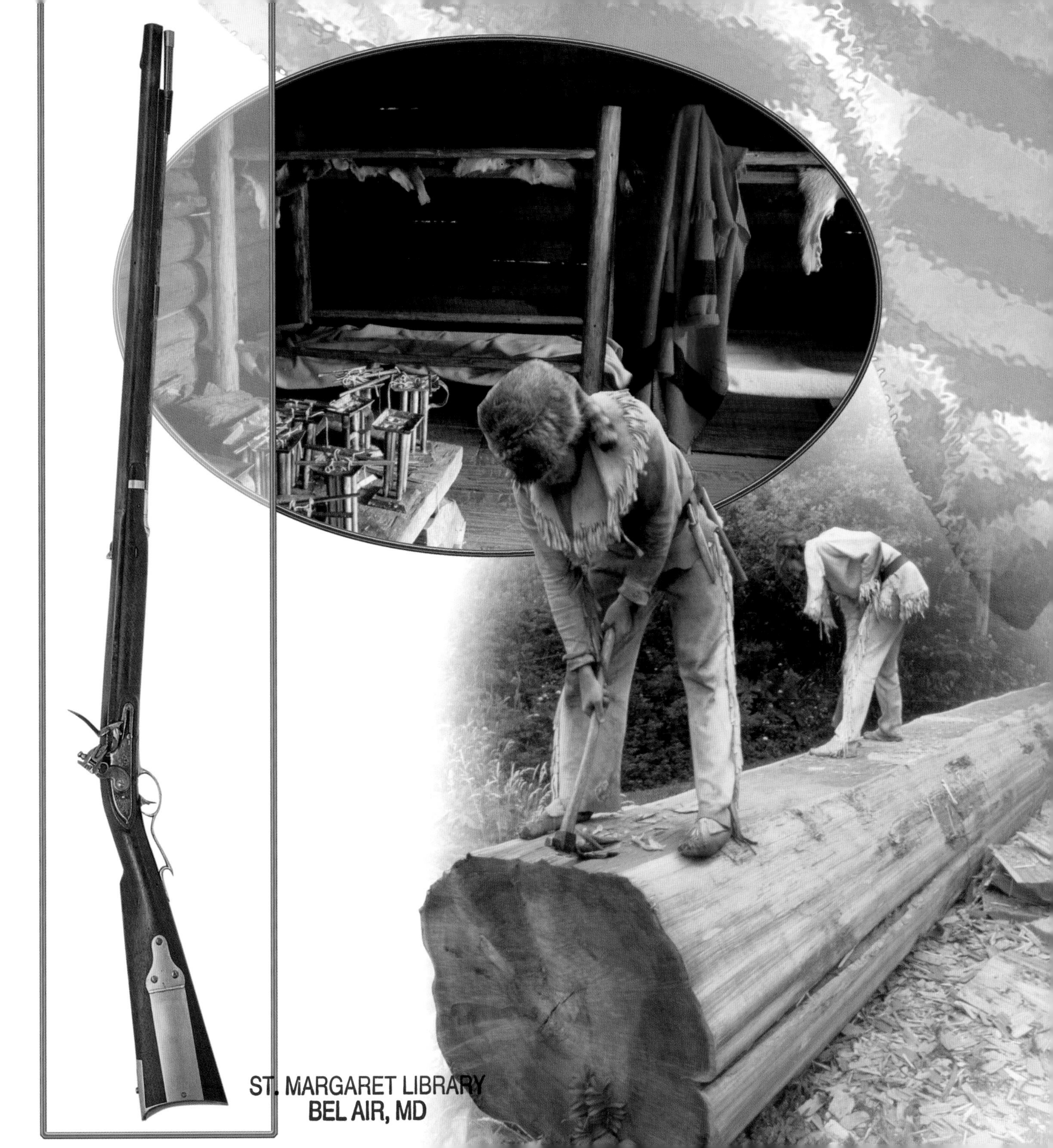

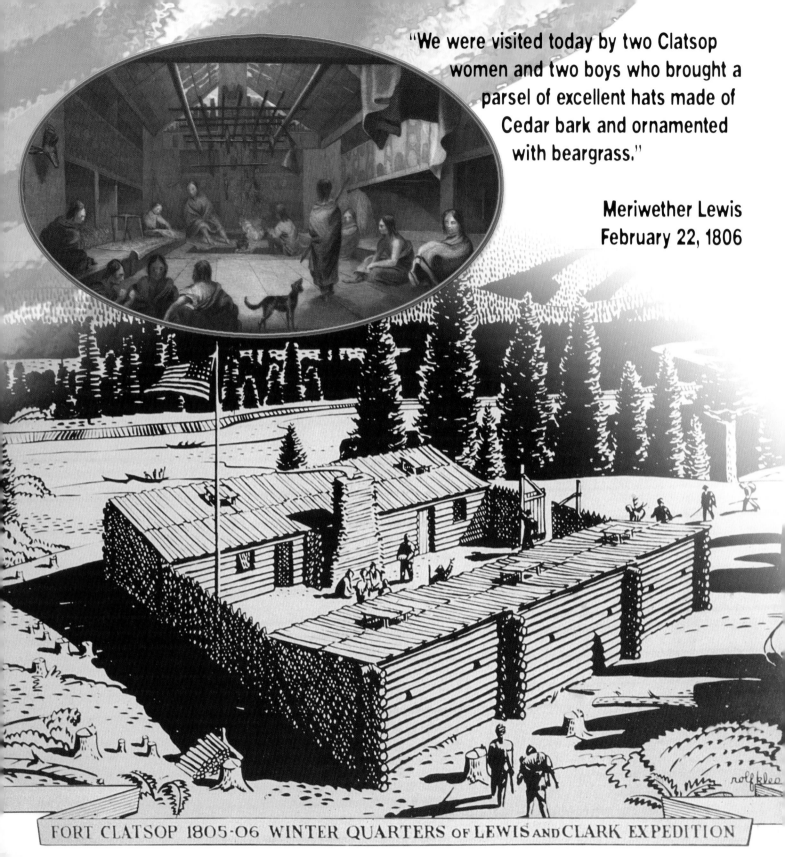

“We were visited today by two Clatsop women and two boys who brought a parsel of excellent hats made of Cedar bark and ornamented with beargrass.”

Meriwether Lewis
February 22, 1806

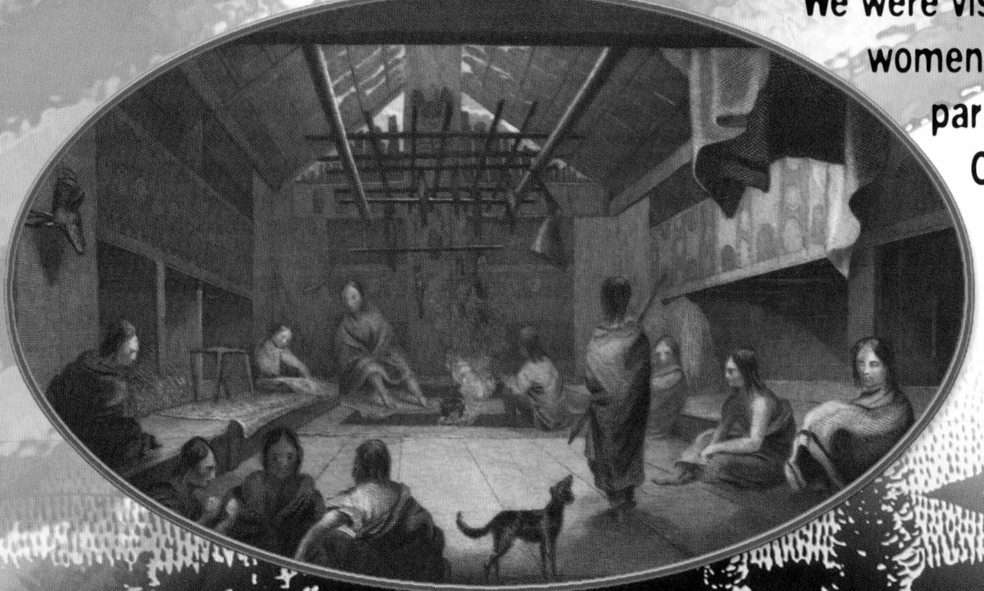

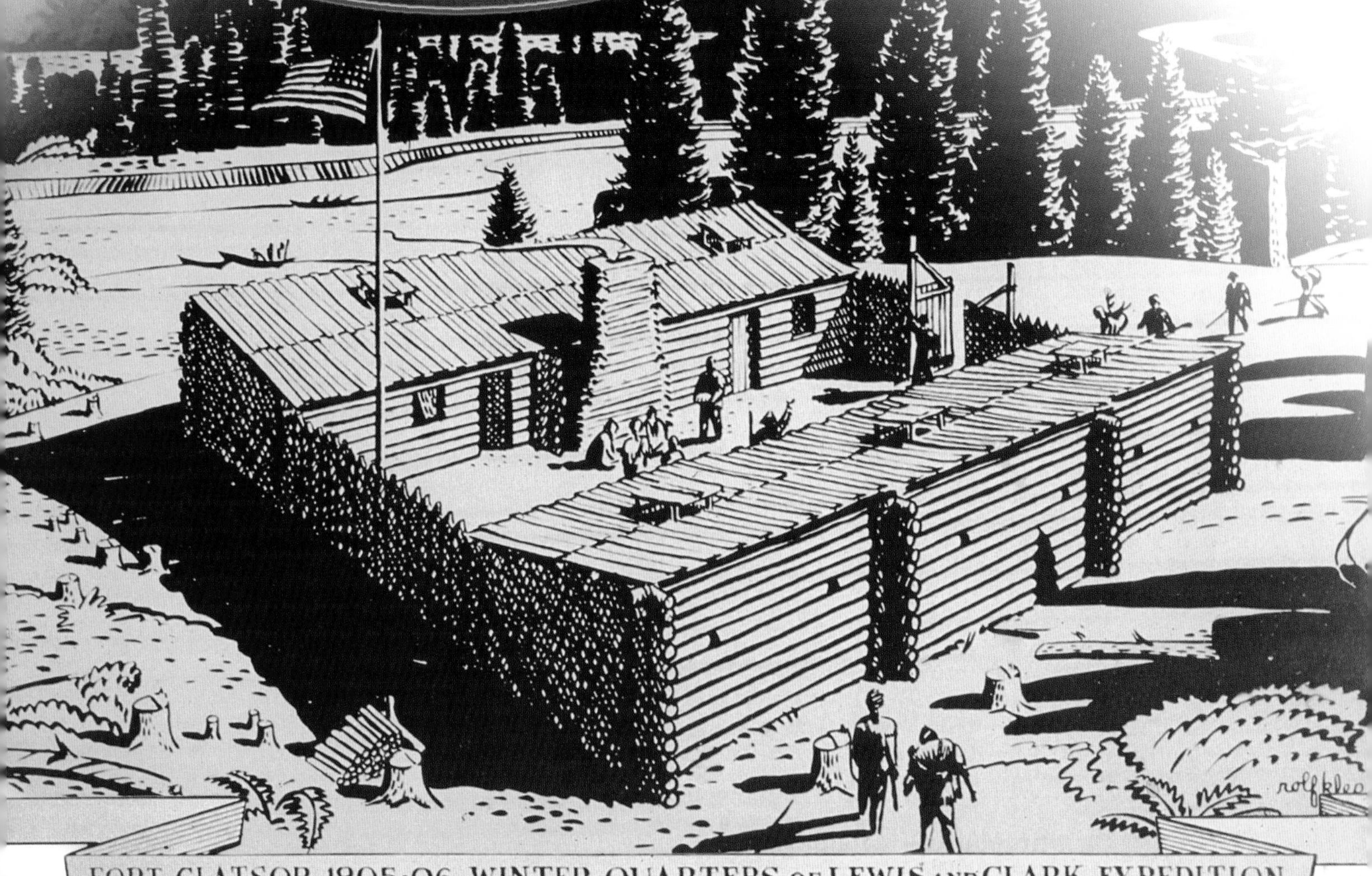
rolf klep

FORT CLATSOP 1805-06 WINTER QUARTERS OF LEWIS AND CLARK EXPEDITION

Native American Neighbors

The Clatsop, Chinook, and Tillamook peoples lived near Fort Clatsop. All skillfully canoed over the rough waters of the ocean, rivers, and streams in handcrafted dugout canoes. At first the members of the expedition could talk to them only by using signs. The explorers studied the native languages to learn a few words. The Native Americans often visited the small fort to trade fish, dogs, berries, and wapato roots for beads, knives, and other goods. Also, the Clatsop women traded beautiful handwoven hats and cedar bark baskets.

The Lewis and Clark expedition learned about the area from the neighboring Clatsop and Chinook peoples. Without the support of the local people and other Native American people along the journey, the expedition never would have reached its goal.

Top: *This picture shows a Chinook family and the interior of a Chinook lodge from the early 1840s. The Chinooks were one of many Native American peoples with whom Lewis and Clark traded.*
Bottom: *During the winter stay at Fort Clatsop, the men worked to make candles, cure elk meat in the smokehouse, and sew clothes. They spent most of the winter preparing for the long trip back to St. Louis, Missouri.*

17

Recording the Journey

Before Lewis, Clark, and the others had left on the expedition, President Jefferson had asked them to keep detailed **journals** of the entire trip. Several of the other men also kept daily records. During the gloomy days Lewis, Clark, and some of the other men wrote **observations** of their travels. Clark carefully worked on detailed maps of the journey west. Lewis wrote and drew descriptions of plants, animals, and places seen along the way, as well as those around Fort Clatsop. The two men also described the many Native American tribes they met.

In reviewing their notes and Clark's maps at Fort Clatsop, they decided to return home by different routes. They spent much time planning and preparing for the return trip. Eager to depart for home, the expedition left Fort Clatsop in March, two weeks earlier than planned.

Top: These pages from Lewis and Clark's journals included their notes about salmon, shrubs, Native Americans, and birds. Bottom: The original Fort Clatsop no longer stands. The fort (seen here) was rebuilt in 1955.

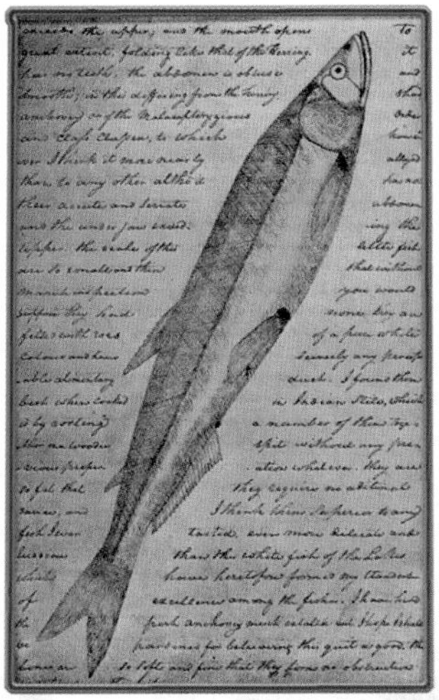

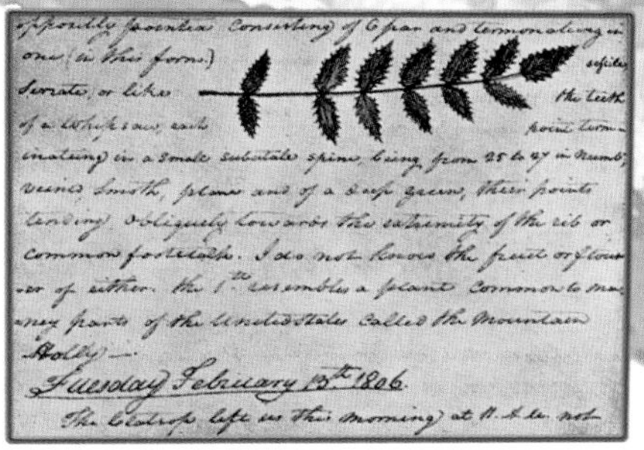
Tuesday February 18th 1806

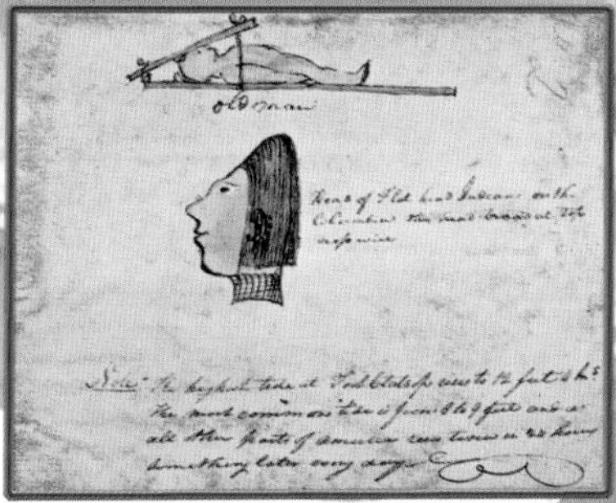

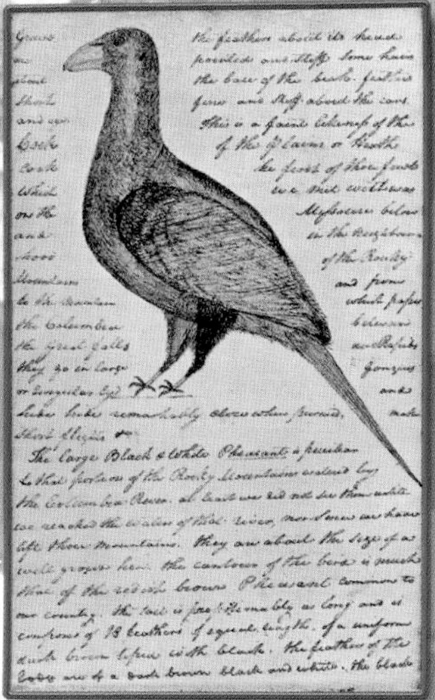

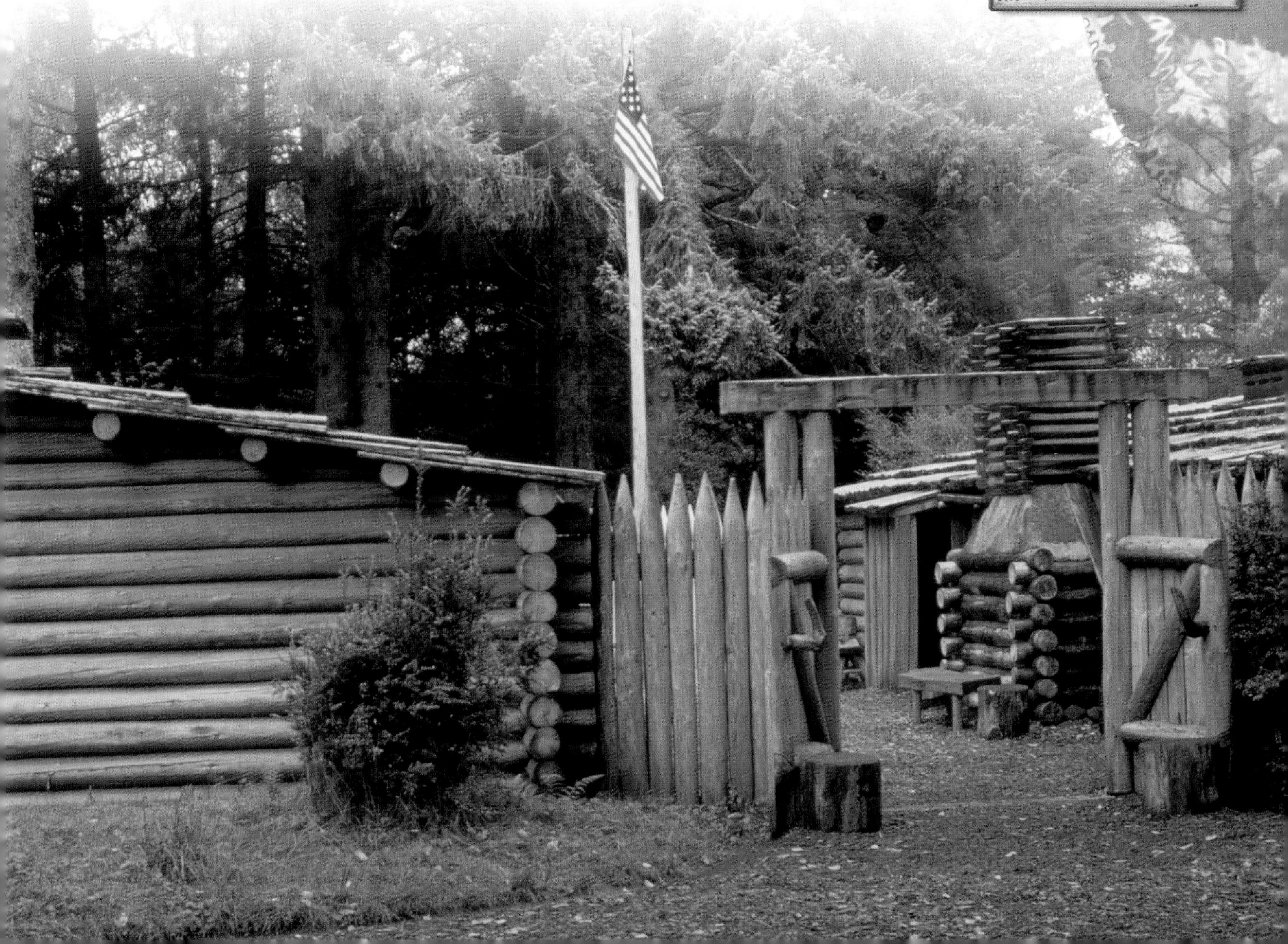

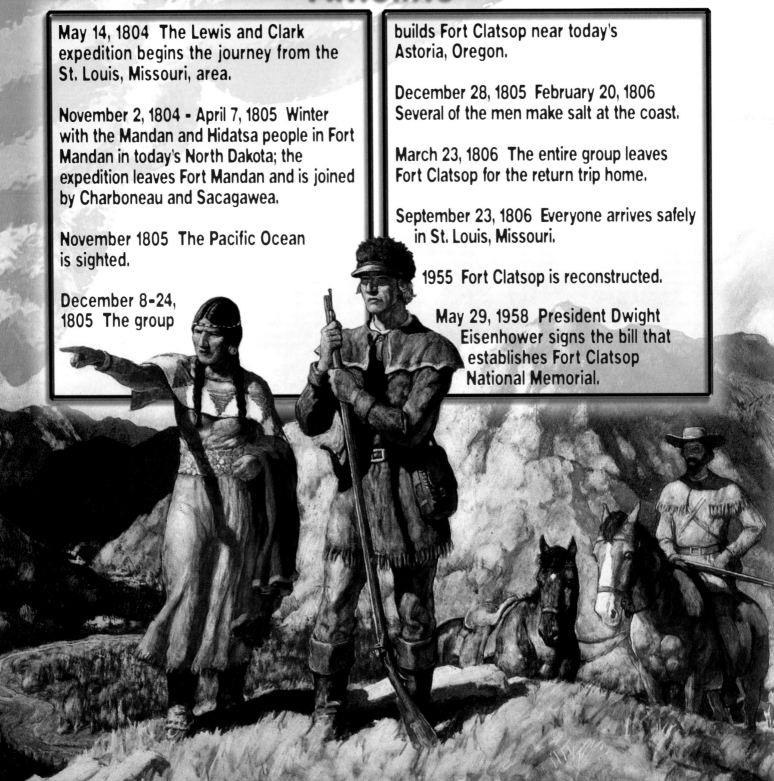

Timeline

May 14, 1804 The Lewis and Clark expedition begins the journey from the St. Louis, Missouri, area.

November 2, 1804 - April 7, 1805 Winter with the Mandan and Hidatsa people in Fort Mandan in today's North Dakota; the expedition leaves Fort Mandan and is joined by Charboneau and Sacagawea.

November 1805 The Pacific Ocean is sighted.

December 8-24, 1805 The group builds Fort Clatsop near today's Astoria, Oregon.

December 28, 1805 February 20, 1806 Several of the men make salt at the coast.

March 23, 1806 The entire group leaves Fort Clatsop for the return trip home.

September 23, 1806 Everyone arrives safely in St. Louis, Missouri.

1955 Fort Clatsop is reconstructed.

May 29, 1958 President Dwight Eisenhower signs the bill that establishes Fort Clatsop National Memorial.

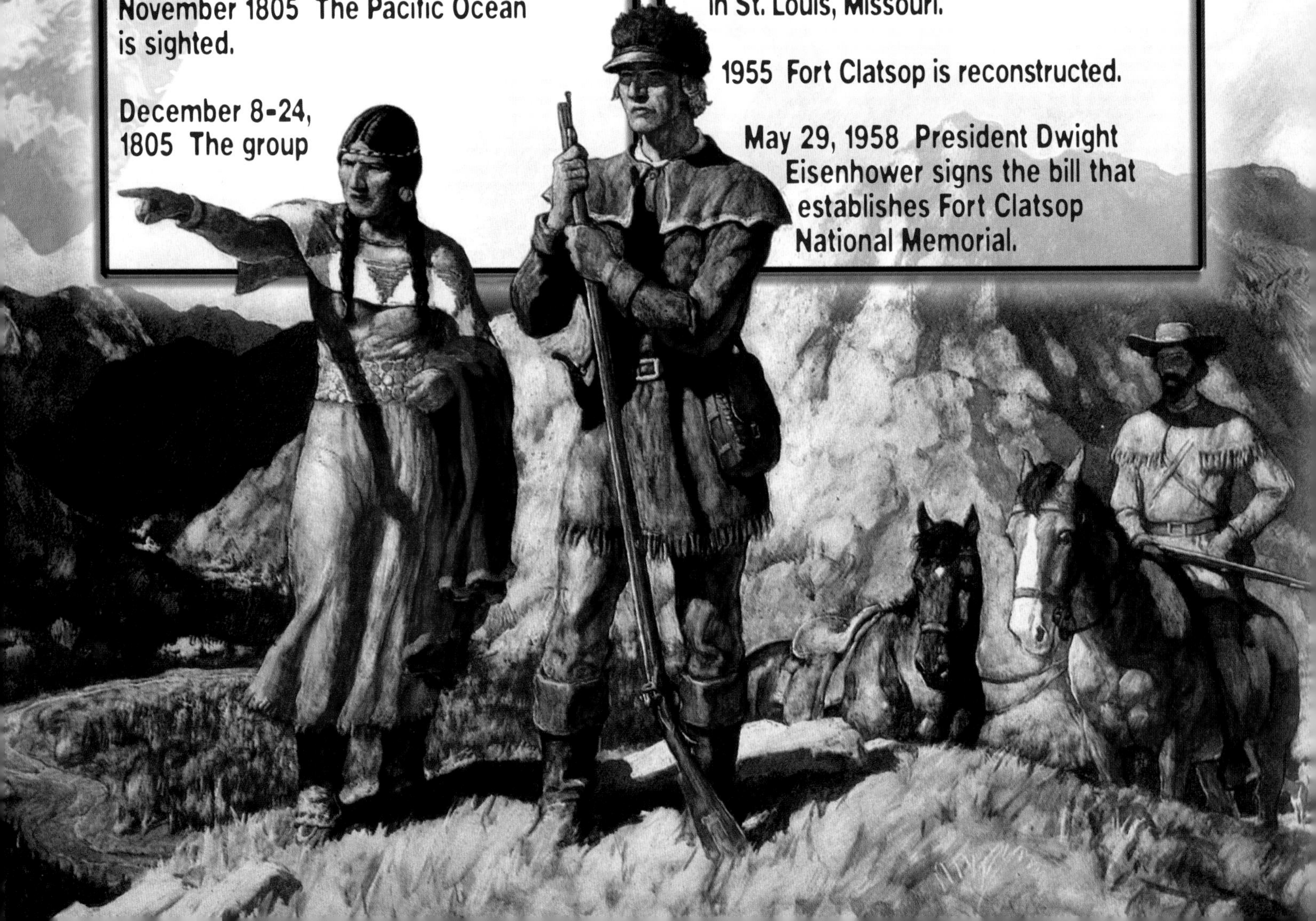

"We Proceeded On...."

The phrase most written by Lewis and Clark in their journals is "we proceeded on." These words prove that the explorers would not give up as they traveled across America. The group moved slowly up rivers, over high, snow-covered mountains, and down swift streams. They met many Native American people. Fort Clatsop on the Pacific coast housed the small group for one rainy winter during the difficult journey.

In 1940, artist N. C. Wyeth painted this picture of Sacagawea traveling with the Lewis and Clark expedition.

Fort Clatsop Today

The Lewis and Clark expedition left Fort Clatsop on March 23, 1806, to return to St. Louis. In the following years, the small log structure crumbled and rotted away.

The site of the old fort was located from Clark's good maps and Lewis's careful descriptions. Settlers founded the town of Astoria just five years after the explorers left the area. These settlers and the Clatsop knew where the fort had once stood. In 1955, local people used drawings made by Clark to rebuild it. A visitor center near the fort displays **exhibits** about the explorers and the local Native Americans. The **reconstructed** fort became the Fort Clatsop National Memorial, a unit of the National Park Service, in 1958, by an act of Congress. Park rangers in historic clothing make the winter stay of 1805–06 live again. **Demonstrations** are given of how the people lived and worked at Fort Clatsop and the saltworks. Today's visitor truly can walk in the footsteps of the famous explorers.

Glossary

adventures (ad-VEN-cherz) Unusual or exciting things to do.

blubber (BLUH-ber) The fat of a whale, penguin, or other sea animal.

demonstrations (deh-mun-STRAY-shunz) Showing people how to do something by acting it out.

dugout canoes (DUG-owt kuh-NOOZ) Narrow boats made from hollowed-out logs that move through the water by paddling.

exhibits (ig-ZIH-bits) Objects or pictures set out for people to see.

expedition (ek-spuh-DIH-shun) A trip for a special purpose such as scientific study.

journals (JER-nuhlz) Notebooks in which people write their thoughts.

interpreter (in-TER-preh-ter) A person who explains the meaning of one language with another.

keelboat (KEEL BOHT) A large boat with a long piece of wood running from the front to the back under the boat. Oars and sails move the boat.

moccasins (MAH-kuh-sinz) Native American shoes made of leather and often decorated with beads.

observations (ahb-sur-VAY-shunz) The acts of looking at something carefully.

pirogues (pi-ROHGZ) Large, canoelike boats.

preserved (prih-ZURVD) To have kept something safe from abuse, weather, and rot.

reconstructed (ree-kun-STRUK-ted) To fix up something that needed to be repaired.

specimens (SPEH-sih-mins) Samples.

wapato (WAH-pah-toh) A plant with an edible root similar to a potato.

Index

Web Sites

To learn more about Fort Clatsop and the Lewis and Clark expedition, check out these Web sites:

www.lewisandclark.org
www.lewis-clark.org
www.nps.gov/focl/home.htm
www.pbs.org/lewisandclark